Richard Crashaw

AND THE

SPANISH GOLDEN AGE

R. V. YOUNG

YALE UNIVERSITY PRESS
NEW HAVEN AND LONDON

Published with the assistance of the
Elizabethan Club of Yale University from the
foundation established in memory of
Oliver Baty Cunningham of the
Class of 1917, Yale College.

Designed by James J. Johnson
and set in Fairfield Medium type by The Composing Room of Michigan.
Printed in the United States of America by
Vail-Ballou Press, Binghamton, N.Y.

Library of Congress Cataloging in Publication Data

Young, R. V., 1947–
    Richard Crashaw and the Spanish Golden Age.

    (Yale studies in English ; 191)
    Includes index.
    1. Crashaw, Richard, 1613?–1649—Sources.
2. Crashaw, Richard, 1613?–1649—Religion and
ethics.   3. Spanish literature—Classical period,
1500–1700—History and criticism.   4. Literature,
Comparative—English and Spanish.   5. Literature,
Comparative—Spanish and English.   I. Title.
II. Series.
PR3386.Y6   821'.4   82–1850
ISBN 0–300–02766–4   AACR2

10 9 8 7 6 5 4 3 2 1

Y, a la verdad, si hay debajo de la luna cosa que merezca ser estimada y preciada, es la mujer buena; y en comparación de ella el sol mismo no luce y son obscuras las estrellas.

Fray Luis de León, *La perfecta casada*

Contents

Acknowledgments

The present study of Richard Crashaw's poetry began as a Yale dissertation directed by Louis L. Martz, who provided superb guidance then and has continued to prove an invaluable mentor, friend, and inspiration. In addition, he has continually furnished as noble a model of professional excellence as a young scholar could wish.

A number of others at Yale also helped me while I was a graduate student. Gustavo Correa introduced me to the Spanish mystics and Spanish baroque poets in his seminars, and A. Bartlett Giamatti, Lowry Nelson, and Marie Borroff gave me precious counsel and encouragement. I also wish to remember here the late William K. Wimsatt and the late Richard Sylvester whose example and instruction enriched my scholarly pursuits.

The Carolinas Symposium on British Studies, the Philological Association of the Carolinas, and a summer fellowship with the Southeastern Institute for Medieval and Renaissance Studies gave me opportunities to broaden my knowledge of Crashaw and Renaissance poetry. I also wish to thank the Kairos Foundation for inviting me to teach in its summer program at El Escorial in 1979, thereby enabling me to finish my research in Spain. In addition, the staffs at the Beinecke Library of Yale University, the Perkins Library of Duke University, and the Biblioteca Nacional in Madrid were unfailingly helpful.

I wish to thank Dorothée Metlitzki and the committee for Yale Studies in English, and Ellen Graham, Mary Alice Galligan, and the

Yale University Press for their careful and expeditious handling of my manuscript. Manuel Durán of Yale University and Anthony Low of New York University both read the manuscript and offered crucial suggestions for its improvement with the utmost tact and consideration. I am grateful to Dale Randall of Duke University and the members of his seminar for their insightful comments.

I wish to thank Larry Champion and the executive committee of North Carolina State University, department of English, for their patience. My colleague Tom Hester has furnished good advice and, above all, good comradeship for years. Frank and Dorothy Doggett have given me encouragement and inspiration, usually at long distance, for longer still.

The dedication indicates a debt to my wife that I can neither express nor ever hope to repay. The debt is increased by the joyful assurance that it need not be repaid.

1

Crashaw in Context:
Spain and the Counter
Reformation

CRASHAW," OBSERVES T. S. ELIOT, "is primarily a
European."[1] This judgment has provoked little dis-
agreement over the succeeding years: Crashaw remains
the least "metaphysical" of the Metaphysical poets.
While modern British and American readers are likely to discover in
the religious poetry of Donne or Herbert something that seems familiar, even contemporary (however illusory this feeling may be),
Crashaw is likely to prove a source of discomfort for most. Set against
the English devotional tradition, his passionately exuberant religious
sensibility and his lush imagery and extravagant hyperbole appear
wholly foreign. Scholarly investigation of his work, tending to concentrate on the establishment of his debt to the Italian and neo-Latin
poetry of his time, especially that of Marino and the Jesuit epigram-
matists, has developed an image of Crashaw as a poet of excessive, if
not outrageous, artificiality and luxuriance. Although this emphasis
on foreign influence is all to the good insofar as it makes clear
Crashaw's place in the European baroque movement in literature and
the arts, the results have, nonetheless, failed to be completely satisfactory. A disproportionate attention has been devoted to those poems
with clear marks of Marinist or neo-Latin influence at the expense of
later and decidedly superior pieces, like the Teresa poems and the
various hymns on ecclesiastical feasts. Thus Crashaw's regrettable fate
is to be remembered largely for his most extravagant epigrams and,
especially, for "The Weeper," one of his most Marinistic but least

successful efforts. Moreover, the focus on the more superficial and insistent distinctions—the startling conceit, the fusion of wit, piety, and sensuality—has obscured the truly fundamental differences between Crashaw and his English contemporaries.

In seeking to define this difference, it is important that concrete examples be adduced but equally important that "The Weeper" be avoided. The common assumption that this poem is typical of Crashaw (resulting, no doubt, from its irresistible pedagogical usefulness as an example of "baroque excess") has placed it in the center of most discussions of the poet's work.[2] It is all too easy to trot out the notorious comparison of Mary Magdalene's eyes to "walking baths" and "portable and compendious oceans"[3] and to aver smugly that such horrors are not to be found in Donne or Herbert. This is not strictly true. Allowing for an irreducible element of the subjective regarding what shocks, it is hard to see that anything in Crashaw's verse could arouse more distaste in delicate sensibilities than Donne's lines on the Church: ". . . let myne amorous soule court thy mild Dove, / Who is most trew, and pleasing to thee, then / When she' is embraced and open to most men."[4] Similarly, Herbert is not above depicting his relation to the suffering Lord in the imagery of Petrarchan love poetry:

> Thou art my lovelinesse, my life, my light,
>   Beautie alone to me:
> Thy bloody death and undeserv'd, makes thee
>   Pure red and white.[5]

In any case, even if Crashaw is more inclined to the startling conceit and the luxuriant image, even if he uses them far more frequently than Donne or Herbert, this distinction is still a matter of degree rather than kind. The truly crucial difference is a matter of tone, atmosphere, and essential import; and these elements in turn grow out of the Counter-Reformation religious and cultural orientation which develops in Crashaw in the course of his life.

At a very simple level, it is easy to see the contrast between Crashaw's firmly Catholic approach to a given Christian theme and the Protestant handling of the same theme. Nothing could be more striking than the divergence between Milton's treatment of the Nativity and the Catholic counterpart provided by Crashaw. The latter, as Louis L. Martz notes, "produces a ritual love-song; Milton, a hymn in

praise of the Power and Glory."[6] Even in the limited scope of a lyrical
ode, Milton's "On the Morning of Christ's Nativity" focuses on the
epic action of the Redemption; and until the end of the poem, and then
only in the most cursory fashion, the concrete scene of Christ's birth
never materializes. Crashaw's "Hymn in the Holy Nativity," to the
contrary, is designed to evoke just this concrete scene, complete with
intimate detail, so that poet and reader alike might enter into it
spiritually and emotionally:

> No no. your KING's not yet to seeke
> Where to repose his Royall HEAD
> See see, how soon his new-bloom'd CHEEK
> Twixt's mother's brests is gone to bed.
> Sweet choise, said we! no way but so
> Not to ly cold, yet sleep in snow.
>
> [ll. 65–70]

It is simply unimaginable that Milton could have written these lines;
the chasm dividing the puritan, humanist strain of Protestantism from
Counter-Reformation Catholicism appears with all its dizzying profundity in the contrast between these rival visions of the Nativity.

Interestingly enough, with respect to the grandly heroic tone and
moral focus, it is Milton's treatment of the theme that develops in a
straight line from the classicizing humanism of the earlier, pre-
Reformation Renaissance in Italy. The first of Antonio Geraldini's
twelve eclogues on the life of Christ, *De Salvatoris Nostri Nativitate*
(1485), is a dialogue between "Mopsus," who stands for Alphonso,
Archbishop of Saragoza, to whom the eclogues were dedicated, and
"Lycidas," who is clearly the poet himself.[7] Much of the first half of
the poem's one hundred twenty-eight lines is given over to an effort by
Mopsus to convince Lycidas that he ought to shake off his winter
lethargy and sing: "Quis te torpor habet? dudum mulcere solebas/
Pastorum tetricas blandis modulatibus aures" (ll. 6–7: "What torpor
possesses you? Once you used to soothe the gloomy ears of shepherds
with soft measures"). During the rigors of winter, however, Lycidas
would prefer "to lead sleepless nights in varied play" ("Insomnes uario
noctes deducere ludo," l. 14). Mopsus admonishes him for his interest
in the wanton frivolities of "the mob," of "vain girls," and of "boys
whose concern is the cursed dice box." For us it is fitting to bring forth

other pastimes of achievement, Mopsus maintains: "Shamefastness, the gravity and age of manly devotion allow neither soft worthlessness nor filthy stupidity."[8] Properly chastened, Lycidas offers to sing of a mythical King of Hispania who performed heroic exploits in the distant past, but Mopsus would rather hear of the newly born child whence salvation is arisen; and he calms Lycidas' fears of profaning what is sacred. After some hesitation, the latter proceeds to give an account of several Old Testament types of Christ's virginal birth, including Moses at the burning bush (Exodus, 3:1–6), Aaron's rod that budded (Numbers, 17:8), Gideon's fleece (Judges, 6:36–40), Ezekiel's vision of the shut gate of the temple sanctuary (Ezekiel, 44:1–3), and Daniel's vision of the statue of four metals and clay feet, which is destroyed by a stone uprooted by no human hand (hence the Virgin Birth), with the stone becoming a mountain filling the earth (Daniel, 2:31–35).

The tone and structure of the eclogue are considerably more like Milton than like Crashaw, and it is fairly typical of the neo-Latin Nativity eclogue right through the seventeenth century.[9] The preoccupation with the Christ child's consummating role in the sweep of sacred history is parallel to the epic mood of Milton's account of the silencing of the oracles and the departure of the pagan deities from their shrines in stanzas XVIII through XXV of "On the Morning of Christ's Nativity." In the last of these stanzas, Milton implicitly compared the infant Jesus to Hercules: "Our babe to show his Godhead true, / Can in his swaddling bands control the damned crew" (ll. 227–28).[10] This classical touch is very much in the spirit of Geraldini, who takes advantage of the Vulgate translation of Exodus, which equips Moses with horns,[11] to effect a comparison of the Hebrew lawgiver with Pan: "Cornibus, ut celeri Fauno, frons fulsit eburnis" (l. 57: "like rash Faunus his forehead flashed with ivory horns"); and God the Father is designated by Jove's epithet Tonans, "Thunderer" (l. 120). Finally, as Geraldini's modern editor notes, the eclogue is filled with phrases, images, and figures borrowed from Ovid and Virgil; and, from the latter, the Renaissance poet has drawn more frequently on the Georgics and Aeneid than on the pastoral verse.[12] To be sure, at the close of the poem, there is a moment far more Crashavian than Miltonic:

> Sed cur tam lento passu procedimus? ecce
> Aliger e supera descendit nuntius arce,

Gaudia laeta ferens pastoribus. His quoque, si uis,
Cum boue cumque asino gelida ad praesepia iuncti
Diuinum infantem proni ueneremur uterque.

[ll. 122–26]

[But why do we proceed with such slow step? behold a winged messenger
descends from the vault above, bearing joyous news to shepherds. With these
also, if you wish, joined with the ox and with the ass, all of us bowing down
at the cold manger, let us worship the divine infant.]

But the eclogue never arrives at the scene; and the entire performance
is self-consciously learned and high-minded; and Mopsus and Lycidas,
despite their names, are not shepherds but Renaissance prelate and
poet, lightly disguised after the manner of humanist literati. It is
obvious that the background of Crashaw's Nativity hymn lies elsewhere. His poem is, of course, an imitation of the classical eclogue
form and to that extent humanist, but its gay tone and luxuriant
texture divide it from the formal rigors of Geraldini's strict humanism
and even more from the sterner rigors added by Milton's Protestantism.

Metaphysical poets like Donne and Herbert, however, are by no
means so thoroughly Protestant as Milton, and they have moved away
from the neo-classical refinement he shares with the earlier
humanism. As Louis Martz has shown, their poetry bears the influence of Counter Reformation sources from the continent, especially
treatises on meditation, and expresses a deep reverence for traditional
ceremonies and rituals. [13] Crashaw's verse, nevertheless, stands apart.
If we accept Herbert's *The Temple* as a norm for English devotional
poetry, a very simple comparison reveals how very different *in kind* is
the poetry of Richard Crashaw. First, the two poets rarely write on the
same subject, and then not from the same perspective. A typical title
in *The Temple* expresses a relation between God and the individual in
terms of a moral or emotional category: "Complaining," "Constancie,"
"Content," "Deniall," "Dulnesse." The closest Crashaw comes to
writing such a poem is "Charitas Nimia," and that poem does not
employ the sharply individual focus which distinguishes Herbert. The
latter, for his part, seems almost sedulously to avoid Crashaw's favorite
kind of verse: "To All Angels and Saints" is a poem about why he will
not write a poem to angels and saints. It is clear that Herbert, like
Donne, consciously rejected Roman Catholicism, notwithstanding

Puritan suspicions of the Anglican party.[14] Even when Herbert
undertakes another of Crashaw's favorite themes—an ecclesiastical
feast—his treatment is altogether dissimilar. In Crashaw's "Hymn in
the Holy Nativity," the shepherds are characters in a gay and dazzling
pageant, but Herbert's shepherds, in "Christmas," give way to an
interior drama:

> The shepherds sing; and shall I silent be?
> My God no hymne for thee?
> My soul's a shepherd too; a flock it feeds
> Of thoughts, and words, and deeds.[15]

The movement here and in virtually all of *The Temple,* especially as it
appeals to modern taste, is toward deeply personal reflection. Herbert
finds the significance of the Nativity in its application to an individual
spiritual and moral condition.

Even in turning to Crashaw's Peterhouse colleague and close
friend Joseph Beaumont, who appears to have imitated Crashaw's
conceits and images quite freely,[16] one rarely finds a poem as a whole
which captures the unique configuration of subject, tone, and import
which is distinctly Crashaw's. *Jesus inter Ubera Maria*—"Jesus between Mary's Breasts"—would seem to promise a poem in the manner
and on the subject of Crashaw's Nativity hymn, in which the Christ
child "Twixt's mother's brests is gone to bed" (l. 68); but what in fact
follows the title is a reference to Canticles, 6 (plus a note that the
poem had been set for "a Base and 2 Trebles"), and a six-stanza
allegorical fantasy in which the relation between Jesus and Mary is
subsumed by a vague elaboration of figures from the Song of Songs,
with the concrete event of the Birth largely neglected:

> In ye coolnesse of ye day
> The old Worlds Even, *God* all undrest went downe
> Without His Roab, without His Crowne,
> In his private garden, there to lay
> on spicey Bed
> His Sweeter Head.

> There He found two Beds of Spice,
> A double Mount of Lillies, in whose Top
> Two milkie Fountaines bubled up.

He soon resolv'd: & well I like, He cries,
              My table spread
              Upon my Bed.
                    . . .
       Paradise springs new with you,
Where 'twixt those Beds of Lillies you may see
       Of life ye Everlasting Tree.
Sweet is your reason, then said Wee, come strow
              Your pious showres
              Of Eastern flowres.

              CHORUS
    Winds awake, & with Soft Gale
Awake the Odours of our Garden too;
       by which your selv's perfumed goe
Through every Quarter of your World, that All
              Your sound may heare,
              And breathe your Aire. [17]

The treatment of the poetic material here is reminiscent of poems like
Vaughan's "Regeneration": the slightest fragment of a verse of Scripture becomes a point of departure for an obscure, private meditation
comprising an elaborate embroidery of images, which are not only
enigmatic but virtually incoherent apart from their import as allegory.
As subsequent chapters show, Crashaw, like Beaumont and most of
his religious contemporaries, is quite fond of the traditional allegories
of the Song of Songs; but he generally ties scriptural reference to a
specific human experience or event—for example, the Assumption of
the Virgin or an incident from the life of Santa Teresa. Moreover, his
conceits and images, even at their most extravagant, rarely lose sight of
a concrete scene or action of some sort. [18] No poet was more familiar
with Crashaw's work than Joseph Beaumont, who may have edited
Steps to the Temple; [19] but for all the parallels of phrase and figure,
Beaumont is finally closer to Herbert and Vaughan in the tone and
structure of his poetry.

    In a fairly typical discussion of the subject, Earl Miner identifies
the "private mode" as the "chief 'radical' of metaphysical poetry." [20]
There are certainly grounds in Herbert's poetry for such a statement, and it seems still more germane to Donne, Vaughan, and,
in some respects, Marvell (not to mention Gerard Manley Hopkins).

The personal quality of such poetry suggests sincerity and genuine individual commitment; in addition, no matter how ingeniously witty, or anguished and impassioned, it may become, it retains an air of quiet restraint because of its personal intimacy, and because the poem is circumscribed by an immediate, individual situation. Since modern Anglo-American culture is more disposed to accept the expression of emotion in private circumstances, a poet will be more accessible to current readers insofar as his work partakes of this "private mode." The same critic adds as a second important characteristic of the Metaphysicals the rubric "dramatic" (a term which in the twentieth century is more evaluative than descriptive): "Again and again we are convinced that someone definite is speaking somewhere, sometime, to someone."[21]

Routinely judged by these same criteria, Crashaw inevitably emerges as a Metaphysical poet manqué: missing is the quiet but moving voice of Herbert's personal conversations with God, or the anguished cry of Donne, working out his salvation in fear and trembling. The speaker in Crashaw's poems is, in fact, almost always impersonal. True, the Nativity hymn is a dialogue (but with a "chorus"), and to that extent "dramatic," but Thyrsis and Tityrus are virtually interchangeable; and the same may be said of the three Kings in the Epiphany hymn. Crashaw's "sometime" is usually eternity, and his "somewhere" is constantly shifting, if located at all: although his poems generally evoke a more specific scene than Beaumont's, it is very often the transformation of that scene with which the poem deals. The whole purpose of the sequence of paradoxical conceits and lush images in the Nativity poem is to signify the metamorphosis of a shabby stable and dreary winter night in Bethlehem into the transcendent realm of God himself:

> WINTER chidde aloud; and sent
>   the angry North to wage his warres.
> The North forgott his feirce Intent;
>   And left perfumes in stead of scarres.
> By those sweet eyes' persuasive powrs
> Where he mean't frost, he scatter'd flowrs.

>   [ll. 24–29]

Similarly, the "Hymn to Sainte Teresa" moves from Avila during Teresa's childhood to her visionary experience as a nun, and finally to heaven; "To the Name of Jesus" occurs beyond the confines of space and time. When Crashaw addresses someone, Santa Teresa for example, it is almost always in the mode of apostrophe: there is no sense that he is expecting a reply. Even the apparent exceptions—his poems to the Countess of Denbigh, to Mrs. M. R., to "a gentlewoman"—in which individual women (at least one of them a historical personage) are urged to take up the religious life or to convert to Catholicism, do not so much as *suggest* a dialogue: the poet speaks in the authoritative voice of the Church in terms that apply to anyone of wavering faith or commitment. In short, although he deals with persons, Crashaw does not deal with specifically individual or private experience; and although he is often interested in a particular place, as in the Nativity and Epiphany hymns, he almost never defines a truly dramatic setting.

To treat Crashaw simply as a Metaphysical poet is to assume that he is imitating Donne and Herbert rather badly. But the fact is that Crashaw is doing something different from the other Metaphysicals, so different that it cannot be accounted for merely in terms of personal style and temperament. Crashaw's poetry is essentially public: the poet is a participant in a ritual, in a celebration of the Church.[22] If the personal note is foremost in Herbert, in Crashaw the essence is impersonality. He is interested in Teresa more as a saintly pattern for the faithful than as an individual: there is nothing "psychological" about his treatment of her raptures. Even the mysticism of the dark night of the soul is characteristically linked by Crashaw to a celebration of a Church feast in the Epiphany hymn. And it is no accident, in contrast again to Herbert and Donne, that so many of Crashaw's most memorable poems are written in honor of saints or feasts. As the "Divine Epigrams" follow the New Testament, so the great hymns or odes, which crown his career, seem to follow the Christian calendar. Crashaw writes what then might be called "sacred occasional verse," but since the "occasions" are not only renewed each year but indeed represent the transfiguration of time by the ingression of eternity, his poems escape the usual limitations of this sort of poetry. Crashaw's own poems, like the medieval hymns he translated, aspire to be, in spirit if not in fact, a part of the liturgy.

Plainly the difference between Crashaw and most other English devotional poets is not simply a matter of Marinist and neo-Latin

influence. Witty conceits and lush images are not the most important
or distinctive features of Crashaw's poetry; a contrasting popular element of humor, innocence, and childlike wonder pervades his work
and is explicitly indicated in the Nativity hymn:

> WELCOME, though not to those gay flyes.
> Guilded ith' Beames of earthly kings;
> Slippery soules in smiling eyes;
> But to poor Shepheards, home-spun things:
> Whose Wealth's their flock; whose witt, to be
> Well read in their simplicity.
>
> [ll. 91–96]

If this is not the accent of Herbert, neither is it the exotic sophistication associated with Marino. In any case, the Italianate style was
available in England before Crashaw (indeed, before Marino) began to
write. As A. Alvarez observes, "The elements of Crashaw's style are
there in Southwell and Giles Fletcher; he also has qualities in common
with Francis Quarles. Yet nobody worries about *them*."[23] In other
words, elaborate rhetorical artifice is not what sets Crashaw apart.
"There would be no difficulty with Crashaw's poetry," Alvarez quips,
"if it were not as good as it is."[24]

The fundamental incompatibility between Crashaw's tone and
purpose and the work of Marino and the neo-Latinists may be observed
in a progressive slackening of their influence in Crashaw's finest and
most mature poetry. Mario Praz's study of Crashaw and the notes in
the editions by George Williams and L. C. Martin cite numerous
parallels to and borrowings from Italian and continental Jesuit sources
in Crashaw's epigrams, "The Weeper," and many of the earlier
poems.[25] In addition there are translations of Marino, other Italians,
and various neo-Latinists. But when we turn to the sacred poems
identified by Martin as among Crashaw's last compositions, there is a
dramatic diminution in these analogues and, in fact, a dramatic
change in the character of the poetry:

The poems which were added to *Steps to the Temple* in 1648 show that, apart
from the continued preoccupations with "divine" subjects and the continued
and perhaps increased fostering of an exalted religious sense, Crashaw's style
was now developing away from the clearly apprehended imagery and precise
metrical forms of his earliest poetry towards a freer verse and more complex

metaphorical utterance, in which the images, as in Shakespeare's later style, seem to follow each other in quicker succession without always being clearly conceived or fully exploited.[26]

Crashaw's most astute critics have noticed this change in the character of his work and point out that it involves a growth beyond Marinism. Even Mario Praz, who was first to stress the Italian influence, gives certain indications that it is an inadequate explanation for many aspects of Crashaw's poetry. He praises the translation of *Sospetto d'Herode* at the expense of Marino's original, commends the naturalness of Crashaw's conceits in contrast to Marino's mechanical effects, and finally suggests that similarities between Crashaw and Marino are largely superficial:

It would be unfair to call Crashaw a Marinist just because he was trained to turn surprising *concetti* in Marino's school: Crashaw's poetry, in its more peculiar aspects, is the literary counterpart, though a minor one, to Rubens's apotheoses, Murillo's languors and El Greco's ecstasies.[27]

The extent of Marino's influence on Crashaw and other English writers is also questioned in a major study of the Italian poet. James V. Mirollo observes that, with few exceptions, "similarities of theme or imagery between Crashaw and Marino cannot be safely attributed to the direct influence of the Italian, who in many instances worked with the same materials in Latin and Italian poetry that Crashaw knew." According to Mirollo, Marino's general impact has often been exaggerated:

In truth, the elements of Marino's verse that appealed to Crashaw were available as early as the poetry of Robert Southwell, whose poem on Saint Peter (1595), translated out of Tansillo's *Lacrime di San Pietro* (1585), may be said to mark the arrival in England of the continental neo-Catholic style. . . . if the Marinesque style is to be identified exclusively with post-Tridentine poetry, then we should have to say that it all began before Marino wrote a word. In short, Crashaw was concerned with a minor part of Marino's output, with those elements of his style which are least original with him, hence the Italian's influence was important but not crucial.[28]

Crashaw, quite evidently, stands apart from the Metaphysical poets despite obvious affinities of theme and style, but at the same time his peculiarity cannot be accounted for and dismissed by merely referring it to the seductive influence of Marino and neo-Latin rhetoric. It has become commonplace to call Crashaw's poetry baroque, but very often this is a verbal evasion rather than an explanation. Douglas Bush, for example, calls Crashaw "the one conspicuous English incarnation of 'baroque sensibility,'" but he proceeds to close an unedifying circle by defining baroque poetry as "poetry like Crashaw's."[29] Various scholars have drawn illuminating parallels between Crashaw's verse and baroque music or plastic arts, or Counter-Reformation mystical or liturgical symbolism, but comparisons among the various arts are always vague and full of qualifications. This apparent impasse, which forces us to regard Crashaw's later poetry as sui generis and utterly remote, is the result of assuming that baroque literature was virtually all written in Italian or Latin and thus ignoring one of the most fertile sources of the European baroque movement: the Spanish *siglo de oro* or Golden Age. In the later sixteenth and earlier seventeenth centuries, baroque art, both visual and literary, was nowhere stronger than in Spain; and, of more importance, nowhere were the forces of the Counter Reformation stronger among poetic talents of the first order.[30] It is, then, to Spain that we must turn in seeking to provide a literary home for England's poetic outcast, in seeking to place Crashaw in context.

II

For a variety of reasons, the Spanish Golden Age provides not only a source of religious inspiration for Crashaw (most notably in Santa Teresa), but also a background, a literary frame of reference, which contributes to an apprehension of the full significance of Crashaw's poetry. Perhaps the readiest entry into this complex subject is by way of Ruth Wallerstein's comment on the overall character of Crashaw's later poems: "They relate Crashaw more deeply than do previous poems to the medieval tradition, and to that tradition as it was carried forward in the renewed religious impulse of the Counter Reformation, in such a life as Teresa's."[31] No one would contest the notion that the Counter Reformation, insofar as it modified and revitalized the medieval tradition, is a crucial factor in Crashaw's poetic, as well as spiritual, development; and in her reference to Santa Teresa, Wallerstein suggests the third component, Spain. Culturally, ecclesiastically, and politically, Castile was as much the dynamic center of the Counter Reformation as Rome. The armies of Phillip II fought the Protestant heretic in the north and the Moslem infidel in the south. A Spaniard, San Ignacio de Loyola, founded, in Spain, the spiritual army of the Counter Reformation, the Society of Jesus.[32] The characteristic saints of the period are predominantly Spanish, and the driving moral force at the Council of Trent was provided by Spanish theologians and ecclesiastics.[33] This preeminent role of Spain in the Counter Reformation is in large measure a result of its retention of what, as Wallerstein indicates, is a fundamental element of that movement: the medieval tradition. "The originality of the Spanish Golden Age, within the European Renaissance," says Dámaso Alonso, "consists in being a fusion of the medieval and the renaissance."[34]

Although Spain's importance as a center of political power and religious influence during this era is widely acknowledged, there is another aspect of the Golden Age which generally goes unrecognized among students of English literature: the sixteenth and seventeenth centuries witnessed in Spain a magnificent flourishing of lyric poetry. Dámaso Alonso maintains that only in England was a comparable lyric production to be found during this period.[35] The terms of this comparison must not escape notice: there is reason to believe that the relationship between the Spanish and English literature of the baroque age is far more significant than has usually been suspected, and that Crashaw's poetry is a plenary example of this relationship. (It is notable that the three painters to whom Crashaw is compared by Mario Praz were all subjects of the Spanish Crown.) That a possible influence of Spanish poetry has been neglected can be attributed to a general neglect of the Spanish language, literature, and culture in England and America. Scholars have long been aware of Crashaw's fascination with Santa Teresa, and translations of her works and those of her protegé, San Juan de la Cruz, have been available for many years, facilitating comparisons of their teachings with the content of Crashaw's poems. Translations of the Spanish poetry of the period, however, are few in number and not well known; they also suffer from the basic impossibility of effectively rendering lyric poetry in another language—especially for the purpose of a critical examination of imagery, versification, and tone. Such difficulties are a likely cause for the

neglect of the interesting parallels between Crashaw's poetry and that
of San Juan, the only Spanish poet of the Golden Age to have been
frequently translated in recent years.

It is especially unfortunate that the literary importance of the
Spanish mystics is not commonly known among critics of English
literature. Not only did Santa Teresa and San Juan de la Cruz both
write verse (the latter has left a small body of poetry of the highest
order), but the surge of mysticism and ascetic piety, of which they
were the culminating figures, had a substantial impact on succeeding
generations of Spanish poets. The beatification of Teresa, for example, inspired scores of poems, and her life furnished a model for a
poetry of ecstatic devotion. The influence of the Spanish mystical
writers on Crashaw can thus be understood best in the light of the
literature of the siglo de oro as a whole. This approach provides for the
comparison of Crashaw's poems to those of other poets who were
directly influenced by the mystics, and who lived and wrote in the
same milieu: the establishment of such a literary context, at the very
least, acts as a check on needlessly obscure, hieratic readings of
Crashaw (see n. 2, this chapter); and, of more moment, offers a firmer
basis than has been previously available for interpreting and appreciat-
ing his work.

A question immediately arises regarding Crashaw's knowledge of
Spanish and the availability of the pertinent texts. With respect to the
former, the evidence is small but there is no reason to doubt it. Who-
ever wrote the preface for *Steps to the Temple* (1646, 1648) tells us that
Crashaw knew Spanish (*Complete Poetry*, p. 651), and the poet himself seems to imply that he had read the works of Santa Teresa in the
original language in "An Apologie for the Fore-Going Hymne":

> What soul so e'er, in any language, can
> Speak heav'n like her's is my souls country-man.
> O 'tis not spanish, but 'tis heav'n she speaks!
>
> [ll. 21–23]

Spanish does not seem to have been an uncommon acquirement among
Englishmen of the seventeenth century. Edward M. Wilson has called
attention to various editions of Spanish poetry left to the Emmanuel
College library by Archbishop Sancroft, including an edition of Lope
de Vega's *Rimas sacras*. Some of these volumes include marginalia in

the archbishop's own hand. Likewise, there were Spanish books in the library of Bishop Ken; and William Drummond, Richard Fanshawe, Thomas Ayres, and Thomas Stanley all translated or imitated Spanish poetry. "John Donne, George Herbert, and Richard Crashaw," adds Wilson, ". . . almost certainly knew and read Spanish."[36] James V. Mirollo has presented evidence that George Herbert's brother Edward, Lord Herbert of Cherbury, was also familiar with the poetry of Lope de Vega.[37] Crashaw's travels carried him into areas where he would have had little difficulty developing any nascent interest in Spanish: parts of the Netherlands and Italy were or had been under Spanish control, and Spanish was evidently a common second language in France. The remark by Cervantes, that "In France neither man nor woman fails to learn the Castilian tongue," is doubtless an exaggeration; nevertheless, the French, especially after the marriage of Louis XIII to the Spanish-born Anne of Austria in 1615, were widely familiar with the Spanish language.[38] Finally, Kenneth J. Larsen has discovered that all the entries in Crashaw's bank account during his stay at the English College in Rome were either in English sterling or in Spanish pistoles, "which might," he adds parenthetically, "suggest a visit during his travels to the Spain of his 'Admirable Sainte Teresa.'"[39]

Obviously the preceding remarks, presented to support the assumption that Crashaw could read Spanish, indicate a fortiori the availability of Spanish books. The evidence accumulated by Wilson shows that they were obtainable in England, but even this is not a crucial point. Crashaw left England, probably late in 1643, because of the growing power of the puritan revolutionaries. The sole extant piece of English prose from his hand—indeed, our only Crashaw autograph—is a letter from Leiden dated February 1644, and he turns up again in Paris in 1645. Austin Warren supposes that Crashaw returned to England between these two dates, but this is only speculation: he could have been wandering about the continent during the entire period.[40] In any case, the availability of Spanish books would have presented no problem in the Netherlands and in France. Editions of Teresa's works in the original language were published in Antwerp in 1630 and 1649. The first complete Spanish edition of the works of San Juan de la Cruz appeared in Brussels in 1627, and Lope de Vega's *Pastores de Belén* ("Shepherds of Bethlehem") was printed in Brussels in 1614 and in Rouen in 1616. The availability of Spanish works in France is also attested by Corneille's *Le Cid* (1636), Rotrou's *St. Genest* (1646), and Moliere's *Dom Juan* (1665), all based on Spanish plays by Guillén da Castro, Lope de Vega, and Tirso de Molina respectively.[41] Perhaps even more important was the impact of Spanish mystical writing and devotional practice on the religious life of France. Of special significance were Santa Teresa and the reformed Carmelite order, whose influence is manifest in the founding of thirty-eight reformed convents in France between 1610 and 1630.[42]

The period when Crashaw began his travels into areas where Spanish books were readily available, where the influence of Spanish devotional practice and Spanish culture generally had made an even deeper impression than in England, seems to have coincided with the composition of the poems in which he moves away from the style of Marinism and the neo-Latin poets.[43] But it is unlikely that the coincidence *is* mere coincidence. An estimate of the impact of Spanish literature on the change that comes over Crashaw's style in his last years demands a reconsideration of the nature of literary influence, of the relation between the individual poem and literary tradition and convention, between the individual poet and his cultural background.

III

Wellek and Warren issue a stern warning to the scholar who would seek to establish relationships of influence and parallel between specific works of literature:

Parallel hunting has been widely discredited recently: especially when attempted by an inexperienced student, it runs into obvious dangers. First of all, parallels must be real parallels, not vague similarities assumed to turn, by mere multiplication, into proof. Forty noughts still make nought. Furthermore, parallels must be exclusive parallels; that is, there must be a reasonable certainty that they cannot be explained by a common source, a certainty attainable only if the investigator has a wide knowledge of literature or if the parallel is a highly intricate pattern rather than an isolated "motif" or word.[44]

Having asserted this point, however, they then concede the value of the method: "The relationships between two or more works of literature can be discussed profitably only when we see them in their proper place within the scheme of literary development. Relationships between works of art present a critical problem of comparing two wholes, two configurations not to be broken into isolated components except for preliminary study."[45] It is precisely from a failure to heed this last injunction that Crashaw's reputation has suffered. Because it is not difficult to locate extravagant conceits in Crashaw, and because there are such conceits in Marino, it has been all too easy to dismiss the English poet as Italianate without ever considering the poetic design which his conceits—and all the other aspects of his poetry—serve. In the light of such observations, it is hardly to the purpose to demonstrate that a given phrase or figure or image in a poem by Crashaw comes not from Marino but rather from, say, Góngora, even if this should prove often enough to be true.

But there is more to literary comparisons than merely showing that a poem by author X derives certain elements from a poem by author Y: "When the comparison is really focused on two totalities, we shall be able to come to conclusions on a fundamental problem of literary history, that of originality."[46] Paradoxically, it is only by setting Crashaw in a literary context, into a sympathetic tradition, that his originality may be perceived. If Crashaw is "foreign" when viewed in terms of the English devotional tradition, then—to keep to the metaphor—it is necessary to find his literary homeland. To call him "European" or "continental" ultimately will not suffice, because these terms are vague where precision is required. They force one to fall back on scattered parallels to Crashaw's conceits, images, classical allusions, and so forth, which of course may be found in England. What really is needed is a group of works which evince similar patterns of outlook and tone, which employ details of style in creating similar literary worlds. To be sure, the aim of placing a poet in a given literary tradition is not to judge his work simply according to the extent of his conformity or rebellion, but rather to see more clearly what he is doing. Without the background of English Petrarchism, it would be very difficult to grasp—still more to evaluate—the following lines from Donne's "Canonization":

> Alas, alas, who's injur'd by my love?
>   What merchants ships have my sighs drown'd?
> Who saies my teares have overflow'd his ground?
>   When did my colds a forward spring remove?
>   When did the heats which my veines fill
>   Adde one more to the plaguie Bill?[47]

By the same token our awareness both of the first sonnet of *Astrophil and Stella* and of the complex style of Donne's *Divine Poems* (even without assuming that the latter is a specific object of reproof) adds immeasurably to our response to Herbert's "Jordan" (II):

> When first my lines of heav'nly joys made mention,
> Such was their lustre, they did so excell,
> That I sought out quaint words, and trim invention;
> My thoughts began to burnish, sprout, and swell,
> Curling with metaphors a plain intention,
> Decking the sense as if it were to sell.[48]

Likewise, a knowledge of *The Temple* in reading Vaughan is even more important, because, for all his undeniable originality, Vaughan's echoes of Herbert are constant and crucial.

If, in these three examples, the obvious is belabored, it is precisely because the traditional relationships they illustrate are so widely recognized, so obvious; and because this set of relationships breaks down with Crashaw. For him the Metaphysical background has proven inadequate, and the assumption that he was trying to write like Donne has elicited no small number of irrelevant commentaries: "It is doubtful whether a poet in whom the senses and the emotions were so much more active than the intellect, was well-served by the metaphysical style."[49] It is in order to find for Crashaw a more congenial literary context that we turn to Spain. In terms of historical fact, he spent the last years of his life in exile; but, if we take his flight from England symbolically, he was going home. Crashaw reacted, in a far more fundamental way than the Anglicans associated with Archbishop Laud or the Little Gidding community, against the liturgy, theology, and general devotional temper of what the Puritans conceived as the ongoing Reformation.[50] And although historical circumstance took him to Italy, what he was seeking was the heart of the Counter Reformation, and that was in Spain.

It was, moreover, in Spain that the Counter Reformation enjoyed its most outstanding literary success, and it is a literary background— this cannot be too strongly emphasized—which is necessary for an adequate critical appraisal of Crashaw's poetry. It is quite possible that Crashaw read, absorbed, and even imitated some of the Spanish works adduced in this study for comparison (besides those of Santa Teresa, whose direct influence is undeniable); in some instances the probability seems very high. But this aspect is not of primary importance. Although there is an intrinsic interest in establishing immediate literary relationships, it is very difficult to reach assured conclusions of this kind without substantial external evidence. In Crashaw's case, external evidence of any sort is rather sketchy; critical value lies not in demonstrating particular one-to-one relations but in defining a literary milieu. Such a procedure cannot determine critical standards nor replace the direct confrontation of the poems themselves, but it can prepare us as readers by enabling us to perceive more exactly the character of the work we are dealing with. Hence the examination of detailed parallels between Crashaw's poems and a variety of Spanish works in the chapters which follow are ordered to one purpose: to place the English poet in the context of the Spanish Golden Age insofar as the latter is the consummate literary expression of the Counter Reformation. Only through such a comparative examination will the essential nature, and thus the intrinsic value, of Crashaw's poems emerge.

2

Crashaw and Sacred Parody: Human Love *a lo divino*

*A*LEADING SOURCE OF MISUNDERSTANDING in the poetry of Richard Crashaw is the crucial role of sacred parody in almost all of his mature devotional pieces. Indeed, without a minimum awareness of this technique no wholly adequate assessment of his work is possible. A factor in his religious poetry from the first in *Epigrammata Sacrorum Liber* (1634), sacred parody is pervasive in the late hymns which are the focus of the present study, and it endows them with a sensuousness unique in English devotional poetry. Bruce W. Wardropper has demonstrated that sacred parody is virtually as old as Christendom itself, and that it has flourished throughout Western Europe and America.[1] The greatest outpouring of such poetry—its broadest, most varied, and most intense development—occurred during the siglo de oro in Spain, and it was in this country, toward the end of the sixteenth and in the early decades of the seventeenth centuries, that sacred parody became a vehicle for consistent literary excellence.[2] Probably this phenomenon may be attributed to the convergence of two powerful forces: the expansion of Iberian literary culture under the impact of the Italian Renaissance and the fervid devotion, somewhat medieval in character, of the Counter Reformation. In any event, Crashaw's particular style of sacred parody finds its only real parallel in Golden Age Spanish literature.

Sacred parody may assume a variety of appearances, but in its simplest form, termed "divinization of texts" by Dámaso Alonso,[3] it requires the alteration of just enough of a work of literature to change its overall significance from secular to sacred. An early example may be found in the Middle English of *The Harley Lyrics:* editor G. L. Brook maintains that "The Way of Christ's Love" is just such a reworking of "The Way of Woman's Love."[4] Throughout the Middle Ages and the Renaissance, the procedure was widespread, with members of the lower clergy, monks, and friars (especially the Franciscans—"God's minstrels") assuming the major burden of the work.[5] Although popular, anonymous love songs were the usual source of material for the sacred parodists, during the sixteenth century more cultivated and literary poets were also rewritten with the intention of adapting their profane charms to the service of religion. The poet most frequently subject to divinization was Petrarch. The rewriting of his entire opus was first and most successfully undertaken in 1536 with *Il Petrarcha spirituale* by a Franciscan monk, Gerolamo Malipiero. In Spain one of Petrarch's sonnets (*Rime* 298) was converted a lo divino by both Lope de Vega and Fray Luis de León, though probably indirectly through Garcilaso de la Vega's secular imitation. Lope also wrote a monumental poem, *Triunfos divinos,* which is a straightforward divine imitation of Petrarch's *I Trionfi.* Likewise in Spain, the complete poetic works of that country's first two masters of Italian Renaissance style were rewritten a lo divino by Sebastián de Córdoba in *Las obras de Boscán y Garcilaso trasladadas en materias Christianas y religiosas* . . . (1575).[6] This last work serves to exemplify the influential vogue of sacred parody in the siglo de oro;[7] although it is of small literary value in itself, Córdoba's work apparently served, in some measure, as an inspiration for the poetic achievement of San Juan de la Cruz (1542–91).

To San Juan belongs the distinction of having produced truly first-rate poems by parodying, simply and directly, secular verse. As a rule the straightforward divinization of texts, as might be anticipated, results in mediocre poetry, but Dámaso Alonso has shown that the great mystical poet adapted at least two of his most moving sacred poems, "Tras de un amoroso lance" ("After an amorous cast") and "Un pastorcico" ("A little shepherd"), from rather nondescript anonymous love songs.[8]

The heart of San Juan's work, however, lies in a more subtle and sophisticated realm; hence a realm of sacred parody which has more literary import: the "divinization of themes." Largely because of the

research of Alonso, the profound influence on San Juan of the poetry of
Garcilaso de la Vega and of Garcilaso's parodist, Sebastián de Córdoba,
is now generally recognized.[9] Apparently the saint was inspired by
Sebastián's sacred parody, which awakened memories of a youthful
acquaintance with Garcilaso's own verse, to create the haunting pastoral landscapes of his most exquisite mystical poems, especially *Noche
oscura* ("Dark night") and *Cántico espiritual* ("Spiritual canticle"). But
despite important parallels in imagery, phrasing, and tone, San Juan's
poetry is by no means simply a parody or imitation of Garcilaso after
the fashion of Sebastián de Córdoba. It is probably too much even to
call Garcilaso his model; this title belongs rather to the Song of Songs.
What San Juan has gained from his acquaintance with his secular
counterpart is a field of images and motifs, a high artistic finish, a
general atmosphere of intense beauty, and—above all—a resonance
generated by the mere fact of the profane associations of the poetic
conventions he uses. In short, this divinization of themes is not a
matter of mere borrowing, but rather of challenging the erotic poetry
of the day and thereby drawing deliberately on the spiritual tension of
his contemporaries.

   In San Juan de la Cruz, then, the significance of even the most
mediocre of the sacred parodists becomes manifest: these pious ver-
sifiers, uninspired as most of them usually were, fed the hunger of a
people caught up in the renewed devotional surge of the Counter
Reformation yet still attracted by the artistic flowering of the Renaissance. Nowhere was the tension between sacred and profane, between
ascetic and sensual, so acute as in Spain; hence it is not surprising that
Spain was the most fertile ground for sacred parody, and that in Spain
this literary fashion culminated in a number of fine poetic works. Fray
Luis de León (1527–91) wrote many odes in which the form and mood
of Horace's verse are captured for Christianity;[10] he and San Juan are
followed by Luis de Góngora y Argote (1561–1627) and Lope Félix de
Vega Carpio (1562–1635), to mention only the most distinguished
writers, who adapt the genuinely rustic pastoralism of Spain's traditional popular poetry, as well as the Petrarchan love lyric, to sacred
ends. Góngora and especially Lope are remarkable in that they employ
both the simple divinization of texts and the more subtle divinization
of themes in creating a devotional literature marked by a constant
interplay of religious and secular motifs.

In time the element of sacred parody began to play an important role in English literature. As Louis Martz observes, the return of Robert Southwell after years of exile on the continent, where he was educated as a Jesuit missionary, appears to be a turning point for English poetry: "first came Robert Southwell, seeking to reform English poetry by bringing to it certain arts that he had found flourishing on the Continent: the practice of religious meditation, and *the conversion of the methods of profane poetry to the service of God*" (emphasis added).[11] Southwell's preliminary, often shaky steps were to be succeeded by the fine devotional poetry of Donne and Herbert, whose "conversion of the methods of profane poetry" is precisely what Alonso calls divinization of themes. Bruce Wardropper suggests that this is the constant method of Herbert's *The Temple,* and that Donne's poetry "strikes a balance on the edge of a knife between the sacred and the profane. In the poetry of Donne there is a complete interpenetration of secular and religious images."[12] Evidently Wardropper has in mind such things in Donne as the religious conceits in "The Canonization" and the erotic metaphor which closes the holy sonnet, "Batter my heart." The elements of sacred parody in Donne's divine poems, however, are generally used in discrete passages for startling effects, and in Herbert the suggestion of profane motifs, though constant, tends to be subdued, producing a quietly ironic undertone. It is in the work of Richard Crashaw that English poetry finds its most pervasive, insistent, and unblushing use of sacred parody; in this Crashaw reflects the mood and style and, quite probably, the influence of Spain.[13] He pushes the parallels between the rapture of divine love and human erotic experience further than any other English poet, in striking similarity to San Juan de la Cruz and Lope de Vega. In addition there is an ingenuous gaiety in the tone of his devotional poetry (an aspect of it not generally noticed) that resembles nothing so much as the traditional, popular features of the religious verse of San Juan, Lope, and Góngora.

II

The importance of considering the pervasive element of sacred parody in Crashaw's poetry cannot be overemphasized: no other feature of his work poses such an obstacle for appreciation and com-

prehension. Some modern critics, like Crashaw's contemporary puritan antagonists, are offended by elaborate forms of worship which
appeal to the senses; moreover, it would seem that the typically
modern and typically Protestant sensibilities share a distaste for an
emphasis on the details of the Passion, especially if, as in Crashaw's
verse, the sexual implications of passion are played off against the
sufferings of Christ through the techniques of sacred parody. Hence,
among Joan Bennett's *Five Metaphysical Poets,* Crashaw is the only one
who receives a largely unsympathetic treatment. One senses a palpable
Freudian shudder in the following comment:

> Crashaw loves to elaborate sensations. Moreover, his sensations are peculiar
> and sometimes repellent. The collocation of torture and erotic emotion . . . oc-
> curs repeatedly in Crashaw's poetry from first to last. There can be no doubt
> that the conjunction of physical torture with sensual love was to him pleasura-
> ble and inevitable . . . [14]

Happily, this is a decidedly inaccurate account of the poetry; in fact it
is really an account of the critic's distaste for the personality of the
poet (or what she believes to be his personality) in which the poems are
merely pseudo-clinical evidence in a case study of repressed and sublimated masochism. In the first place, "On the wounds of our
crucified Lord," which is adduced to support the generalization quoted
above, does not "elaborate sensations" ("peculiar" or otherwise). The
figurative language moves as rapidly as possible away from the concrete, physical world of the senses: in the space of twenty lines the
wounds in Christ's feet are turned into mouths that may kiss, then
into roses, and finally into "blood-shot eyes" that "weep" rubies. To be
sure, Crashaw employs sensual images, but hardly in the furtive manner of the sexual neurotic; the imagery is rather the stuff of a fantastic
metamorphosis, expressing devout wonder before the mystery of the
sacrifice of the incarnate God. The poet consciously and deliberately
raises the erotic implications of the wounds, like mouths, repaying the
Magdalene's kisses, in order to show how the sinful woman's physical
love is transmuted into a different realm of being through contrition,
where the marks of human grief become "pearls," and the marks of
human suffering, "rubies."

    Such is the constant purpose of sacred parody: it is a literary
technique for dramatizing the tension between sacred and profane

inherent in the paradox of the Incarnation. But in our era there is a constant temptation to engage in a diagnosis of the putative condition of the poet's psyche rather than in an examination of the poem, and it is Crashaw's fate to suffer such handling even among apparently sympathetic critics. Robert M. Adams, for example, contends that Bennett's opinion is, in effect, right: Crashaw's poetry is repellent—a seething kettle of latent sexual perversion. But this, he argues, is its purpose. A characteristic sample of his reading is the following comment on Crashaw's epigram on Luke 11:27, "Blessed be the paps which thou hast sucked":

> The Poet here comes close to a direct statement that the Incarnation was a revolting joke on Jesus and Mary; incest, perversion, cannibalism, and the extra incongruity of "tabled at thy Teates" make the quatrain a little gem of encrusted grotesquerie. [15]

To be sure, the epigram is a rather poor one: clarity, the characteristic feature of a "gem," is precisely what it lacks; but it does not at all come close to anything which would faintly justify the construction Adams imposes upon it. His interpretation rests on the assumption that it is really the expression of sublimated sexual impulses; in other words, poor Crashaw, assuming naively that he is writing religious verse, is merely giving vent to assorted repressions and neuroses. But in fact there is no evidence that Crashaw was unaware of the erotic suggestion of his imagery and included it accidentally. Anyone not hopelessly adrift on the dreary sea of amateur psychology ought to notice that the epigram explicitly develops a contrast between the comparatively weak and harmless passion of the mother in nursing and the pierced side of Christ's Passion which feeds the whole world with the blood of the Eucharist:

> Suppose he had been Tabled at thy Teates,
> Thy hunger feels not what he eates:
> Hee'l have his Teat e're long (a bloody one)
> The Mother then must suck the Son.

The grotesque wit of "Tabled at thy Teates" and the overt sensuality of the mother sucking the Son are a deliberate and pointed means of stressing the radical and shocking transformation of every aspect of day-to-day life by the fact of the Incarnation. Among other things,

these lines assert in the harshest possible terms the scandalous origin
of the Eucharist and the startling nature of taking communion—that
is, the relation established between man and Christ. The use of the
witty conceit and the sensuous image is not here altogether successful
in artistic terms, but we have no grounds for assuming that the "in-
congruity" proceeds from the poet's deviancy, or from anything more
disturbing than a temporary lapse of skill.[16] Indeed, a principal purpose of this study is to show how an acquaintance with Spanish literature furnished Crashaw with more effective models for devotional
expression in his later poetry.

Objections to the effects of sacred parody in Crashaw's verse may,
of course, emerge from an altogether different critical viewpoint. In
his last book, the late Yvor Winters numbers Crashaw among the
corrupters of English verse. An essential element in Winters's critique
is his rejection of Crashaw's divinization of profane love in order to
portray mystical love:

Crashaw is, first of all, fascinated with the mystical experience, or at least
with the theory of it. This experience, the mystics tell us, is supra-rational, is
intuitive in the theological sense of the term, and is essentially unrelated to
human experience; and since human language is the tool of discursive reason
and functions in time rather than in eternity, the mystical experience cannot
really be discussed. Its nature can be suggested by analogies with human
experience, and the analogical experiences can be described. In the older
Christian tradition, the common analogy is that of sexual union. . . . I cannot
see any way to defend poetry which purports to deal with the mystical experience in itself, for by definition one cannot deal with the experience and the
poetry is bound to be fraudulent. . . . the poet who insists on dealing with the
mystical experience and who becomes involved emotionally in the sexual analogy runs the risk of corrupting his devotional poetry generally with sexual
imagery. It is not that the sexual experience is "immoral"; but it is irrelevant
to the religious experience, and, in so far as it is introduced into the religious
experience, can result in nothing but confusion.[17]

This is hardly the proper context for a thorough critique of Winters's
theory of language, or of the epistemology implicit in this passage. We
can, however, examine his comments about mysticism per se and its
relation to poetry. First, although mystics would agree that their experience is "supra-rational," it is doubtful that any Christian
mystic—and certainly none who influenced Crashaw—would concede

that it is "essentially unrelated to human experience"; quite to the contrary, they would insist that it is the ultimate fulfillment of the human potential for experience.[18] And such a claim is supported by the central tradition of Christian theology; the quest for mystical union with God is simply an attempt to realize fully the Augustinian concept of charity:

This is the divinely instituted rule of love: "Thou shalt love thy neighbor as thyself," He said, and "Thou shalt love God with thy whole heart, and with thy whole soul, and with thy whole mind." Thus all your thoughts and all your understanding should be turned toward Him from whom you receive these powers. For when He said, "With thy whole heart, and with thy whole soul, and with thy whole mind," He did not leave any part of life which should be free and find itself room to desire the enjoyment of anything else. But whatever else appeals to the mind as being lovable should be directed into that channel into which the whole current of love flows.[19]

Mysticism, then, is the intensification of Christian love for God, differing in degree and in means, rather than in essence, from the ordinary Christian's experience. Furthermore, St. Augustine gives explicit approval to the expression of sacred ideas and feelings in human terms:

If what I said were ineffable, it would not be said. And for this reason God should not be said to be ineffable, for when this is said, something is said. And a contradiction in terms is created, since if that is ineffable which cannot be spoken, then that is not ineffable which can be called ineffable. This contradiction is to be passed over in silence rather than resolved verbally. For God, although nothing worthy may be spoken of Him, has accepted the tribute of the human voice and wished us to take joy in praising Him with our words. In this way He is called *Deus*. Although He is not recognized in the noise of those two syllables, all those who know the Latin language, when this sound reaches their ears, are moved to think of a certain most excellent immortal nature.[20]

This passage from St. Augustine is the *reductio ad absurdum* of Winters's contention that mystical experience is by definition beyond the range of human reason and hence also of poetry. According to this line of thinking, as Augustine indicates, *all* religious poetry would be equally prohibited. Of course religious poetry is not about God in his essence, but about man's experience of God. Mystical experience is

especially intimate and intense and, according to mystical doctors,
engages spiritual faculties which ordinarily remain dormant; but it is
not for all that "unrelated to human experience." After all, it is a
human being who undergoes the experience in question.

Equally untenable is Winters's assertion of the irrelevance of
sexual imagery to religious experience. His critique is founded upon a
curious view of the mind as compartmentalized and assumes that
experiences are necessarily discrete: "If it [the mystical experience] is
real, it is quite as distinct from sexual union as from any other experience."[21] But such a stricture cannot logically be confined to mysticism: metaphor must be entirely eliminated from poetry. Clearly
Burns's "love" is quite as distinct from a "red, red rose" as from, say, a
turnip; but here the mind rebels. As C. S. Lewis observes, "the *Romance of the Rose* could not, without loss, be rewritten as the *Romance
of the Onion*."[22] Obviously distinctions among various categories of
experience are neither absolute nor uniform: a given state of mind may
be profitably compared with one thing, but not with another. As for
the specific analogy between sexual and mystical union, perhaps the
wisest course is to honor "the older Christian tradition" which Winters so casually dismisses. It is hard to think of a better analogy for
mystical union than erotic union, provided, that is, a willingness to
accept the principle of analogy at all. Freudians would crush all
distinctions—mysticism, poetry, science, and everything else are really sublimated sexual drives; Winters, their polar opposite, would
erect all distinctions into ironclad barriers. Neither position is helpful
in dealing with a poet who works in the Christian tradition, which
adds to the ancient classical tradition of universal harmony and the
great chain of being, the dogma of the Incarnation.

There is a final objection which, although its formulation does
not touch on Crashaw, must be met, because it centers on sacred
parody as such; moreover, the argument employed suggests that the
objection grows out of a misunderstanding—or at least a severely limited view—of the nature of sacred parody. Rosemond Tuve, in a long
article on Herbert's "A Parodie," attempts to show that this poem is
not a sacred parody, as suggested by F. E. Hutchinson, Louis Martz,
and others, nor in fact a *literary* parody at all; but instead that it is a
musical parody, with virtually no semantic relationship to the secular
poem, "Soul's Joy," which has merely furnished the musical setting for

the new devotional poem. Tuve's technical argument relating to Renaissance music is not germane to the present discussion; likewise, the
specific status of "A Parodie" and the meaning of its title are of little
immediate concern. Her argument that Herbert generally avoids sacred parody because it is poetically crude and theologically and morally
narrow is of greater moment.

Tuve first points out that, contrary to Martz's notion, sacred
parody did not originate in continental Counter Reformation circles
toward the end of the sixteenth century, but rather among the reformers associated with both Calvin and Luther. Moreover, these parodies
are simple, straightforward "substitutions" which are intended to
"displace" secular poetry completely. Finally, "convinced 'sacred
parodists' anxious about the substitution of the sacred . . . have either
reformers' aims or else the narrowly moral fervor of puritanical piety,
Catholic or Protestant. Herbert's religious verse smacks of neither."
For these reasons it would diminish the reputation of Herbert—and
presumably that of any other poet—to attribute the use of sacred
parody to him:

Surely it somehow lessens Herbert as a poet to conceive of him as narrowly
anxious to convert whatever hinted at the power and interest of love between
human beings to pious uses. If this be true, it has very real connections with
his theology, particularly with his conception of the definition of the love of
God, the center of a Christian life as of a Christian theology. Such interpretations do not seem to me to square with the rest of his poetry, nor with his
notably sane and balanced understanding of the close relation between
heavenly love and all the many kinds of human love which he dealt with,
knew, and apparently wove into a life distinguished for its practice of loving-
kindness. [23]

Now sacred parody, as the first part of this chapter has shown, no
more began with the Reformation than with the Counter Reformation:
it began in the earliest Christian centuries. The point of Martz's
observation regarding Southwell and the Counter Reformation is that
a new kind of sacred parody was emerging which, intimately con-
nected with formal meditation, emphasized the interpenetration of
flesh and spirit, of the senses and the intellect. Tuve seems mes-
merized by the associations of the word "parody," which in the Renaissance as well as in our own time usually implies mockery or burlesque;
but the term "sacred parody" is simply a rather awkward modern term

for a literary phenomenon which seems to have lacked an English designation in the sixteenth and seventeenth centuries. In Spain the term *poesía a lo divino* implies neither ridicule nor absolute disapproval of the converted secular sources. San Juan de la Cruz, for example, was neither missionary nor moralist in Tuve's limited sense—he dwelt in a far more sublime range; and Lope de Vega, an altogether different sort of man (to say the least), was equally adept as a poet both of secular and sacred love and converted a number of his own love lyrics a lo divino. No one acquainted with siglo de oro poetry could see sacred parody merely as an outgrowth of the "narrowly moral fervor of puritanical piety." The study of contemporary Spanish poetry for this reason alone offers an enriched understanding of English poetry of the later Renaissance. Finally, there is the matter of Tuve's crudely biographical interpretation of the concept of poetic tension. She automatically assumes that any interest (on the part of poet or critic) in the tension generated by the juxtaposition of sacred and profane love is necessarily a psychological interest, and towards the end of the essay the tension has been simply equated with a personal, self-conscious anxiety on the part of the poet.[24] It will be the principal business of the remainder of this chapter to show, by adverting to the rich a lo divino tradition of Golden Age Spain, that sacred parody in the hands of a skilled poet—specifically in the work of Richard Crashaw— indicates a far more subtle and complex poetic vision than most commentaries in English would indicate.

III

It will be helpful, if somewhat perverse, to begin with a poem in which Crashaw is not altogether successful with the technique of sacred parody, in which the secular poetic conventions and images do not altogether mesh with the devotional purport; that is, sacred and profane love remain polarized, rather in the manner assumed by Winters and Tuve to be inevitable, rather than unified in a single poetic effect. "Ode on a Prayer-book," one of Crashaw's most explicit attempts to treat the intimate relation between God and the soul in the manner of secular love poetry, is, in my judgment, a rather interesting failure, although it has been extravagantly praised as "an expression of mystical experience" superior not only to Crashaw's later poems on

Santa Teresa, but even to the writings of the saint herself in some respects.[25] But in fact the poem strays away from Santa Teresa's concept of mystical union in ways which damage it, because the proper relation between profane and sacred elements is not maintained. Its method is to convert in toto the situation of secular love poetry into a devotional situation: God is simply substituted for a human lover. The danger here is not that the poetry will be too sensual or erotic, but that the tone of the poetry will be self-consciously fastidious, and its theology will be no more than a simple dualistic opposition between body and soul.

This problem is painfully apparent in the following passage from "Ode on a Prayer-book," in which the divine Spouse is depicted merely as a rival among earthly lovers:

> But if the noble BRIDE GROOM, when he come
> Shall find the loytering HEART from home;
>   Leaving her chast aboad
>   To gadde abroad
> Among the gay mates of the god of flyes. . . .
>
> Doubtlesse some other heart
>   Will get the start
> Mean while, and stepping in before
> Will take possession of the sacred store. . . .
>
> [ll. 47–51, 61–64]

This conception of mystical love, involving the notion that the devout soul must forswear earthly lovers (or earthly affections in general) and desire only God, may be matched among the Spanish mystics of the sixteenth century, complete with erotic and courtly motifs, as in these lines by Santa Teresa:

> Hirióme con una flecha
> Enherbolada de amor
> Y mi alma quedó hecha
> Una con su Criador;
> Ya yo no quiero otro amor,
> Pues a mi Dios me he entregado.[26]

[He wounded me with an arrow / Anointed with love / And my soul was left / As one with its Creator; / Now I want no other love / Since to my God I have given myself.]

The idea that the soul must remain pure, giving itself only to God, is likewise found in the *Noche oscura* of San Juan de la Cruz, where the divine Spouse sleeps "on my flowering breast, which I kept whole only for Him."[27] Throughout Lope de Vega's *Soliloquios amorosos de un alma a Dios* ("Amorous soliloquies of a soul to God"), the poet laments precisely the sin about which Mrs. M. R. is admonished by Crashaw: "¡Qué de veces os negué/por confesar mi locura/a la fingida hermosura!" ("What of the times I denied you by confessing my madness for a feigned beauty").[28] There are, however, serious discrepancies between these passages and the poem by Crashaw. Apart from any knowledge of Lope's own erratic life, it is clear in context that his poem is penitential: a man who has pursued "feigned beauty" promiscuously and adulterously is turning back to God with dust and ashes on his head. In the poems by the two Carmelite mystics, there is no literal comparison of secular and divine love; in their situation as cloistered contemplatives, they are swept away in the latter. The implied references to sexual love are a means of suggesting how the human faculty for love is transformed and intensified by the power of grace. Neither of these situations obtains, however, in Crashaw's address to Mrs. M. R.; she appears to be neither a grave sinner nor a religious ecstatic. Hence the figurative language of the poem is not really appropriate to the situation it treats; it seems to imply that different souls are in competition for God's favors, which evidently are assumed to be in short supply. This is not only unsound theology, but also a serious artistic flaw in Crashaw's ode. The circumstances of a secular love poem are evoked too literally; God is, in effect, represented as being on the same plane of existence as potential human lovers, equally finite and equally fickle. The divine love affair is localized to the extent that the erotic elements are in no way transformed by or subsumed in the divine theme of the poem, but rather jostle against it incongruously. The fault, then, is not the inclusion of amorous motifs, but the failure to control them.[29]

Crashaw's attempts to establish an interaction between sacred and profane in "Ode on a Prayer-book" are, compared with San Juan and Teresa, crude; the poem's greatest successes come in passages of purely sensuous evocation of rapture:

> Words which are not heard with EARES
> (Those tumultuous shops of noise)

Effectual wispers, whose still voice
The soul it selfe more feeles then heares;

Amorous languishments; luminous trances;
SIGHTS which are not seen with eyes;
Spiritual and soul-piercing glances
Whose pure and subtil lightning flyes
Home to the heart, and setts the house on fire
And melts it down in sweet desire.

[ll. 65–74]

The effect of breathlessness which is attained in this rapid accumula-
tion of "hidden sweets and holy joyes" is rather impressive; the alliteration and general preponderance of liquid and sibilant sounds produces a
chanting, hypnotic quality. Such a description of ecstasy is very much in
the manner of the mystical writing of Spain. Crashaw's list of "joyes" is
reminiscent of a list of *favores* granted to San Juan de la Cruz, in the
account of a seventeenth-century biography, as a reward for the rigor-
ous spiritual purgations he had endured. Among these graces are "high
and sudden communications, delectable sentiments . . . ardors, amorous meltings . . . raptures, suspensions, ecstasies and assimilations in
God; ravishments, flights and excesses of spirit, visions, revelations,
interior speeches, and Divine Oracles."[30]

"Ode on a Prayer-book" is important despite its shortcomings. The
above-quoted passage, together with the conclusion, attempts a mystical
tour de force and introduces something new in the English devotional
poetry of the seventeenth century, although, as Allison points out, the
imagery owes something to Thomas Carew's very profane poem, "A
Rapture."[31] Instead of simply drawing attention to the lamentable fact
that men's wit and passion are largely expended in praises of carnal
rather than spiritual beauty, instead of using amorous terms only as a
base for largely abstract comparisons,[32] Crashaw actually attempts to
explore the experience of God's mystical presence by way of the concrete
details of love poetry:

O let the blissful heart hold fast
Her heavenly arm-full, she shall tast
At once ten thousand paradises;
    She shall have power
    To rifle and deflower
The rich and roseal spring of those rare sweets

>   Which with a swelling bosome there she meets
>   Boundles and infinite
>   Bottomles treasures
>   Of pure inebriating pleasures.
>   Happy proof! She shall discover
>   What joy, what blisse,
>   How many Heav'n's at once it is
>   To have her GOD become her LOVER.
>
>   [ll. 111–24]

This passage, too, is not wholly satisfactory. The disappointment is partly owing to the failure of the poem as a whole to prepare adequately for this conclusion, but it also stems from an excessive fleshliness in the imagery: Mrs. M. R.'s "swelling bosome," for instance, contributes nothing to the specifically devotional import of the poem. The ode deals with the paradox that the rapturous pleasures of mystical love grow out of ascetic self-denial, but the latter half of the paradox is not convincingly presented. It is not, again, that there is anything intrinsically improper about the inclusion of a "swelling bosome" in a sacred poem; here, however, this detail, like many of the other images, fails to coalesce into a thematic unity. Perhaps this accounts for the air of self-conscious cleverness in the triumphant synthesis of "GOD" and "LOVER" in the last line. Nevertheless, "Ode on a Prayer-book" is significant as a step in Crashaw's development toward the memorable representations of mystical ecstasy in the "Hymn to Sainte Teresa," "The Flaming Heart," and his other mature hymns, and the use of sacred parody in the poetic treatment of this theme is among Crashaw's distinctive features.

IV

Stanley Stewart has traced a late Renaissance tradition of scriptural commentary, through its manifestations in a number of relatively obscure, mostly recusant, English poets, in which the erotic imagery of the Song of Songs is valued not merely as an allegorical veil for sacred mysteries, but as a rehabilitation of human passion and desire—as a demonstration that divine love both fulfills desire and stimulates it further. Thus it leads not to the negation, but rather to the ultimate consummation of the human erotic nature.[33] Indeed, this treatment of the Song of Songs is not new in the Renaissance; St. Bernard of Clairvaux, in his eighty-fourth sermon on the Canticles, is emphatic in his view that love of God does not diminish erotic desire but transfigures it: "Is the consummation of joy extinction of desire? It is rather to it as oil poured upon a flame: for desire is, as it were, a flame."[34] But, notwithstanding Stewart's investigations among certain minor figures of the earlier seventeenth century, the tradition is not strong in Reformation England. Crashaw's interest in the poetic depiction of mystical union in terms of a passionate reading of the Song of Songs seems to coincide with his discovery of Santa Teresa.[35] For this fascinating woman became the center not only of religious veneration, but also of a compelling literary movement.

In Golden Age Spain the close connection between the Song of Songs and secular love poetry, and hence between divine and human love, was a familiar idea in religious literature of all sorts. In the prologue to his Spanish translation of and commentary on the Song of Songs, Luis de León describes the scriptural book as "a pastoral eclogue wherein, with the words and language of shepherds, Solomon and his Bride, and sometimes their companions, speak as if they were all country villagers."[36] This remark gives a clear indication of the reciprocal influence of the Bible and Humanist literary conventions. More important, the stated purpose of the exposition is to set forth the *literal* sense of the Song of Songs, the "amorous compliments" under which "the Holy Spirit expounds the Incarnation of Christ, the deep love which He always has for his Church, and other mysteries of great secrecy and great weight" (*Obras,* I, 72). What is noteworthy here is that the literal sense—"the amorous compliments" and "the passion of love"—are deemed worthy of inquiry in their own right as fitting vehicles for the spiritual sense. Frequently Fray Luis refers to the customs of lovers and love poets in explaining his sacred text, as in his comments on Canticles 2:8–9: "Finally, the nature of love is such that it produces works in him in whom it reigns quite different from the common experience of men . . . and hence it results that authors who treat of love are badly understood and judged as authors of vanity and nonsense" (Ibid., pp. 104–05). Fray Luis then produces a quotation from Ausias March (d. 1460), "the Spanish Petrarch," to support his interpretation of the Song of Songs.

Santa Teresa habitually discusses the presence of God in terms of the Bridegroom of the Canticles, and her language, as in this passage from *Moradas del castillo interior* ("Mansions of the interior castle"), 6, 3, is frequently impassioned:

Our Lord is also accustomed to have other manners of awakening the soul, which at an odd hour, while praying vocally and unattentive to anything interior, it seems a delightful inflammation comes, as if suddenly there came a fragrance so great, that it were communicated through all the senses... or something of this sort, only to make one feel that the Spouse is there; it moves [in] the soul a savory desire to enjoy Him, and with this she remains disposed to great acts and praises for our Lord. [*Obras completas,* p. 409]

A sudden "inflammation," a pervasive synesthetic "fragrance," a "savory desire" to "enjoy" the "Spouse"—this is the language of profane love, consecrated by the Song of Songs.

Nowhere does it find such exquisite and rapturous expression as in the poetry of San Juan de la Cruz, whose *Cántico espiritual* is the ultimate fusion of the Song of Songs, Renaissance pastoral love poetry, and personal mystical experience. Even as Crashaw's "Ode on a Prayer-book" seems to have borrowed tone and atmosphere from Carew's "Rapture," so San Juan's poem employs the lush imagery and languorous mood of Garcilaso de la Vega. In the following lines, Garcilaso describes a magic spring in which one is able to see one's true love:

> En medio del invierno está templada
> el agua dulce desta clara fuente,
> y en el verano más que nieve helada.
>
> ¡Oh claras ondas, cómo veo presente,
> en viéndoos la memoria de aquel día
> de que el alma temblar y arder se siente!
>
> En vuestra claridad vi me alegría
> escurecerse toda y enturbiarse;
> cuando os cobré perdí mi compañía.[37]

[In the midst of winter the sweet water of this clear spring is warm, and in summer more icy than snow.

Oh bright ripples, how I see as if present, in seeing you, the memory of that day on which I felt my soul tremble and burn!

In your clarity I saw my joy darken completely and become turbid; when I gained you I lost my companionship.]

In the *Cántico* San Juan depicts a similar spring:

> 11. ¡Oh cristalina fuente,
> si en esos tus semblantes plateados
> formases de repente
> los ojos deseados
> que tengo en mis entrañas dibuxados!
> 12. Apártalos Amado,
> que voy de buelo.
>
> [*Vida y obras*, p. 628]

[11. Oh crystalline spring, if in your silvered surfaces you suddenly shape the longed-for eyes that I hold within my bowels drawn!
12. Take them away, Beloved, for I am going to take flight.]

These two passages are similar in their exotic imagery and tone of erotic languor. But San Juan's poem is distinguished from Garcilaso's—and this is also what sets it apart from Crashaw's prayer-book ode—by its constant allusion to and paraphrase of the Song of Songs, and by its delicate transformation of the passionately erotic motifs:

> 9. ¿Por qué, pues has llagado
> aqueste corazón, no le sanaste?;
> y, pues me le has robado,
> ¿por qué así te dejaste
> y no tomas el robo que robaste?
> 10. Apaga mis enojos,
> pues que ninguno basta a deshacellos,
> y véante mis ojos,
> pues eres lumbre dellos,
> y sólo para ti quiero tenellos.
> 11. Descubre tu presencia,
> y máteme tu vista y hermosura;
> mira que la dolencia
> de amor, que no se cura
> sino con la presencia y la figura.
>
> . . . .
>
> 22. Entrado se ha la esposa
> en el ameno huerto deseado,
> y a su sabor reposa,
> el cuello reclinado
> sobre los dulces brazos del Amado.

23. Debajo del manzano,
    allí conmigo fuiste desposada,
    allí te di la mano,
    y fuiste reparada
    donde tu madre fuera violada.

[*Vida y obras*, p. 628]

[Why, since you wounded / this heart, do you not heal it?; / and since you have robbed me, / why do you depart thus / and not take the prize you robbed? / Quench my sorrows, / since nothing is sufficient to undo them, / and let my eyes behold you, / since you are their light, and only for you do I wish to have them. / Disclose your presence, / and let the sight of you and your beauty kill me; / behold, for the suffering / of love is not cured / save by your presence and form. . . . The bride has entered / into the pleasant desired garden, / and reposes at her pleasure, / her neck reclined / upon the sweet arms of the Beloved. / Beneath the apple tree, / there you were betrothed to me, / there I gave you my hand, / and you were redeemed / where your mother was violated.]

The first three stanzas quoted above are virtually indistinguishable, out of context, from a passage of Petrarchan love poetry, say by Garcilaso, but the latter two stanzas, without diminishing the passionate tone, are closely parallel to verses in the Song of Songs (i.e., 2:6; 6:3; 8:3, 5). The judicious intertwining of biblical motifs with the conventional features of the Renaissance erotic pastoral is an important factor in San Juan's transformation of the secular material; moreover, he avoids the occasional coarse imagery of "Ode on a Prayer-book"—Crashaw's excessive preoccupation with "The gay mates of the god of flyes" and with Mrs. M. R.'s "Bosome"—and the ode's didactic, chiding tone. Instead San Juan endows his imagery with a remarkable delicacy and mystery. The action of the poem is lifted out of mundane chronology and any recognizable setting, and thus the *Cántico* evokes the ineffable—and untranslatable—air of remote, dreamlike vision.

A similar striving, to transform the motifs of Renaissance Petrarchism into an expression of mystical devotion without sacrificing their sensuousness and emotive power, is pervasive in Crashaw's sacred poetry. Such a metamorphosis of the conventional attributes of the Petrarchan lady is a recurrent device of "The Weeper," and, though I judge the poem as a whole unsatisfactory, it has moments of shimmering beauty enlivened by admirable wit:

VIII

The deaw no more will weep
The primrose's pale cheek to deck,
The deaw no more will sleep
Nuzzel'd in the lilly's neck;
Much reather would it be thy TEAR,
And leave them Both to tremble here.

. . . .

XIV

Well does the May that lyes
Smiling in thy cheeks, confesse
The April in thine eyes.
Mutuall sweetnesse they expresse.
No April ere lent kinder showres,
Nor May return'd more faithfull flowres.

XV

O cheeks! Bedds of chast loves
By your own showres seasonably dash't;
Eyes! nests of milky doves
In your own wells decently washt.
O wit of love! that thus could place
Fountain and Garden in one face.

In addition to the witty echo of Campion's "There is a garden in her face" in the last couplet, the generally resonant texture of these stanzas, and of many others in "The Weeper," results from the tension between their dominant devotional current and the erotic undertow of imagery which frequently recalls profane love poetry. It is in this delicate balancing of divergent forces—the fruit of sacred parody—that "The Weeper" resembles the *Cántico* of San Juan de la Cruz.

The *Cántico espiritual* is among the more successful examples of the most rarefied form of sacred parody: the divinization of theme with close reference to a specific, sophisticated, or literary poet. By far the most fertile source of inspiration for the Spanish devotional poet was the vast number of poems (often little more than refrains) preserved in the popular Iberian oral tradition, reaching back into the Middle Ages.

These poems or songs (most were intended, at least originally, to be sung) were necessarily anonymous, passed on by word-of-mouth among the common people, often in several versions. By the time of Ferdinand and Isabel (1479–1504), such poems were beginning to be collected, along with imitations and revisions by courtly poets, in *cancioneros* (song-books). This interaction of popular and cultivated verse increased steadily throughout the sixteenth century. As one historian of Spanish literature writes, "the song [had] a fecund life in the music, the poetry, and the theatre of the sixteenth and seventeenth centuries from Juan de Encina and Gil Vicente to Lope and his contemporaries."[38]

It is not difficult to see how a body of poetry so rooted in the tradition of the populace, so pervasive in the national literature, would be attractive to the sacred parodist; Dámaso Alonso has pointed out that Spanish poets were converting poetry "of the traditional type" a lo divino as early as the fifteenth century.[39] Although the more cultivated poets of literary pretension in the early sixteenth century kept to the imported Italian forms under the classicizing influence of humanism, toward the end of the century the major baroque poets, like Lope de Vega and Góngora, became masters in the composition of every form of Spain's popular verse, writing either completely original poems or borrowing from and revising traditional ones. This is an especially intriguing facet of the poetry of Góngora, who is famous for the sophistication and esoteric obscurity of his verse in *arte mayor* (compositions in the Italian forms). It was not uncommon for these poets to convert their own poems of the traditional type a lo divino. Góngora, for instance, produced a secular version of a pastoral *romance* (or "ballad") in 1613 and turned it into a Nativity poem seven years later. Here is the opening of each version:

> ¡Cuántos silbos, cuántas voces
> la nava oyó de Zuheros,
> sentidas bien de sus valles,
> guardadas mal de sus ecos!
> Vaqueros las dan, buscando
> la hermosa por lo menos,
> cerrera, luciente hija
> de el toro que pisa el cielo.
> 1. *¿Qué buscades, los vaqueros?*

2. *Una, ay, novilleja, una,*
que hiere con media luna
y mata con dos luceros.

[How many whistles, how many cries/heard the hollow of Zuheros,/ perceived well by its villages, / badly guarded by their echoes! Cowherds make them, seeking/the beautiful, at the least, / untamed, shining daughter / of the bull that treads the sky. 1. *What seek you, herdsmen? / 2. A young heifer, alas, one, /that wounds with the half moon, / and kills with two bright stars.*]

Cuántos silbos, cuántas voces
tus campos, Bethlen, oyeron
sentidas bien de sus valles,
guardadas mal de sus ecos,
pastores las dan buscando
el que, celestial Cordero,
nos abrió piadoso el libro
que negaban tantos sellos.
¿ *Qué buscáis los ganaderos?*
—*Uno, ay, niño, que su cuna*
los brazos son de la Luna
si duermen sus dos luceros. [40]

[How many whistles, how many cries, / your fields, Bethlehem, heard perceived well by their villages, / guarded badly by their echoes, / shepherds make them, seeking/the one who, celestial Lamb, / mercifully opened for us the book / which so many seals were denying. / *What are you herdsmen seeking? / —A child, oh, whose cradle is the arms of the Moon, / if his two bright stars are sleeping.*]

In the first version Góngora praises or flatters (*lisonjea*) the daughter of the Lord of Zuheros in the guise of a heifer (presumably she *was* flattered), her suitors depicted as cowherds seeking a mythical prize creature, daughter of the constellation Taurus.[41] In the sacred self-parody the celestially born heifer becomes the heavenly Lamb which opens the seals on the Book of Life in Apocalypse (chapter 5); the cowherds become shepherds; and the heifer's horns, figured as the crescent moon, are readily identified with the crescent moon as a traditional symbol from the Apocalypse (chapter 12) associated with the Blessed Virgin, especially in Spanish paintings of the Immaculate Conception.[42] The Christ child of course retains the dazzling eyes which are a conventional feature of the Petrarchan lady, and thus Góngora's poem anticipates the last lines of Crashaw's Nativity hymn:

"Till burnt at last in fire of Thy fair eyes, / Our selves become our own best SACRIFICE" (ll. 107–08). Lope de Vega, even more than Góngora, is given to the technique of sacred parody based on the popular verse of the cancioneros. Examples of his use of the traditional poetry in this manner are countless; let it only be noted here that one very old anonymous song, *Velador que el castillo velas* ("Watchman who watches over the castle"), is found imitated twice among Lope's works: once in a secular version and once a lo divino.[43]

England has no tradition of popular, oral poetry even vaguely comparable in scale and influence to that of Spain, but the song-books of the late sixteenth and early seventeenth centuries occupy a position in the English Renaissance somewhat similar to that of the can-cioneros of the siglo de oro. It is interesting, therefore, to find Crashaw adapting the verse of the song-books in the manner of Lope and Góngora in his "Hymn in the Glorious Assumption."[44] Much of this poem consists of a lyric in the style of the song-books combined with imagery from the Song of Songs. This triangular relation among a secular love poem, the Song of Songs, and sacred parody which fuses the two is also reminiscent of San Juan de la Cruz:

> She's calld. Hark, how the dear immortal dove
> Sighes to his sylver mate rise up, my love!
> Rise up my fair, my spotlesse one!
> The winter's past, the rain is gone.
>   The spring is come, the Flowrs appear
> No sweets, but thou, are wanting here.
>   Come away, my love!
>   Come away, my dove!
>   The court of heav'n is come
> To wait upon thee home; Come, come away!

> [ll. 7–16]

The immediate context of this passage is, of course, Scripture; the Virgin Mary is traditionally associated with the dove that returned to Noah's ark with the olive branch (signifying the abatement of God's wrath), and the whole passage closely parallels the Song of Songs, 2:10–13:

My beloved speaks and says to me: "Arise, my love, my fair one, and come away; for lo, the winter is past, the rain is over and gone. The flowers appear on the earth, the time of singing has come, and the voice of the turtledove is

heard in our land. The fig tree puts forth its figs, and the vines are in blossom;
they give forth fragrance. Arise, my love, my fair one, and come away.

"Hymn in the Glorious Assumption" clearly has a much firmer biblical
and theological basis than "Ode on a Prayer-book." The Assumption
poem, employing the Catholic interpretation of the Song of Songs, in
which the Bride is identified with the Virgin as well as the Church
and the Christian soul, wholly escapes the oversophisticated but often
awkward cleverness of Crashaw's admonitions to Mrs. M. R.

This does not mean, however, that the Assumption poem is any
less sensuous in its imagery. Moreover, Christ the Spouse sings a
madrigal to the Queen of Heaven as lush in tone and atmosphere as
any of the song-book lyrics. A significant analogy to Crashaw's
poem—not only in the song form and commonplace "Come away"
motif, but also in the general content of the imagery—is John Dowland's "To his Love," in *England's Helicon* (1600):

> COME away, come sweet Love,
> The golden morning breakes;
> All the earth, all the ayre,
> Of love and pleasure speakes. . . .
>
> Come away, come sweet Love,
> The golden morning wasts:
> While the Sunne from his Sphere
> His fierie arrowes casts,
> Making all the shadows flie,
> Playing, staying in the Groave;
> To entertaine the stealth of love.
> Thither sweet Love let us hie
> Flying, dying in desire:
> Wing'd with sweet hopes and heavenly fire.[45]

Crashaw's hymn shares with this Dowland song a sense of nature's
ravishing beauties, which are instigations to love, and the intense,
masculine impatience of the lover—an aspect which is not particularly
marked in the Song of Songs. In addition, Crashaw shrewdly and
effectively emphasizes the flight motif (Dowland's song concludes,
"Hast then sweet Love our wished flight"), which takes on an extra
significance because of its very literalness in the context of an Assumption poem.

It is precisely such direct echoes of the tone and strategy of secular love poetry which distinguish Crashaw's and San Juan's use of the Song of Songs from typical treatments of the same material by contemporary neo-Latin poets of the continent. The famous Jesuit Casimire Sarbiewski, for example, entitles a number of odes *Ex sacro Salomonis Epithalmio* but, as the following passage reveals, he tends to handle the scriptural references in a way that is primarily allegoric, in contrast to the immediacy and personal intensity of Crashaw and San Juan de la Cruz. This ode is headed by an epigraph from one of the most sensuous moments in the Song of Songs (2:10ff.), yet here the broad, general description of an idealized landscape which merges the Canticles with the prophecies of Isaiah (11:6), has the effect of attenuating the concrete sensuousness of erotic images:

> Fallor? an Elysii laeva de parte Sereni
>   Me mea vita vocat?
> Surge soror, pulchris innectito lora columbis;
>   Pulchrior ipsa super
> Scande rotas, Libanique, levem de vertice currum,
>   Has, age, flecte domos.
> Ad tua decidui fugiunt vestigia nimbi,
>   Turbidas imber abiit:
> Ipsa sub innocuis mitescunt fulmina plantis,
>   Ipsa virescit hiems.
> Interea sacris aperit se scena viretis
>   Sub pedibusque tibi
> Altera floret humus, alterque vagantia late
>   Sidera pascit ager.
> Hic etiam trepidi pendent e rupibus hoedi
>   Praecipitesque caprae;
> Hinnuleique suis, passim dum flumina tranant,
>   Luxuriantur aquis.
> Et leo cum Pardo viridis de colle Saniri
>   Mitis uterque regi,
> Cumque suo passim ludunt in montibus agno
>   Exsuperantque juga.[46]

[Do I err? Or is my life calling me from the propitious region of clear Elysium? Arise sister, join the reins to the beautiful doves, yourself more beautiful by far (;) mount the wheeled car, drive your light chariot, and turn from the summit of Libanus to these mansions. At your descent the traces of storm clouds flee, the wild rain departs; lightning itself grows mild beneath your innocent soles, winter itself grows green. Meanwhile a scene unfolds in sacred greenery. Another soil flowers underfoot for you; another field widely culti-vates wandering stars. Here also nervous goats hang with their kids from the steep sides of cliffs; and fawns as they swim the streams frisk in their waters. And the Lion with Leopard, gentle and tamed from the hill of green Sannus, play each with his own lamb among the mountains and skip over the ranges.]

Casimire's treatment of the Canticles imagery resembles the work of Beaumont discussed in chapter 1. The images have meaning here only as symbols. The poem is, in effect, an allegorical verse commentary on the Song of Songs: the interpolation among the erotic images of the messianic theme from Isaiah—the lion and the leopard "playing" with the lamb—is a means of expounding the spiritual significance underly-ing the nuptial passion of the Song of Songs. As Maren-Sofie Roestvig observes, "Much of Casimire's poetry is . . . best understood as a con-scious effort to apply the allegorical technique of Canticles to the classical *beatus ille* themes."[47] Crashaw, like San Juan de la Cruz, does not offer so much a meditation on the scriptural passage, as an application of the traditional allegory of the Song of Songs to a specific situation: the Spanish mystic embodies personal spiritual experience in terms of Canticles imagery; Crashaw, the communal experience of the faithful upon a feast commemorating an event in the life of the Church. But in each instance the scriptural reference is a basis for ordering the concrete experience to which it is tied, while Casimire's collocation of scriptural imagery with classical form and attitude serves as a means of ordering or explaining the otherwise obscure symbolism of the Canticles. Hence Roestvig rightly terms his kind of poem "philosophic lyric."[48]

In addition to Casimire's handling of the imagery, he also differs from Crashaw in his use of the Horatian ode.[49] To be sure this does represent, in a sense, the conversion of a profane form to sacred purposes, and hence a kind of sacred parody. But the relation between sacred and profane elements in Casimire's ode is very different from that which obtains in Crashaw's love song or madrigal a lo divino. The latter emphasizes the elements of ecstatic mysticism cum eroticism of the Canticles, evoking a fruitful tension between carnal and spiritual desire, with each transforming and vivifying the other. The cool re-straint of the ode used by Casimire, like his introduction of Isaiah's

messianic prophecies, tends to suppress, or at least to dissipate, the
rapturous aspects of the Song of Songs. It is as if Casimire were
seeking to filter out the suggestions of profane sensuality, while
Crashaw, again like San Juan, fuses them with the sacred elements
into a single unified poetic effect. For all his stature as an exemplar of
the continental neo-Latin baroque, there is a refinement, an incipient
neoclassicism in Casimire, which disqualifies him as a model for the
passionate release which marks Crashaw's later hymns.

As the comparison with Casimire's ode clearly demonstrates,
Crashaw's "Hymn in the Glorious Assumption" is an accomplishment
of consummate literary tact and delicacy: it is charged with a sensuous, passionate energy that the Latin poem lacks, but it avoids the
indecorum of Crashaw's own poem to Mrs. M. R. In addition to its
firm anchoring in Scripture, what most sets the Assumption hymn
above the prayer-book ode is the role assumed by the speaker vis-à-vis
the Blessed Virgin. Here the poet adds to the festivity of the Assumption a tinge of grief since the occasion represents a loss for men. There
is no suggestion, however, of competition between God and man, only
of the innate limitation and sadness of the condition of fallen humanity. The poet as spokesman for a people at once rejoicing and lament-
ing is surely preferable to Crashaw playing John Alden to God's Miles
Standish with Mrs. M. R. This very situation causes the speaker to
become—as Yvor Winters warns—excessively involved in Mrs. M.
R.'s quasi-sexual passion.[50] But the Assumption is an occasion requir-
ing consolation; hence the rapturous description of the Virgin's Coronation that closes the poem is tempered by sadness:

> LIVE, rosy princesse, LIVE. And may the bright
> Crown of a most incomparable light
> Embrace thy radiant browes. O may the best
> Of everlasting joyes bath thy white brest.
> Live, our chast love, the holy mirth
> Of heavn; the humble pride of earth.
> Live crown of woemen; Queen of men.
> Live mistresse of our song. And when
> Our weak desires have done their best,
> Sweet Angels come, and sing the rest.

>   [ll. 60–69]

V

Crashaw's most famous use of erotic imagery comes, of course, in the poems to Santa Teresa de Jesús: "A Hymn to Sainte Teresa" and "The Flaming Heart." Although these poems do not derive from particular secular models, but rather from Teresa's own life, they are still classic examples of sacred parody—specifically, of the divinization of themes. In these poems the sexual analogy for the transcendent raptures of mystical experience is explicit, but the same analogy is continuously latent and frequently bursts forth in most of Crashaw's mature hymns. "To the Name of Jesus" is, among other things, a love song to Jesus' saving name which is sweet like honey (ll. 151–58) and fragrant like perfume (ll. 173–82), and which can "fill the senses" in "balmy showres" of "condensed sweets" (ll. 167–70). "Hymn in the Glorious Epiphany" sets the mystic love of Christ against the adulterous worship of heathen idols in explicitly sexual terms, and the Magi promise to seek Christ by the *via negativa* and become "amorous Spyes / And peep and proffer at thy sparkling Throne" (ll. 224–25). In both the "Hymn for New Year's Day" and the "Hymn in the Holy Nativity," the infant Jesus is accorded the bewitching charm of the Petrarchan lady, especially her dazzling eyes; and the latter poem, as noted in chapter 1, presents a sensuous vision of the Blessed Virgin as both tenderly maternal and warmly passionate.

Robert G. Collmer has pointed out that the erotic imagery of Crashaw's poems derives principally from the nuptial symbolism of Catholic mysticism, not from profane love poetry, and that the religious motif, not the sexual, is the controlling element in the poem. "It is wrong," Collmer maintains, "to view the parallels with physical love in Crashaw's poems which ostensibly deal with religious themes as products of a celibate's 'Peeping Tom' attitude toward sex."[51] This admonition is permanently valuable as a corrective to facile generalizations about Crashaw, but at the same time we must not lose sight of the real use which mystics make of the tensions inherent in the relation of sacred and profane love. Such a bold conquest of the conventions of secular love poetry, as Helmut Hatzfeld observes, is especially characteristic of the Spanish mysticism which influenced Crashaw:

Spanish mysticism appears late in the western tradition at a moment in which Socratic introspection and self-analysis were able to comprehend and express the psychological side of metaphysical experience and when Spanish poetry, with its Italianate tendency and its popular tradition, had prepared a set of symbols and metaphors that mysticism could use in a most surprising manner, although in accordance with a form that literary historians customarily call *a lo divino*. [52]

Hence it is justifiable to regard all of Crashaw's major hymns, insofar as they employ "the symbols and metaphors" of secular poetry "in a most surprising manner," as examples of sacred parody. But since sacred parody is only the means, and the end of these poems is the representation of mystical experience, it will be more convenient to consider their use of the imagery of profane love in more detail in a general treatment of mysticism in Crashaw's poetry in chapter 4.

One short lyric, however, associated by theme, diction, imagery, and—in all the early editions—by position with the Teresa poems provides an especially interesting example of the ramifications of sacred parody. Moreover, "A Song" is one of Crashaw's finest short pieces:

> LORD, when the sense of thy sweet grace
> Sends up my soul to seek thy face.
> Thy blessed eyes breed such desire,
> I dy in love's delicious Fire.
>   O love, I am thy SACRIFICE.
> Be still triumphant, blessed eyes.
> Still shine on me, fair suns! that I
> Still may behold, though still I dy.

> [ll. 1–8]

This "Song," like the Assumption poem, suggests the verse of the song-books. As George Williams points out, the poet here echoes a conventional figure of Petrarchan love poetry in which the lady's eyes are likened to suns which consume the lover in their radiant heat. [53] But the most striking single feature in the quoted stanza is the use of the word "dy" with its tangle of associations. It is a commonplace to observe that, during the Renaissance, an accepted slang meaning of the word linked it with erotic longing and even sexual intercourse; however, for men of Crashaw's background and interests there was, most certainly, a quite different set of associations with the word which would come into play in this poem: "I protest by your rejoicing which I have in Christ Jesus, our Lord, I die daily" (1 Cor. 15:31). It would seem, then, that Crashaw is quite consciously playing the trite Petrarchan conventions, especially the erotic overtones of "dy," against various biblical echoes. The mystical significance of "dy" derives from the convergence and clash of these two divergent sources of meaning. This point is clearly established by the second and final stanza:

> Though still I dy, I live again;
> Still longing so to be still slain,
> So gainful is such losse of breath,
> I dy even in desire of death.
>   Still live in me this loving strife
> Of living DEATH and dying LIFE.
> For while thou sweetly slayest me
> Dead to my selfe, I live in Thee.
>
> [ll. 9–16]

This tissue of paradoxes finds a pattern in Romans, 6:1–13, of which for comparison only the eighth verse is quoted: "Now if we be dead with Christ, we believe that we shall also live with him." By embodying the doctrine in the lilting sweetness of the Elizabethan song, Crashaw highlights and enhances the inherent mystical aspects of the Pauline epistle.

This little poem—which first appears in the 1648 edition of *Steps to the Temple*—is of particular interest because it seems to be of Spanish provenance, and because it illustrates how deeply embedded was Crashaw's art in the tradition of poesía a lo divino. In a note to "A Song" in his edition, Williams remarks that it is "perhaps inspired by St. Teresa's *Interior Castle,* VI, Mansions" (p. 65). This citation probably refers to the eleventh chapter of *Moradas sextas,* which "treats of certain desires so great and impetuous that God gives to the soul of enjoying Him, that they place [it] in danger of losing its life; and of the benefits that remain from this grace which the Lord grants." The principal theme of this chapter is the paradox that the more the Spouse grants the soul the favor of His mystical presence, the more the soul languishes and suffers, for it desires all the more intensely to be wholly at one with Him. At times the soul is brought to such straits that "it is dying to die [se muere por morir] when it presses so much, that now it seems that it lacks almost nothing of leaving the body . . ." (*Obras,* pp. 434–37). To be sure, this passage closely resembles Crashaw's poem, but there is yet a closer parallel in her versification of the same theme. Among Santa Teresa's poems is a lyric based on the refrain, "Vivo sin vivir en mi / Y tan alta vida espero / Que muero porque no muero" ("I live without living in myself, and I hope for life so high, that I die because I do not die"—*Obras*, pp. 498–99).[54] Crashaw's "Song" could well be a development of this refrain,[55] in which case he has, for once, far outdone his heroine, whose poem rambles on—never getting anywhere—through fourteen stanzas. Crashaw, with admirable critical insight, has perceived that the value of the central conceit is in its compression, and he manages the essentially verbal play with deftness and brevity.

The ultimate interest of the comparison, however, lies in the source of the Spanish poem. Dámaso Alonso has shown that Santa Teresa's "Muero porque no muero" (and a poem on the same refrain by San Juan de la Cruz) is based on a long tradition of love poetry with both popular and courtly roots. Even the key refrain is matched almost exactly in at least three secular love poems.[56] Quite possibly Crashaw's "A Song" is a variation upon, or if you will, a parody of Spanish sacred parody. For this reason the poem sums up very concisely Crashaw's debt to the poesía a lo divino of Spain. First, Spanish verse furnishes a source of concepts, imagery, even phrasing: compare "Muero porque no muero" to "I dy even in desire of death." Second, and more important, Spanish poetry provides a pattern for the conversion of secular English poetry, like that of the song-books, to devotional purposes. It was through the model of Spanish authors that Crashaw found his own way to resolve the dilemma posed by George Herbert: "Who sings thy praise? onely a skarf or glove / Doth warm our hands, and make them write of love."[57]

3

Crashaw and the Comic Spirit: Pastoral Innocence and Sacred Joy

ERHAPS THE LEAST APPRECIATED FACET of Crashaw's sacred poetry is the skillful handling of tone in his mature hymns—a skill won with great effort through the practice of such uneven poems as "Ode on a Prayer-book" and "The Weeper." To some extent this complexity may be attributed to the technique of sacred parody, pervasive in his devotional verse: while the conversion of profane themes to sacred uses suggests an element of naiveté in its implicit confidence that human desires can be so totally directed to their proper end, at the same time the tension generated by the juxtaposition of secular poetic conventions and religious contexts necessarily indicates a certain literary sophistication. This mingling of contrary elements, which furnishes the distinctive feature of Crashaw's devotional poetry, also embodies one of its distinctive purposes: to produce a tone which answers to the wonder and mystery which Crashaw perceives at the heart of the Christian faith. This same paradoxical tone, compounded of equal measures of popular piety and mystical profundity, of light-hearted wit and spiritual earnestness, is a constant feature throughout the works of Santa Teresa de Jesús, undoubtedly the single most important influence on the later poems of Richard Crashaw.

Tone is the most conspicuously distinctive factor in these poems. For example, the various English and Latin counterparts to Crashaw's "Hymn in the Holy Nativity," examined in the first chapter, all differ from his poem in tone: they reflect the magnificence of miniature epic, the gravity of philosophic allegory, or the urbane polish of classical imitation; none stress the paradoxical conjunction of Christian theme and classic form as Crashaw does, and they wholly lack his marked blending of popular gaiety and theological wit.

If a completely unique poem were possible, it would probably be unintelligible, and Crashaw's "Hymn in the Holy Nativity" is by no means unique. There are a multitude of possible models in the literature of the Spanish siglo de oro. Santa Teresa, for example, wrote several *villancicos* on the Nativity in which the speaker of the poem is one of the shepherds, and in some instances there is an exchange of questions and responses which resembles the rustic dialogue of Crashaw's hymn:

> Pués ¿como, Pascual,
> Hizo esa franqueza,
> Que toma un sayal
> Dejando riqueza?
> Más quiere pobreza,
> Sigámosle nos;
> Pués ya viene hombre,
> *Muramos los dos.*
>
> [*Obras completas,* p. 504]

[Well, how, Pascual, did he gain that freedom, he who takes coarse woolen, leaving riches? He prefers poverty, let us follow him; since he now comes as man, *let us both die.*]

Villancico is generally translated "carol" or "Christmas carol" and, like its English counterpart, originally referred to a secular dancing song with a refrain (indicated in the above and subsequent quotations by italics in the original Spanish texts). Although the villancico is today usually associated with Christmas, when Santa Teresa was writing it was still a popular secular form, the very use of which involves an element of sacred parody. The refrain, "Muramos los dos," in attributing desire for mystical death to the shepherds, anticipates the close of Crashaw's Nativity hymn: "Till burnt at last in fire of Thy faire eyes, / Ourselves become our own best SACRIFICE." Hence Crashaw's distinctive tone of popular wonder mingled with a longing for mystical rapture has a substantial basis in the work of a great mystical teacher.

Likewise, among the sacred poems of Góngora are several on the

Nativity which share a similar popular flavor with Crashaw's hymn. In the "romance," "Al Nacimiento de Cristo Nuestro Señor," there is a dialogue between one shepherd, Gil, and a group of his fellows who question him about what he has seen in the stable. Like Crashaw's Thyrsis and Tityrus, Gil is amazed by the Infant who provides his own light: [1]

> Tanto he visto celestial,
> tan luminoso, tan raro,
> que a pesar, hallarás claro,
> de la noche, este portal.
>
> [*Obras*, p. 223]

[So much have I seen that is celestial, so luminous, so rare, that in spite of the night you will find this portal bright.]

But the poet who treated the Nativity theme most frequently, and with the most devotion and care, is Lope de Vega; in addition, it is in Lope's work that the most remarkable parallels to Crashaw's "Hymn in the Holy Nativity" are to be found. The Spaniard left verses on the infant Jesus scattered throughout his *comedias, autos sacramentales,* and collections of lyric poetry. The culmination of his preoccupation with the theme lies in his *Pastores de Belén* ("Shepherds of Bethlehem"), a pastoral novel modeled on Sannazaro, Montemayor, and his own *Arcadia* (1598)—only converted a lo divino. First published in 1612, *Pastores de Belén* seems to have been among Lope's most popular works during his lifetime and was reprinted at least a dozen times in the seventeenth century. For our present purposes it is worth recalling that editions of the work appeared both in the Low Countries (Brussels, 1614) and in France (Rouen, 1616), as well as in Spain. [2] Hence it is not unlikely that Crashaw saw a copy of the work during his travels on the continent. If we consider the many similarities, in details of style and in general conception, between the poetry of *Pastores de Belén* and Crashaw's "Hymn in the Holy Nativity," then the likelihood seems even greater.

In the typical fashion of pastoral novels, *Pastores de Belén* is built around the most tenuous of plots. In the first book the shepherd Aminadab, "descendant of the tribe and house of Jacob and kindred to the most holy Joseph," [3] journeys to Bethlehem to obtain some sheep from his uncle Mahol. On his way he reflects upon the prophecies of

the Hebrew Scriptures concerning the Messiah, which he knows—
having been present at the Blessed Virgin's Visitation of St.
Elizabeth—are soon to be fulfilled. As he nears Bethlehem he meets
his cousin Palmira (who later becomes his bride), and they are
gradually joined by various other shepherds and shepherdesses. While
the company proceeds, Aminadab tells the others in great detail the
story of the Virgin Mary—of her Immaculate Conception, of the An-
nunciation, the Visitation, and finally of the birth of a son, John, to
the aged Elizabeth and Zacharias. Aminadab's narrative is, of course,
continually interrupted by songs and epigrams in honor of the Virgin
and by metrical paraphrases of Scripture. Some are his own and some
are spontaneous compositions by the other shepherds accompanying
him. As the first book draws to a close the group has reached the home
of Mahol and agreed to meet the following day so that Aminadab can
finish the story.

Book 2 is thus largely devoted to his account of the justa poética
held in his own village in honor of the birth of John the Baptist.[4]
Aminadab describes the various emblems and hieroglyphs entered in
the competition, as well as reciting or singing the riddles and various
sorts of poems composed for the occasion. He describes even the prizes
awarded to the winners. Book 3 deals with the arrival of Joseph and
Mary in Bethlehem and the Nativity itself. It concludes with a long
section which tells of the return of the shepherds from the scene of the
Birth, singing and rejoicing over what they have witnessed—the very
subject of Crashaw's "Hymn in the Holy Nativity." Book 4 treats of
the Circumcision in a similar way, and book 5 of the Epiphany, ending
with an account of the flight into Egypt. Throughout the work the
lean narrative is larded with digressions into scriptural material and
into classical history and myth, and of course there is an endless
variety of poems and songs. Lope's skill in blending all the essentials of
a pastoral novel into a genuine work of devotional art is truly remarkable.

The most striking similarity between Crashaw's "Hymn in the
Holy Nativity" and Lope's *Pastores de Belén* lies in the area of tone, for
both works are characterized by an air of lightness and familiarity.
Given the nature and lineage of Lope's sacred pastoral, it is not sur-
prising that Lope's shepherds are more native to seventeenth-century
Iberia than to first-century Palestine; however, it is somewhat surpris-

ing, to the reader whose ideas of pastoral are shaped by Sidney's *Arcadia,* that the principal characters are shepherds at all, rather than disguised courtiers. In fact, the shepherds of *Pastores de Belén* bear a marked resemblance to the sturdy peasants depicted so well in the poet's secular comedias. The attitude they manifest toward the momentous sacred events which they witness is based on a simple, unquestioning, yet joyously exuberant faith. In Lope's account the Virgin is but a girl, a niña of fourteen, and the reverent awe of the shepherds is freely mingled with purely human feelings of love and tenderness. Likewise, the Christ child is looked upon not only as the Incarnate Word, but also as an object for compassion: a poor baby, born in a cold stable, surrounded by animals.

The shepherds are also characterized by a love of improvised song and games of wit. As a group of them returns from the scene of Jesus' birth, they play a game, *soldado.* All the shepherds select colors—each with a special significance—in which to dress the Child, the "soldier." When the judge, who proceeds to praise the Christ child, alludes to the corresponding characteristic of Jesus, each shepherd must call out his own color. Anyone who falters or misses his cue is "penalized" by having to sing about the Nativity. All of the scriptural events recounted in *Pastores de Belén* are similarly subject to celebration in songs and dances and games. In addition to providing an easy way to introduce poetry into the story, such diversions also give the work a feeling of gaiety. This tone of familiarity extends to every aspect of the book, pervading Lope's entire conception of his subject. Not only are his shepherds light-hearted in their response to Jesus, they are also marked by their own humorous qualities. Ergasto, for example, is comically eager to display his poetic talents, especially in the eyes of a particular shepherd girl, but tries rather awkwardly to hide his eagerness. Even Aminadab, the principal personage among the shepherds, is marked by an amusing strain of sententiousness.

Audrey Aaron has suggested that Lope's humor in treating sacred topics—a common feature throughout his poetry—was possible only among a people of deep, unshaken faith.[5] It may well be that the playful joy pervading Catholic worship was an important factor drawing Crashaw to the old religion. Johan Huizinga, in his classic study *Homo Ludens,* recurs several times to the parallels between play and liturgy, to the "overlap" of play and holiness, and Josef Pieper argues the intimate and vital connections between celebration, leisure, and divine worship. "In leisure," Pieper writes, "man oversteps the frontiers of the everyday workaday world, not in external effort and strain, but as though lifted above it in ecstasy."[6] But this play element in religion is antithetical to the general tendency of the Reformation. "Calvin and Luther," Huizinga remarks, "could not abide the tone in which the Humanist Erasmus spoke of holy things. Erasmus! his whole being seems to radiate the play spirit."[7] As R. H. Tawney remarks, "Puritanism, not the Tudor secession from Rome, was the true English Reformation . . ."; and "to the Puritan, a contemner of the vain shows of sacramentalism, mundane toil becomes a kind of sacrament."[8] This view of the situation receives contemporary support from the autobiography of Richard Baxter, who notes the importance of the Puritan aversion to "the innovations in the Church, the bowing to alters, the Book of Sports for Sundays," among other causes of the civil war.[9] In Lope's genuinely rustic and popular treatment of the shepherds of the Nativity story, Crashaw could have recognized a kindred spirit, whose gay and joyous celebration of the holiday contrasts markedly with the Puritan suppression of Christmas in England and New England alike.[10]

On the other hand, the games played by Lope's "shepherds of Bethlehem"—their emblems, riddles, and poetic contests—reflect the interests of the cultured classes of Lope's own day in the witty aspects of art and poetry. In the beginning of *Pastores,* we are informed that Aminadab is "studious in the reading of the *Torah*" and "also curious . . . about human histories, of the foundings of the empires of the Assyrians, Greeks, Trojans, and Romans . . ." (*Obras escogidas,* II, 1178). We soon come to realize that he is also well versed in Tridentine theology, and if Aminadab is acknowledged as the most learned among the shepherds, his companions, nonetheless, seem to have little difficulty in following his complex disquisitions. In addition, the various personal relationships are managed with impeccable manners. Evidently Lope's rustic shepherds enjoy all the learning and polish of the ideal Renaissance courtier. Here again there is, incidentally, a notable contrast between Lope's cultured rustics and the usual situation in pastoral novels: real courtiers affecting the life of, or disguised as, shepherds.

The extraordinary character of Lope's shepherds reveals the fu-

sion of two disparate poetic styles, and this fusion defines the unusual
nature of *Pastores de Belén*. Audrey Aaron cites the concluding quatrain of Lope's poetic introduction to the work as a key to its composite
style:

> Los reyes te darán cosas mayores:
> que yo solo te puedo dar, Rey mío,
> frutas del alma y del ingenio flores,
> que por manos tan rústicas te envío.
>
> [*Obras escogidas*, II, 1177]

[The kings shall give you greater things: / for I am only able to give, my
King, / fruits of the soul and flowers of ingenuity, / which I send you with such
rustic hands.]

"Fruits of the soul" and "flowers of ingenuity": *Pastores de Belén* is a
blend of *lo popular* and *lo culto:*

This pastoral, insofar as it is a manifestation of popular religious ingenuous-
ness, independent of the classical influences of the Renaissance, gave the
"fruits of the soul," while the profane pastoral tradition, even reduced to an
artificial framework which had for its original object the admitting of the
shepherds who disguised its blasé sentiments, was now able to put forth
"flowers of ingenuity."[11]

This unusual complex of the popular and rustic joined with the
courtly and sophisticated was possible because of the unique development of Spanish literature during the sixteenth and seventeenth centuries. As noted above in the first chapter, a distinguishing feature of
Spanish Renaissance culture as a whole is the retention in a living
form of much of the medieval heritage which in Italy and France
succumbed to the classical revival, and which in Protestant countries
fell victim to the Reformation. In the realm of poetry, the persistence
of the popular medieval tradition was a major factor, and the common
use of poetic forms and themes from the Middle Ages by the chief
poets made Spanish poetry in this respect quite unusual in the European Renaissance.[12] The greatest poets of the baroque period all wrote
in the common forms of the anonymous verse of the Middle Ages.
What is more, they wrote skillfully and naturally in these forms. The
orally transmitted poetry of the common people was still alive in
sixteenth-century Spain, and the cultivated literary artists breathed it
in with the air. Lope, for example, based countless songs (usually in

his plays) on the popular *estribillos,* or refrains, which could be heard
in the streets. In addition to those he borrowed, Lope often made up
his own, which, in the absence of external evidence, scholars sometimes cannot distinguish from the traditional refrains. [13] In short, the
influence of the literature of the Italian Renaissance was absorbed by
Spanish poets without causing a rupture in the continuity of their
national poetic tradition.

This can be seen in the remarkable variety of genres which appear in *Pastores de Belén:* eclogues, canzones, and sonnets are jux-
taposed with romances, villancicos, glosas, and various kinds of letril-
las. [14] Of more significance than mere diversity is the success attained
by Lope in bringing these different poetic traditions into stylistic harmony. The beautiful lyric simplicity and popular realism associated
with the medieval forms mesh neatly with the rhetorical sophistication
and witty conceits of the baroque style. Audrey Aaron adduces as an
example of this fusion a "lullaby-ballad" sung by one of the shepherd
girls as she returns home after seeing the Holy Family. The Virgin is
depicted as musing upon the poverty of her circumstances; if we lived
in anything but poverty, she says to her baby, "your own heavens
would envy my riches." But the Christ child responds with paradoxical
silence:

> El Niño recién nacido
> no mueve la pura lengua,
> aunque es la sabiduría
> de su Eterno Padre inmensa.
>
> [*Obras escogidas,* II, 1277]

[The newly-born Baby/does not move his pure tongue/although he is the
immense wisdom/of his Eternal Father.]

As Audrey Aaron points out, this "theological conceit" dates back to
St. Augustine's "Verbum infans":

If we consider the ultimate etymology of *infans* ("'child' that does not speak")
we are able to perceive the paradox fully: the Word that does not speak (a
word), and thus the paradoxical disproportion between All-powerful God and a
defenseless child is expressed in the best manner. [15]

Yet for all the evident sophistication of this conception, it does not
clash with the charming lullaby that concludes the poem:

Pues andáis en las palmas,
ángeles santos,
que se duerme mi Niño,
tened los ramos.

[*Obras escogidas,* II, 1277]

[Since you are walking in the palms, / holy angels, / since my Baby is
sleeping, / hold the branches still.]

The reason that the two stylistic tendencies are compatible is that both
are appropriate to the subject: God is made, not only man, but even a
helpless child; and the poet must respond both to the miracle and to
the tenderness of the mother–child relationship. At times rising bril-
liantly to this challenge, Lope creates in *Pastores de Belén* passages of
verse which unite ingenious wit, rich imagery, and a tone of gaiety and
joy.

The key to the tone of familiarity and simplicity, to the frequent
humor in Lope's Nativity poetry, is his skill in combining the popular
Spanish tradition with the cultivated pastoral novel, a product of the
Italian Renaissance. Viewed in relation to *Pastores de Belén,* Crashaw's
"Hymn in the Holy Nativity" seems to share a similar blend of disparate elements. Notwithstanding the hymn's kinship to the Renaissance pastoral eclogue, there is a popular flavor in the use of the
refrain and in the chanting rhythm of the repetitive syntax. An ingenuous quality is particularly evident in passages of the first chorus
where simple syntactical patterns are repeated several times and reinforced by heavy alliteration:

Come we shepherds whose blest Sight . . .
Come lift we up our loftyer Song . . .
Tell him He rises now, too late . . .
Tell him we now can show Him more . . .
Tell him, Tityrus, Where th'hast been
Tell him, Thyrsis, what th'hast seen.

[ll. 1, 3, 9, 11, 15–16]

Crashaw's paradoxical conceits and sensuous imagery are thus embedded in the simplest kind of diction and sentence structure, which is
firmly stressed by reiterated rhetorical patterns and alliteration. It is
not difficult to perceive how this kind of writing resembles the method
of many of Lope's Nativity poems based, as they often are, on popular

refrains and traditional forms. The same kind of repetitive syntax and colloquial diction dominates the following song, one of many such in *Pastores:*

> Zagalejos y pastores,
> de aqueste Niño de flores
> coronad las rubias sienes,
> *pues es quien trajo los bienes*
> *y quien nos quita los males.*
>
> Hacedle, hermosas zagalejas,
> mantillas de vuestra galas,
> y amor de vuestras desdenes,
> *pues es quien trajo los bienes*
> *y quien nos quita los males.*
>
> [*Obras escogidas,* II, 1277]

[Swains and shepherds, / crown with flowers / the blond temples of that Child, / *since it is He who brought us blessings and who quits us of our evils.* / *Make for Him, lovely shepherd girls,* / *swaddling clothes of your finery,* / *and love of your disdains,* / *since it is He who brought us blessings* / *and who quits us of our evils.*]

As a further contribution to simplicity of tone, Crashaw's hymn also contains the same kind of light-hearted humor which is common in Lope's Nativity poetry. This humor often involves personification: Crashaw's shepherds gibe at the sun for "sleeping" too late while the new supernatural "Sun" brings a more brilliant day (ll. 11–12). Lope's shepherds attribute jealousy of the Virgin to the sun because a "greater sun" is in her arms, and in another poem the night of Jesus' birth is likewise subject to the sun's envy:

> De una Virgen hermosa
> celos tiene el sol,
> *porque vió en sus brazos*
> *otro Sol mayor.*
>
> [*Obras escogidas,* II, 1260]

[The sun is jealous / of a beautiful Virgin, / *because he saw in her arms* / *another greater Sun.*]

> Una oscura noche,
> del sol envidia,
> parió la aldeana
> de nuestra villa.
>
> [Ibid., p. 1300]

(One dark night, / the envy of the sun, / a country girl of our village / gave birth.)

Two much discussed stanzas of Crashaw's hymn also involve the same kind of reverent but familiar humor:

> *Tit.* I saw the curl'd drops, soft and slow,
>   Come hovering o're the place's head;
> Offring their whitest sheets of snow
>   To furnish the fair INFANT's bed
> Forbear, said I; be not too bold.
> Your fleece is white But t'is too cold. . . .
>
> *Thyr.* I saw the obsequious SERAPHIMS
>   Their rosy fleece of fire bestow.
> For well they now can spare their wings
>   Since HEAVN itself lyes here below.
> Well done, said I: but are you sure
> Your down so warm will passe for pure?
>   [ll. 51–56, 58–63]

The latter stanza, especially, has proven to be a source of critical consternation. Kerby Neill goes to some lengths to show that the impurity of the seraphim is merely relative—a way of asserting the Virgin's superiority.[16] George Williams speculates that Crashaw found a suggestion of impurity in the rosy color (not "perfectly red") of the seraph-wings. "The alleged impurity of the angels is difficult to understand," he adds. "Mr. Neill presents a recondite source for the idea which Crashaw quite possibly knew, but it seems to me the taint of color is the nearer way."[17] Here the value of the comparison between Crashaw and Lope as a critical tool is quite apparent. The parallel forces us to consider the context of the stanza, the kind of poem Crashaw was writing. Thyrsis, after all, is not Dionysius the Areopagite setting forth the divine hierarchies; his solicitous chiding of the seraphim is nothing more than the innocent banter of a humble shepherd carried away by joy. He and Tityrus both reveal their rustic background by comparing snow and angels' wings alike to "fleece." In short, the entire passage is written in the same spirit in which one of Lope's shepherds compares the angels to multicolored birds;[18] or in which another promises to bring, as a gift for Mary, a drying-stand of willow wood for Jesus' diapers (p. 1255); or in which Mary, in the lullaby (quoted above, pp. 58–59), asks the angels, since they are

62 CRASHAW AND THE COMIC SPIRIT

"walking in the palms" anyway, to hold the branches still so her baby might sleep. For Crashaw and Lope this is a leading significance of the Nativity: since God has sent his Son to dwell among us and to share each prosaic detail of our lives, then man—even the least among us—may speak intimately, even jest with the angels.

Clearly a key element in the tone is the concept of humility, and it is interwoven in the form of the "Hymn in the Holy Nativity." The end of the poem, says Kerby Neill, "is filled with the fusion of Christian symbolism and pastoral convention."[19] Such is indeed the orientation of the hymn as a whole, but toward the conclusion there is a particular stanza (rather curious at first glance) which helps to clarify the significance of the pastoral motif:

> WELCOME, though not to those gay flyes.
> Guilded ith'Beames of earthly kings;
> Slippery soules in smiling eyes;
> But to poor Shepheards, home-spun things:
> Whose Wealth's their flock; whose witt, to be
> Well read in their simplicity.
>
> [ll. 91–96]

We may question what place such a stanza has in a Christmas hymn, unless we are willing, along with Crashaw, to take the pastoral theme quite seriously. The "simplicity" of the shepherds, their innocent, "home-spun" emotions, are explicitly set against the sophistication, cynicism, and hypocrisy of court life. In other words, Crashaw has sought to include all the elements of the pastoral eclogue: dialogue form, a taste of rustic humor and quaintness, rapturous love (here divine), and an allusion to the world of the court or city. This use of pastoral conventions, converted a lo divino, which is a principal source of the poem's tone of innocence and simplicity, is, then, additionally a means of literary realization of the Church's traditional association between the circumstances of our Lord's birth and the virtue of humility and the love of poverty.[20]

Pastores de Belén, as the title implies, is saturated with precisely the same quality. The shepherds—humble, honest country folk of Bethlehem—are overtly contrasted with Herod and his party: "He lives abhorred as a tyrant for being so blood-thirsty, and so his rebuilding of the holy temple of Solomon and other ruins in Jerusalem was partly to cover up such ugly and astonishing murders" (*Obras escogidas,* II, 1238). Herod is not, then, only a tyrant, but a politic hypocrite too. Opposed to his evil rule in Jerusalem (the city) is the rustic life of the shepherds: among the first poems in *Pastores* is an imitation of the Virgilian and Horatian *beatus ille* theme:[21]

> ¡Cuan bienaventurado
> aquel puede llamarse justamente
> que, sin tener cuidado
> de la malicia y lengua de la gente
> a la virtud contraria,
> la suya pasa en vida solitaria!
>
> Dichosa el que no mira
> del altivo señor las altas casas,
> ni de mirar se admira
> fuertes columnas oprimiendo basas
> en las soberbias puertas
> a la lisonja eternamente abiertas.
>
> [*Obras escogidas,* II, 1190]

[Blessed that man / may be justly called / who, without a care / for the malice and the gossip of the crowd, / contrary to virtue, / passes his own life in solitude!

Happy he who does not gaze / upon the high halls of the haughty lord, / nor is amazed by looking at / the great columns oppressing their bases / of the proud gates, / eternally open to flattery.]

This theme—dear to the hearts of siglo de oro poets—is integrated perfectly with the dominant devotional concern of *Pastores de Belén.* Sung by a group of shepherds early in the work, it establishes the atmosphere and tone for the sacred events to follow: the Nativity occurs among rustics because the holy is only accessible to the simple and the pure in heart. The parallel to Crashaw's hymn is unmistakable: "Welcome, though not to those gay flyes... Slippery soules. ..."

Crashaw's emphasis on the holiness and integrity of the rustic shepherds, as opposed to the ruling powers of court, suggests an especially important distinction between his sacred pastoral and the four Christmastide poems of Robert Herrick, whose work most resembles the "Hymn in the Holy Nativity."[22] Leah Marcus has provided a convincing argument that the popular childlike quality of Herrick's

Noble Numbers constitutes a royalist political statement at a time when
not only King and bishops but the traditional liturgical rites and festive
celebrations of Christendom were subjected to the wrath of a
Puritan-dominated Parliament. "Christmas came under particular
censure," Marcus observes, "in part because its emphasis on Christ as
a helpless infant invited jesting dishonor of the majesty of God; in part
because it was the festival most heavily laden with corrupt celebrations."[23] Obviously, a Puritan would have disapproved equally of
the poems of Herrick and Crashaw, but there are important differences. All four of Herrick's Christmas poems are expressly identified as having been "sung to the King in the Presence at White-
Hall"; and one of them ends with an explicit compliment to Charles I:

> Let's blesse the Babe: And, as we sing
> His praise; so let us blesse the King:
> *Chor.* Long may He live till He hath told
>   His New-yeeres trebled to His old:
>   And, when that's done, to re-aspire
> A new-borne *Phoenix* from His own chaste fire.[24]

Such adulation of a reigning earthly monarch in a pastoral Nativity
poem contrasts sharply with the mood of Crashaw's hymn, which
appears to reflect a certain disillusionment with the powers of this
world.

Herrick's mixing of religion and royalism is, of course, central to
the Laudian view of church and crown; and it reflects a policy that
goes back to the reign of Elizabeth, when, as Louis Adrian Montrose
has pointed out, the government developed the use of pastoral pageants
and literature as an instrument of royal propaganda. A principal purpose of this undertaking was to drain the pastoralism of the medieval
Nativity plays of its potentially subversive aspects and assimilate its
affective power to the strengthening of the crown's absolutism:

In the apocalyptic perspective of the cycle plays, the only true king is the King
of Kings; even Christian rulers might be contaminated by Herod's image.
Elements of the inversion and levelling that were explicit in the divine pastoral
of the Nativity texts might subtly infiltrate other pastoral forms. This context
had to be expunged or transformed if pastoral metaphors were to function
effectively as benign images of the stable and rigorously hierarchical social
order which Tudor governments sought to establish and preserve.[25]

At the close of his paper, Montrose suggests that Milton's "On the Morning of Christ's Nativity" demands "a revival and completion of the English Reformation" and "a recovery of the authentic sources and forms of pastoral power."[26] Crashaw's Nativity hymn likewise represents a reaction against the Erastian monarchical expropriation of the sacred pastoral, albeit in a Counter Reformation perspective; and he has arguably come closer than Milton to the recovery of the popular spirit of the Christian pastoral of the Middle Ages, which had been so finely preserved in siglo de oro Spain. In any case, Crashaw's poem, so vibrant with its paradoxically joyous sense of humble triumph, has nothing of the fey "shadow" which, according to Marcus, betrays Herrick's awareness of the "frailty" of the Laudian royalism which the *Noble Numbers* celebrates.[27]

The extent to which Crashaw's vision of the Nativity develops and the importance of the Spanish background for his poetry are both apparent by comparison with the brief treatment of the birth of Christ in Crashaw's translation of the *Sospetto d'Herode*, the first book of Marino's biblical epic, *Strage de gli Innocenti* (1632). In this work, probably dating from 1637,[28] Crashaw takes from Marino's original the depiction of Herod as a bloody tyrant, a theme which anticipates the pastoral contrast between corrupt court and innocent country in the "Hymn in the Holy Nativity. ' Moreover, Crashaw's translation of Marino's epic includes the basic details of the Nativity setting as mirrored in the baleful eyes of Satan:

> Hee saw rich Nectar thawes, release the rigour
> Of th'Icy North; from frost-bound Atlas hands
> His Adamantine fetters fall: greene vigour
> Gladding the Scythian Rocks, and Libian sands.
> Hee saw a vernall smile, sweetly disfigure
> Winters sad face, and through the flowry lands
> > Of faire Engaddi hony-sweating Fountaines
> > With Manna, Milk, and Balm, new broach the Mountaines.
>
> Hee saw how in that blest Day-bearing Night,
> The Heav'n-rebuked shades made hast away;
> How bright a Dawne of Angels with new Light
> Amaz'd the midnight world, and made a Day
> Of which the Morning knew not: Mad with spight
> Hee markt how the poore Shepheards ran to pay

Their simple Tribute to the Babe, whose Birth
Was the great businesse both of Heav'n, and Earth.

[st. 14–15]

Most of the concrete elements of the later Nativity hymn are here,
and, as Claes Schaar observes, this "list of miracles celebrating the
birth of the Saviour" is not original even with Marino; he doubtless
borrowed them from Pietro Aretino's *I Quattro Libri de la Humanita di
Christo* (1539), and the latter is certainly recapitulating a tradition that
begins in the fourth century with Prudentius's *Cathemerinon* and
Apotheosis.[29] But despite the similarity of fundamental motifs,
Crashaw's Nativity hymn is not the same, and the distinguishing
feature is its buoyant tone, which sets it apart even from his own
rendering of Marino. Only in Lope's sacred pastorals, and in some of
the popular poetry of his siglo de oro countrymen do we find its like.
Only in the poetry of Crashaw and his Spanish counterparts are the
terms "poor" and "humble"—as applied to the shepherds—fleshed out
into something approaching a distinctive mood and personality of rustic gaiety.[30]

In the first chapter, I called attention to the epic quality of Antonio Geraldini's attempt at a Nativity eclogue, and the epic spirit of
humanist classicism seems to dominate most of the vernacular, as well
as the neo-Latin, treatments of the Nativity during the Renaissance.
The effects of this classicizing tendency can be gauged through a
consideration of the most famous of the Latin biblical epics, Marco
Girolamo Vida's *Christiados* (1535). Vida begins (of course!) in medias
res, and the birth of Christ is narrated in a flashback. The teller of the
Christmas story is none other than St. Joseph, whom Vida imagines
having gone with St. John the Divine to plead with Pilate for the life of
his foster son. Pilate is depicted in a rather favorable light as a
thoughtful and earnest prince, who deals courteously with the
suppliants because he has been impressed by Jesus' demeanor and
suspects that his lineage is aristocratic if not divine:

Talibus orabat. largo simul imbre rigabant
Ora senis lachrymae, placido quem Pontius ore
Accipit, atque ambos uerbis solatur amicis,
Depositumque senem molli locat ipse sedili.
. . . .
Sollicito mihi cura tui est nunc maxima nati,
Quem tibi mente agito incolumem seruare, furoremque,

> Et rabiem, ut potui, compressi gentis iniquae.
> Fare age (nanque mihi haud nunc primum uenit ad aures)
> Quae fortuna uiro, unde domo, quo sanguine cretus.
> Ede tuum, matrisque genus. non ille creatus
> Stirpe humili, mihi si uerum mens augurat. ut se
> Incessu gerit! ut uultuque et corpore toto est
> Humana maior species! ut lumina honorum
> Plena! ut regifici motus! uerba inde notaui,
> Nil mortale sonat. sensi illo in pectore numen.
> Aut certe Deus ille, aut non mortalibus ortus. [31]

[In such wise he beseeched. At the same time tears in copious flow watered the face of the old man whom Pontius received with gentle countenance, and consoled them both with friendly words, and he himself placed the despairing old man on a soft chair. . . . I am vexed and my greatest concern now is for your son, whom I am reckoning how to keep unharmed for you, and I have restrained, as much as I have been able, the wrath and fury of this spiteful nation. Come, speak (for indeed now is hardly the first time he comes to my ears) the lot of the man, whence his house, of what blood sprung up. Declare your race and his mother's. He is not come of humble stock, if my mind perceives aright. How he bears himself in pace! And how completely in countenance and body he is greater than humankind! How full of nobility his eyes! Of what kingly movement! Thereupon I took note of his words; they sounded not at all mortal. I sensed deity in that breast. Either he is certainly a god, or not of mortal origins.]

Such a positive depiction of Pilate, with the additional emphasis on the princely aspect of Christ, is diametrically opposed to the popular rustic flavor cultivated both by Lope and Crashaw. Moreover, a Christ so transparently divine serves to diminish the paradoxical tension of the Incarnation which Crashaw and his Spanish counterparts stress.

Given this setting, it is not surprising that when St. Joseph comes to describe the Nativity scene itself in Vida's poem, his account is rather different from that of Lope's and Crashaw's shepherds. To be sure, many of the same motifs are present. The divine star gilds the shabby stable with supernatural radiance, the humble shepherds show up strewing garlands and playing reed pipes, and their eyes are dazzled by the splendor of the holy Infant's countenance (III, 571–633). While Crashaw and Lope emphasize the ironic contrast between the absolute sovereignty of God and the lowly conditions He has deigned to endure for man's benefit, thereby mingling theological subtlety with a sense of childlike wonder and joy, Vida, in effect, suppresses this

paradox, preferring to highlight Christ's majesty, circumstances notwithstanding, in order that the grave decorum of the epic not be
diminished. Nowhere is this striking contrast more prominent than in
the solemn treatment of the angels by Vida's shepherds:

> His moniti uicinam oculos torquemus ad urbem.
> Ecce autem uolucer pictis exercitus alis
> Coelestes supra pueri toto aethere uisi
> Nubibus impositi liquidas equitare per oras,
> Et mirum in morem celeri proludere coetu.
> Atque ubi ter coelum ternis toto agmine uersi
> Lustrauere choris, ter lustrauere choreis,
> Concentu petiere polum. longe ardua Olympi
> Responsat. laetis dissultat plausibus aether.[32]

[With these admonitions (of the angel) we turned our eyes to the nearby city.
Behold now a flying army of heavenly boys with painted wings seen above
throughout the sky rode through the clear regions astride the clouds, and in
amazing fashion practiced formations with their swift company. And then
with the whole group converged in three choirs, they circled heaven three
times, circled three times dancing, seeking the zenith with harmony. The
heights of Olympus resounded. The upper air trembled with joyful clapping.]

Here is certainly wonder, yet lacking the humble intimacy and rustic
gaiety which are such marked features of the Nativity poetry of
Crashaw and Lope de Vega. It is hard to imagine Vida's shepherds
referring to the angels as multicolored birds (as Lope's do), or teasing
them about the purity of their wings (as Crashaw's do). It appears,
then, that the classicizing tendencies inherent in the composition of
neo-Latin poetry presented virtually insuperable barriers to the at-
tainment of the tone of devout comedy which Crashaw shares with
siglo de oro poets like Lope.[33]

II

The phenomenon I have scrutinized in the Nativity poem is a
particular species of wit, recognized as such by Crashaw and serving
as a distinctive feature in his style, present throughout his work, but
not fully developed except in the hymns of his poetic maturity. The
exact orientation varies, of course, from poem to poem, but its fundamental effect is to generate a resonance of seemingly opposed yet

convergent attitudes and emotions. This is not a matter of semantic ambiguity or equivocation—there is little question over what Crashaw's poems are about, or what they mean—but rather of emotional ambience. The dogma of the Incarnation, albeit a paradox, is clear enough in its content, and the issue of theological doubt never arises in Crashaw's poems; nevertheless, it is not clear how a human being is to regard the dogma or himself confronting it. Sacred parody, with the particular sort of wit which characterizes it, is a poetic means of coping with the problematic response called for by very God's putting on and sanctification of human flesh. As we have observed in the second chapter, Crashaw's Assumption poem is marked by a combination of passionate languor, delicate eroticism, and devout wonder; and it is this striving to hold in harmonious solution an impossibly divergent complex of attitudes and emotions which defines the tenderness and wit of Crashaw's hymns. The "Hymn in the Epiphanie," that profound celebration of mystic darkness, is laced with a humorous irony bordering on satire in the long passage (ll. 8off.) in which the lasciviousness of pagan worship is contrasted with the purity of Christ's love; even in the "Hymn to the Name of Jesus," especially in the lines on the martyrs, there is a high-spirited gaiety: "It was the witt of love o'reflowed the Bounds / Of WRATH, and made thee way through All Those WOUNDS" (ll. 223–24). The blood of the martyrs, which necessarily is the focus of such contradictory feelings, is thus formulated by Crashaw as the "witt of love";[34] and it is because his poems all rest on the edge of Christian paradox that their tone is so subtle and strange.

Nowhere is Crashaw's combination of tenderness and irony, of witty gaiety and sensuous delicacy, more pronounced than in his poems about Santa Teresa; and nowhere are the resemblances of his work to Spanish poetry and the influence of Teresa herself more marked. A consideration of the parallels between Crashaw's treatment of Santa Teresa and the Spanish poems offered in her honor suggests the powerful impact of Teresa's own witty, comic sense. This is an especially important point, because Crashaw's Teresa poems, perhaps even more than the others, have often been thoroughly misunderstood through a failure to interpret his tone correctly. Yvor Winters, for example, refers to "A Hymn to Sainte Teresa" as "a fairy-tale of childish pietism," evincing no little scorn for Crashaw's presumed

naiveté.[35] But it is difficult to see how such an attitude can be maintained if the poem is carefully examined.

"A Hymn to Sainte Teresa" falls into three sections, the first of
which occupies sixty-four lines.[36] In this opening part of the poem,
Crashaw uses Teresa's childhood desire for martyrdom as a means of
setting her in the context of Church history, of comparing her to the
early Christian martyrs:

> Those thy old Souldiers, Great and tall,
> Ripe Men of Martyrdom, that could reach down
> With strong armes, their triumphant crown,
> Such as could with lusty breath
> Speak lowd into the face of death
> Their Great LORD's glorious name. . . .
>
> [ll. 4–9]

The immediate purpose of the comparison is to create wonder: here is
a small child (and female) who would dare the fate of the Church's
first heroes: "'Tis LOVE, not YEARES or LIMBS that can / Make the
Martyr, or the man" (ll. 33–34). To be sure, the traditional idea of
martyrdom is finally set in contrast to the subtle, exalted "death more
mysticall and high" (l. 76) that Teresa will endure as an adult:

> SWEET, no so fast! lo thy fair Spouse
> Whom thou seekst with so swift vowes,
> Calls thee back, and bidds thee come
> T'embrace a milder MARTYRDOM.
>
> [ll. 65–68]

The effect of this transition is, of course, to establish a relation between the tradition of the Church Militant and the extraordinary,
personal experience of Santa Teresa. The hymn thus pursues the
poet's usual interest: the juxtaposition of apparently divergent kinds of
experience.

The motif which informs the first section of Crashaw's poem, a
comparison and contrast of Teresa and the ancient martyrs, also appears in a poem by Lope de Vega, written for a contest in honor of the
Saint. Lope compares Teresa to an early Spanish martyr, San Hermenegildo, son of King Leovigildo (A.D. 567–86), by whom he was put
to death for opposing the Arianism of his father and stepmother.[37]

Lope's poem, "A San Hermenegildo," concludes by giving Santa Teresa's response to the death of Hermenegildo, which is described in terms as extravagant and lurid as anything ever ventured by Crashaw:

> Déjale el golpe la frente
> como una granada abierta,
> porque fruta coronada
> bien es que de reyes sea.
>   Los granos vueltos granates
> bordan entre el oro, y perlas
> la talar túnica, y vuelven
> púrpura la blanca tela.
>   Este espectáculo vivo
> mirando estaba Teresa;
> Teresa, mujer de chapa;
> Teresa, madre y doncella.
>   Del hacha tenéis codicia;
> pues, Madre, tened paciencia:
> que habéis de ser un hacha
> que alumbra toda la Iglesia.
>
> [*Obras escogidas*, II, 234]

[The blow leaves his forehead like an open pomegranate, since it is proper that a crowned fruit be for kings. The seeds turned into garnets embroider the flowing tunic between the gold and pearls, and turn to purple the white cloth. Teresa was gazing at this vivid spectacle; Teresa, woman of judgment; Teresa, mother and maid. You are covetous of the axe; well, Mother, have patience: for you are to be a torch that illuminates the whole Church.]

As in Crashaw's hymn, the actual course of Teresa's life is seen as an alternative to the martyrdom which she desired at an early age—a divinely ordained alternative.

Baltasar Elisio de Medinilla (1585–1620) also compares Teresa with the ancient martyrs, as well as other saints of the past, again in a poem written for a contest. Medinilla begins his "Introducción del Certamen y Justa literaria" by praising the wonder of God who produces saints in every age. In the youth of the Church during heathen times, there were martyrs: "Como de vn grano mill produce sanctos / la púrpura bertida y templa el cielo / con Vida el Fin y con placer los LLantos"[38] ("As from one seed, spilt purple [i.e., blood] produces a thousand saints and heaven tempers the End with Life and with pleasure the laments"). Next the poet mentions the saints of wisdom (Augustine, Gregory, Jerome) and then those of asceticism (Francis, Anthony); but the equal of all those in the past has come in this age:

> Oy en la senetud del tiempo miro
> vn Monstruo raro en cuyas alabanzas
> del Temor al Espanto me rretiro
> vna muger si a tantas esperanzas
> puede llegar Muger, muger que pudo
> exceder las humanas confianzas.[39]

[Today in the old age of time I behold a rare Wonder (or "Monster") in whose praises I shrink back from Fear to Astonishment, a woman, if Woman can fulfill such great hopes, a woman who was able to exceed human assurances.]

In his emphasis on the wonder that a woman could accomplish the feats of Santa Teresa, Medinilla recalls the heading of the later editions of Crashaw's hymn: "A / WOMAN / for Angelical height of specu-lation, for / Masculine courage of performance, / more than a woman" (p. 53). Medinilla, like Crashaw, also observes that Teresa must be "love's victim" rather than a martyr in the usual sense:

> Opusose tanbien contra la Muerte
> pues solo Amor bastó a quitar la Vida
> a quien le dio el dominio de su suerte.[40]

[She also withstood Death since Love alone was sufficient to take the Life of her who gave it dominion of her fortune.]

It should be clear, then, that Crashaw is working within a tra-ditional interpretation of Santa Teresa's life with a clear rationale—an interpretation which, as we shall see, originates with the saint herself. Moreover, the "fairy-tale" quality of the story and the "childish pietism" it manifests are handled in a way that is at once admiring and gently humorous; the ironic, though altogether sympathetic tone is unmistakable:

> FAREWEL then, all the world! Adieu.
> TERESA is no more for you.
> Farewell, all pleasures, sports, and joyes,
> (Never till now esteemed toyes)
> Farewell what ever deare may bee,
> MOTHER'S armes or FATHER'S knee

> Farewell house, and farewell home!
> SHE's for the Moores, and MARTYRDOM.
>
> [ll. 57–64]

The skipping rhythm alone, especially as it is comically underscored by heavy-handed alliteration ("Farewell *h*ouse, and *f*arewell *h*ome") ought to be sufficient to reveal that Crashaw is not so sentimental and simple as often supposed by his less than sympathetic critics.

The same wry tone also pervades Lope's "San Hermenegildo" (in fact, it is excessive in this poem), although the puns in the passage quoted above are obscured by translation: *granada* ("pomegranate"), *grano* ("seed"), and *granate* ("garnet"); *hacha* ("axe") and *hacha* ("torch"). But there can be no doubt, even in translation, concerning the mood of the two stanzas which close the poem, following immediately upon Lope's counsel that Teresa be patient in her desire for martyrdom:

> Que a morir vos de siete anos,
> no hubiera esta tarde fiesta
> en el convento del Carmen
> ni tanto poeta hubiera.
> Tanto, que los hijos vuestros,
> si no es que Dios lo remedia,
> como a otros comen piojos,
> se han de comer poetas.
>
> [*Obras escogidas*, II, 234]

[For had you died at seven years of age, there would not be this afternoon festival in the convent of the Carmelites nor would there have been so many poets. So many, that unless God remedy it, these children of yours, as others are eaten up by lice, will be eaten up by poets.]

The last stanza is especially pertinent as a comic suggestion of the great multitude of poets who were writing about Santa Teresa, and of the general atmosphere of the poetic contests. There is similar extravagance in Baltasar de Medinilla's reference to the saint as a "Monstruo" who frightens and astounds him, and in his exposition of her reform work in military terms:

> Formó campo, hizo gente, intentó guerra
> contra los vicios cuyo ymperio fuerte
> al mismo ynfierno con su Rey destierra.[41]

[She formed the ranks, marshalled her people, undertook war against the vices whose strong empire she exiles to the same hell with their King.]

Perhaps the most extreme manifestation of this light-hearted, comic approach to Santa Teresa is to be found in Luis de Góngora's "En la beatificación de Santa Teresa." This romance was written for a justa poética held in honor of Teresa's beatification in Córdoba in May 1614. As a contemporary account of the contest says, the poem is "of a mixed style, serious at times, and comical" (*Obras de Góngora*, p. 1111); however, the comic parts are by far the more prominent. The characteristic feature of the poem is the pun:

> Moradas, divino el arte,
> y celestial la materia,
> fabricó, arquitecta alada,
> si no argumentosa abeja.
> Tanto y tan bien escribió,
> que podrá correr parejas
> su espíritu con la pluma
> del Prelado de su Iglesia,
> pues abulenses los dos,
> ya que no iguales en letras,
> en nombre iguales, él fue
> Tostado, Ahumada ella.
>
> [*Obras de Góngora*, p. 192]

[A winged architect, if not an argumentative bee, she built mansions, the art divine, celestial the material. So much and so well she wrote, that her spirit could run even with the Prelate of her Church, for both were natives of Ávila; although not equal in letters, their names were equivalent: he was Tostado, she, Ahumada.]

The "mansions" built by Santa Teresa are, of course, her book, *Moradas del castillo interior* ("Mansions of the interior castle"); and, although they are not spelled alike, her family name, Ahumada, is equivalent to the Bishop's, Tostado, because the two mean, respectively, "smoked" and "toasted." Another major element in Góngora's poem is extreme hyperbole: Santa Teresa is a "Patriarch" of two families (reformed Carmelite nuns and friars); "half nun and half friar / sister Angel and friar Teresa," Góngora calls her, and, now that she is to be beatified, "she is threefold in condition, and one / if not

unique, in essence." After thus comparing her implicitly to the triune
Godhead, the poet proceeds to compare her to Moses and Elisha, and
to describe her work in this fashion:

> Baja, pues, y en pocos años
> tantas fundaciones deja,
> cuantos pasos da en Espana,
> orbe ya de sus estrellas.
>
> [*Obras de Góngora*, p. 191]

[She descends (from Mt. Carmel) and in a few years leaves as many foun-
dations as she makes steps in Spain, the sphere, now, of her stars.]

The extravagant conceits, the paradox and hyperbole of the first
sixty-eight lines of "The Flaming Heart," which Austin Warren describes as "for the most part a work of unfired ingenuity,"[42] may be
taken reasonably to represent Crashaw's attempt to compete with the
kind of exaggerated wit represented by Góngora's romance. The witty
ironic treatment of Teresa's masculinity, which is noticed in a more
restrained fashion in "A Hymn to Sainte Teresa," is especially reminiscent of Góngora: "One would suspect thou meant'st to paint / Some
weak, inferior, woman saint" (ll. 25–26). Like his Spanish predecessor
who calls her "friar Teresa," Crashaw has made a joke out of the
common idea that the Carmelite saint was more than a woman. Of
course, the joke has a purpose: it is the miracle of sanctity to obliterate
the standard categories of human thought, such as male and female.

In order to explain this element of extravagant wit and fantastic
hyperbole, the best recourse is to pause and consider briefly the common feature of the Spanish poems about Teresa: all were written for
poetic contests. Throughout the major cities of Spain, festivals were
sponsored by the Jesuits and by the Discalced Carmelites in honor of
the beatification of their respective founders, San Ignacio and Santa
Teresa. Apparently such contests were ordinary occurrences in
seventeenth-century Spain. Probably the grandest of these events was
the festival held in 1622 by the city of Madrid in honor of its newly
canonized patron, San Isidro (not to be confused with St. Isidore of
Seville, famous for the *Etymologies*). We are fortunate in having a good
account of the proceedings, since Lope de Vega was commissioned to
write a history of the festival, *Relación de las fiestas en la Canonización*

de San Isidro (*Obras escogidas,* II, 977–96). In addition, Lope was charged with providing two comedias, performed as part of the celebration, and with being a judge in the poetic contest in which one hundred and thirty-two poets participated. Prizes were given in a variety of categories including sonnets, ballads, "hieroglyphics" (or emblems), and canciones (first prize in the last category was won, incidentally, by Lope himself). The winning poems were read in the main plaza of Madrid, decorated for the occasion with massive "pyramids," figures of saints and martyrs "gilded with fine gold," and altars set up by various religious orders. Although the festival in Madrid was undoubtedly more elaborate than most, it nevertheless gives some idea of the circumstances for which many religious poems were written in Spain during the seventeenth century.

It appears, then, that much of the poetry which probably influenced Crashaw was designed for a setting more like the Tournament of Roses than anything in the Anglo-American literary or religious tradition. Poetry composed for recitation at a festive occasion will inevitably partake of its atmosphere; poets in direct competition with one another—especially in an age when wit is prized for its own sake—can be expected to seek spectacular effects of phrase and image. Crashaw's Teresa poems may be read as part of an entire tradition of Spanish poetry prompted by the contests held in the saint's honor. Seen against such a background, Crashaw's poems do not seem extravagant and eccentric to the same extent as when they are compared only with English devotional literature. The Spanish *justa poética* provides, therefore, a context for the Teresa poems, which allows us to see them not simply as private meditations, but rather as attempts to invest the poet's solitude with the gaiety of communal celebration, a facet of religious expression to which Crashaw's own England was at the time growing increasingly hostile.[43]

The frequent references to martyrdom in poems about Santa Teresa and the humorous tone adopted in many of them are further illuminated by taking into account the saint's own work. She gives no warrant for Góngora's extravagances, but her own writings are not wanting in humor and irony. The incident which is the center of the first part of Crashaw's hymn, and to which Lope alludes obliquely in "San Hermenegildo," comes in the first chapter of Teresa's *Vida,* which bears the heading: "In which she treats of how the Lord began to awaken her soul in childhood to virtous things, and of the help which parents are in this matter" (*Obras*, p. 28). But the heading of the chapter which follows reads thus: "She treats of how she was losing these virtues, and of what is important in childhood, to associate with virtuous persons" (*Obras*, p. 30). The little story of running away from home to seek martyrdom is, then, a parable of innocence. Her childhood was virtuous because it was uncorrupted, and it is important in her *Vida* because it contrasts with the sinfulness (in her view) of the succeeding years. She looks back upon the experience with an affectionate but amused nostalgia; it was the deed of a child, and she treats it as such:

And thus I greatly desired to die (not on account of love, which I conceived to hold for Him, but rather on account of the great benefits that I read were there in heaven). . . . The saying that the pain and glory are forever, in what we [Teresa and her brother] were reading, astonished us greatly. Many times we happened to be discussing this, and we took pleasure in saying over again: forever, and ever, and ever! [*Obras*, p. 29]

Santa Teresa's own candid and unaffected treatment of her childhood undoubtedly inspired the comedy in many of the poems dedicated to her. In the lines of "A Hymn to Sainte Teresa," quoted earlier, Crashaw has caught the tone of Teresa's own work perfectly. Moreover, this charming if slight tale has a purpose: in Crashaw's poem, as in Teresa's *Vida*, it serves as a point of contrast. The quaint, though basically admirable longings of the child are set against the profound experiences of the woman, or rather of the saint. The concept of physical martyrdom is spiritualized; the child's vague yearning is realized in the passion of mystical death.

By placing Crashaw's hymns in the context of the sacred litera-ture of the Spanish Golden Age the distinctive tone of his poetry—so different from that of his English contemporaries—emerges as com-plex and purposive rather than merely excessive or confused. Crashaw is seeking to serve a Church which emphasizes in its liturgy and devotions the most startling paradoxes of the Incarnation and mysteri-ous relation of the Virgin Mary and her divine Son. Moreover, in Counter Reformation Spain he had the model of a culture in which mysticism was not the obsession of recluses, like Henry Vaughan, but the formal vocation of entire rejuvenated orders of men and women religious, some of whom came to be not only public figures but eventually national heroes, celebrated in festival and song. Seen against such a backdrop, the most puzzling features of Crashaw's sacred poetry begin to make sense: his nonchalant presentation of the most intimate relations of the soul, the most profound and intensely passionate mysteries of the faith, in a spirit of witty, carnival gaiety.

4

The Wound of Love
and the Dark Night of the Soul:
Crashaw and Mysticism

THAT MYSTICISM IS A CRUCIALLY IMPORTANT concern in Crashaw's sacred poetry is a proposition to which every reader of his work must give assent: in his reference to the pseudo-Dionysius in his Epiphany poem and his depictions of Teresa's mystical raptures in the poems devoted to her, the theme is explicit. Crashaw's treatment of the theme, nonetheless, has proven puzzling to most critics. Austin Warren defends Crashaw as a mystical poet in an early essay, but little of this enthusiasm seems to carry over into the later book.[1] In subsequent years the mystical element in Crashaw's poetry has often been dismissed or simply ignored.[2] And thus, yet another facet of Crashaw's work suffers depreciation by being judged against criteria based on his English contemporaries: Vaughan and Traherne—introspective and individualistic—are the English poets of mysticism par excellence. Critics who miss their distinctive qualities in Crashaw's poems are quick to infer that his preoccupation with mystical union is superficial if not spurious. Crashaw's wry gaiety of tone and the insistent sensuousness of his sacred parody seem antithetic to Vaughan's plunge into the abyss of "deep, but dazling darkness"[3] or Traherne's invocation of childhood innocence. But if we turn to the literature of Spanish mysticism, which obviously furnished Crashaw's most powerful inspiration, then once again he may be seen in a setting in which apparent incongruities converge in a coherent and satisfying pattern. Those aspects of his poetry which have been viewed with most suspicion turn out to be the source of his particular power and unique contribution to English devotional verse.

In part the problem of interpreting Crashaw's mystical poetry is a problem of interpreting the role of mysticism in Christian life. Donald Attwater provides a frequently quoted, standard definition of mysticism as "experimental knowledge of God's presence, in which the soul has, as a great reality, a sense of contact with him. It is the same as passive contemplation or mystical union."[4] As Helmut Hatzfeld points out, this generally accepted Catholic view of mysticism is derived from the work of Santa Teresa's greatest disciple, San Juan de la Cruz, who adds to his deep personal experience of mystical contemplation the advantage of a firm grounding in Thomistic philosophy. Hence Hatzfeld rightly maintains that the Spanish Carmelite school comprises the "classic mysticism" of the Christian tradition.[5] According to San Juan, "mystical theology" may be equated with "infused contemplation"—an unmediated, intuitive awareness of God which transcends the intellect as it fills it: "the contemplation by which the understanding has the highest awareness of God they call *Mystical Theology*, which means a secret knowledge of God, because it is secret to the very understanding which receives it" (*Vida y obras*, p. 410).

It is clear from these definitions that mysticism is a rare and specialized state of contemplative prayer—an unusual gift of God. Nevertheless, it is not a phenomenon wholly removed from the ordinary course of Christian spiritual life and worship. As Joseph Collins points out, Christian mysticism as such is especially distinctive as a result of its focus on the Incarnation: "The Divine Word or Logos assuming human nature and becoming man gives to Christian mysticism that practical basis for its contemplations which is poles asunder from the abstract, intellectual ascent of the Neoplatonists."[6] E. Allison Peers quotes the opening of Crashaw's "Hymn to Sainte Teresa" as an expression of the essence of Spanish mysticism: "Love, thou art absolute sole lord/ Of life and death"; and he ascribes to siglo de oro mysticism "an unmistakable individuality" because "it is concrete, practical, personal, experiential, active."[7] San Juan de la Cruz teaches that he who would be a mystic must, as any Christian, imitate our Lord in his suffering and drink "the chalice which He had to drink":

And thus, I would persuade spiritual persons how this road of God does not consist in myriad meditations, or ways, or means, or pleasures (although this might in its way be necessary to beginners), but rather in a single necessary thing, which is knowing how to deny oneself truly, both within and without, yielding oneself to suffer for Christ and to be utterly annihilated; because, exercising oneself in this, everything else and more is effected and found out, and if this exercise is lacking, which is the sum and root of all, then everything else is beating around the bush and is of no avail, even though one has meditations and communications as high as angels. Because only imitating Christ is of any avail. [*Vida y obras,* pp. 406–07]

In the *Cántico espiritual* San Juan identifies this same "true imitation of the perfection of the life of the Son of God" with the "cave of stone," a mystical figure for the spiritual marriage (*Vida y obras,* pp. 632–33). [8] Hence Spanish mysticism in its highest form, which so fascinated Crashaw, grows from the same root, to use San Juan's figure, as the *imitatio Christi* associated with the *devotio moderna* so popular in the fifteenth and sixteenth centuries. [9]

The relation between mysticism and the Christian mystery of our Lord's life of suffering and sacrificial death, the ideal model for all Christians, is manifest in Santa Teresa's view of her own life, and in the response of Crashaw as well as numerous Spanish poets. In the preceding chapter attention is drawn to Crashaw's gently comic treatment of Teresa's childhood attempt to become a martyr at the hands of the Moors; in "A Hymn to Sainte Teresa" this event is followed by an impassioned depiction of her mystical martyrdom at the hands of a seraph. This juxtaposing is not a gratuitous piece of wit on the part of the poet. Such a transformation of the conventional idea of martyrdom finds precedent repeatedly in Santa Teresa's own works: "Perfect martyrdom not only happens when blood is spilled, but martyrdom also consists even in true abstinence from sin and in the exercise and keeping of the commandments of God. True patience in adversity also makes a martyr" (*Obras,* pp. 1127–28). In the twenty-first chapter of the *Vida* she imagines that among the saints, "in whom this fire of love for God had grown so great," the longing for union with him "must have been a continuous martyrdom" (p. 98); and in chapter seventeen of *El camino de perfección* ("The way of perfection"), she adds, "For, do you not know, sisters, that the life of the true religious, or one who wishes to be among the near friends of God, is a long martyrdom?" (p. 230). The *Moradas,* or "Mansions of the interior castle," is especially full of references to martyrdom. In the fourth chapter of the sixth "mansion," she describes divine ecstasy in which "it seems that the body changes something in itself and breathes only to die again, and to give greater life to the soul." In such a state, she continues, the soul sees that "the martyrs did not do much in the torments they suffered—for with this help on the part of our Lord, it is easy..." (p. 416).

As manifest in the final quotation, martyrdom and mystical ecstasy are associated in the writings of Santa Teresa; hence, the transition between the first and second parts of Crashaw's hymn has a clear basis in her work. In the middle section of the poem (ll. 65–117), Crashaw turns abruptly from the episode of the saint's childhood to draw upon the most famous and dramatic scene of her *Vida:* her vision of an angel piercing her heart with a dart.[10] Not surprisingly, this vision of an angel was also a favorite among Spanish poets. Lope de Vega devotes to it the third of eight sonnets on Santa Teresa, published with *Triunfos divinos* (1625). In this sonnet the dart wielded by the seraph bears the touch of the divine Spouse and unites the saint to him:

> Seraphin cazador el dardo os tira,
>   para que os deje estática la punta,
>   y las plumas se os queden en la palma:
> Con razón vuestra ciencia el mundo admira,
>   si el seráphico fuego al Dios os junta,
>   y quanto veis en él, translada el alma.[11]

[The hunting Seraph shoots you with the dart so that the point might leave you ecstatic, and the feathers remain in your palm; the world rightly admires your science, if the seraphic fire joins you to God, and your soul transcribes all that you see in Him.]

Crashaw likewise emphasizes that the dart conveys a knowledge of Christ, a direct intuition of the divine Word, or name:

> His is the DART must make the DEATH
> Whose stroke shall tast thy hallow'd breath;
> A Dart thrice dip't in that rich flame
> Which writes thy spouse's radiant Name
> Upon the roof of Heav'n; where ay
> It shines, and with a soveraign ray
> Beates bright upon the burning faces
> Of soules which in that name's sweet graces
> Find everlasting smiles....

> [ll. 79–87]

Crashaw proceeds to describe the dart as "th'immortal instrument" of mystical death and the employment of the seraph as "archerie"; a similar stress on the ferocity of divine love appears in an account of Teresa's vision by Cristobalina Fernández de Alarcón (1576–1646):

> Y por dar más perfección
> a tan angélico intento,
> el que bajó de Sion,
> con el ardiente instrumento
> la atravesó el corazón.
> Dejóla el dolor profundo
> de aquel fuego sin segundo
> con que el corazón le inflama,
> y la fuerza de su llama,
> viva a Dios y muerte al mundo. [12]

[And to give more perfection to such an angelic purpose, he (the seraph) who came down from Zion, pierced her heart with the burning instrument. He left her the profound pain of that fire without second with which he inflames her heart, and the force of its flame, alive to God and dead to the world.]

Among the more prominent aspects of these lines is the emphasis on the "profound pain," bringing at once life and death, exquisite joy and terrible suffering. This motif also appears in Lope's sonnet: "la fuente de vida que os aguarda, / tambien es fuego, y de abrasar no cessa" ("the fountain of life that keeps you is also fire and never ceases to burn"); and in the preceding sonnet, when Christ and Teresa are "betrothed" (*desposado*), He presents her with a nail, "so that now my wounds are knit to your palm with this nail." [13] Such notes all find echoes in Crashaw's poems on Santa Teresa; his response to the Spanish saint is in perfect harmony with that of her countrymen. A poem especially close to Crashaw's sensibility is Baltasar de Medinilla's "Canción"; it includes numerous detailed parallels to the ecstatic central section of "A Hymn to Sainte Teresa" and to the conclusion of "The Flaming Heart":

> En extasis de Amor de Amor herida
> Rosas pidiendo por remedio y flores
> dulcemente mortal Teresa yace
> y anhelando a la vnion de sus Amores
> exala al fuego de su Autor la Vida
> en olocausto que de el Alma hace
> al Amor no a la Muerte satisface

el Tributo forzoso
porque es tan poderoso
que a morir fuerza al que muriendo nace
que donde tanto yncendio se yntroduce
la Vida ynferior fuego
respecta su esplendor luego y no luce.
   No siendo a tanto ardor capaz el Pecho
que es el humano espacio esphera breue
a la del Cielo liberal grandeza
redunda Amor diuino y l'Alma beue
Oceanos de llamas que al estrecho
sobran mortal y anegan su velleza.[14]

[In an ecstasy of Love by Love wounded, asking for Roses and flowers as a remedy, sweetly mortal Teresa lies, and yearning for union with her Love, she exhales her Life into the Fire of its Author. In the holocaust which she makes of her soul, the necessary Tribute satisfies Love not Death, because it is so powerful that it forces her to die, who dying is born; for where such a conflagration gains access, Life, an inferior fire, respects its splendor then and does not shine. The Breast not being capable of such ardor, for the human extent is a brief sphere to the liberal grandeur of Heaven, divine love overflows, and the Soul drinks Oceans of flames which surpass mortal limits and inundate its beauty.]

The striking image in the last few lines of the soul drinking fire is likely to bring immediately to mind the similar imagery in the famous closing passage of Crashaw's "Flaming Heart":

> By thy larg draughts of intellectual day,
> And by thy thirsts of love more large then they;
> By all thy brim-fill'd Bowles of feirce desire
> By thy lasting Morning's draught of liquid fire.

[ll. 97–100]

An even closer, overall parallel to Medinilla's detailed account of the process of mystical death occurs in the central section of Crashaw's "Hymn to Sainte Teresa":

> O how oft shalt thou complain
> Of a sweet and subtle PAIN.
> Of intolerable Joyes;
> Of a DEATH, in which who dyes
> Loves his death, and dyes again.

>   And would for ever be so slain.
>   And lives, and dyes; and knowes not why
>   To live, But that he thus may never leave to DY.
>   How kindly will thy gentle HEART
>   Kisse the sweetly-killing DART!
>   And close in his embraces keep
>   Those delicious Wounds that weep
>   Balsom to heal themselves with.

[ll. 97–109]

The essence of this passage is the paradoxical conception that love and death imply one another (and the corollary joining together of joy and pain). Such a linking of love and death is continually reiterated in Medinilla's "Canción":

> ... conque deliquios regalados prueba
> que como aspira a vnirse en su discurso
> muere, que ay desta suerte
> del Amor a la Muerte breue curso...
>
> ... que quien Amando viue
> ya a empezado a morir en el deseo
> que es deuda Amor y compensarla ymporta
> y fuera diuidida
> para tan grande Amor la vida corta.
>
> ... pues goza de la flor del campo hermoso
> Amante siempre que muriendo quiere
> yrse de amor preciando
> que muere bien quien bien amando muere.[15]

[... and so she experiences delicate raptures, for as she aspires to be united in her discourse, she dies, for in this manner there is a brief course from Love to Death ... for she who lives Loving already has begun to die in desire, for Love is a debt and it is fitting to pay it, and her short life was measured out for such a great Love ... since a Lover always enjoys the flower of the beautiful field who, dying, wants to go on glorying in love, for he dies well who dies loving well.]

Several important considerations emerge from the texts brought together thus far in this chapter. First, since a number of Spanish poems on Teresa stress a paradoxical blending of pain and joy, of death and life, and employ very sensuous imagery, we have further evidence

that such elements in Crashaw's verse are not the product of a pecu-
liarly morbid sensibility. Such Spanish parallels provide additional
evidence for Robert G. Collmer's contention that Crashaw's visions of
ecstatic "death" cannot be regarded as sublimated references to sexual
union. [16] At the same time, these parallels further establish the pervasiveness of sacred parody as a means of handling the theme of mystical
rapture in poetry—a means grounded in the writings of the mystics
themselves. Viewed in the context of Spanish literature and compared
to a wide range of poems of similar theme and style, Crashaw's poems
no longer seem especially outré; it is possible, therefore, to judge them
on their merits as literary representations of mystical experience.

A crucial issue in this regard is the degree to which Crashaw and
his Spanish predecessors alike were influenced by Teresa's own interpretations of her mystical experiences. The vision of her transverberation by the seraph is the kind of concrete, dramatic incident from
the *Vida* that one would expect to find in poems about Teresa, and this
episode does turn up frequently; but her work also exerted an influence of more subtlety and depth. The recurrence of certain details in
various poems about the saint is not the result of mere poetic whim;
Crashaw, as well as the Spanish poets, clearly took a genuine interest
in her work, and the meaning of their poems grows out of, and is
consonant with, Teresa's ideas about the nature and significance of
mystical experience. [17] Passages of the *Moradas,* for example, are quite
illuminating with respect to Crashaw's reiterated stress upon "death"
in "A Hymn to Sainte Teresa" (or Medinilla's in his "Canción"). The
pain which is desired, the repeated deaths, have a basis in the eleventh
chapter of the sixth "mansion"; in addition Teresa explains the reason
for the suffering:

God save me, Lord, how you seize on your lovers! But all is little for what you
give afterwards. It is good that great things cost greatly; so much more, for if it
is to purify this soul in order that it may enter the seventh mansion—as those
that are to enter heaven are cleansed in purgatory—, this suffering is as little
as a drop of water would be in the sea. . . . The soul feels that this pain is of
such value, that it understands very well that it is not able to merit it, only this
feeling in no way alleviates anything, but with this it suffers with very good
appetite, and it would suffer all its life if God were served by it, although
it would not be to die at one time, but rather to be always dying, for truly it
is no less. [*Obras,* p. 436]

In the doctrine of the mystics expounded here and in other passages by Santa Teresa is the source of Crashaw's pain/pleasure oxymora and of his paradoxical references to a series of "deaths." In a passage of which the hesitant wordiness seems to embody her own awe, Teresa identifies two "dangers of death" in this "spiritual way": the natural weakness of the body in the presence of God, and the "very excessive pleasure and delight which is in so very great an extreme, that it truly seems that the soul swoons in such a way that it lacks very little of completely leaving the body . . ." (*Obras*, p. 437). The Christian mystic seeks to suffer and be exalted according to the pattern of Jesus' Passion. When every faculty is concentrated on God's presence, his absence is felt more acutely; given a taste of heaven in this life, the mystic must also bear purgatory—a comparison made by Teresa herself (*Obras*, pp. 435–36). In a sense, then, mystic death is simply death to this world, a concept which is at least as old as the Sermon on the Mount ("he who seeks to save his life shall lose it"), and which is echoed by St. Augustine: "For they are able to see only insofar as they are dead to this world; insofar as they live in it, they do not see."[18]

But mystic death is intimate and personal: it is the paradox of the voluntary surrender of the will, and it culminates in a specific spiritual condition in the individual. It involves the body, but it does not result from physical causes. Hence, Santa Teresa both compares and contrasts her own experiences with martyrdom, and Crashaw rightly juxtaposes mystic death and the martyr's death in his hymn to her. By the same token, the heart of mystical experience has a definite, nonphysical nature: "It is a rapture of the senses and faculties," writes Santa Teresa, "for all that does not . . . contribute to feeling this affliction. . . . this feeling is not in the body . . . but rather in the interior of the soul" (*Obras*, p. 435). Careful scrutiny of the structure of Crashaw's imagery reveals that it is appropriate to the spiritual nature of mystical experience. There are, to be sure, sensuous elements in his verse—the sexual overtones of "dart" and "die" for instance; however, Crashaw manages his material in such a way that the suggestion of erotic sensation is very slight. The sensations encountered in profane love poetry are often sweet and sometimes painful, but rarely as "subtle" as Teresa's pain in Crashaw's hymn, (ll. 97–99). The physical gestures and objects in Crashaw's depictions of mystical ecstasy are too general in reference to serve as images for visualized actions or local sensations.[19] What the poem gains from the sexual metaphor is a sense of intensity and of surrender to an overpowering force, but the sensations are immaterial and the force all but disembodied: "How kindly will thy gentle HEART / Kisse the sweetly-killing DART! / And close in his embraces keep." The antecedent of "his" in the last line is ambiguous: grammar would seem to suggest (at most) the wielder of the dart but that is merely the seraph, while the saint is intended for the "embraces" of Christ the Spouse. Similarly, the conceit of the wounded heart "kissing" the dart which pierces it is a figure which defies visualization, and the entire passage refuses to take shape as a scene. Crashaw's purpose is to take advantage of the rapturous and pleasurable associations of sensuous, erotic language, but to subvert its usual, specifically physical references.

The effect of Crashaw's ambiguously expanded metaphors is augmented by the poet's technique of versification. The key words, or variations on them, are repeated in an interlocking alliterative pattern (DEATH, dyes, Loves, death, dyes, lives, dyes, live, DY). Throughout "A Hymn to Sainte Teresa," Crashaw creates an atmosphere of ritual incantation by means of the repetition of syntactical patterns, as well as words and sounds, without becoming monotonous. This feat is accomplished primarily through the artful introduction of variations; the shift from tetrameters to a single hexameter line to round out a verse paragraph is a good example: "And lives, and dyes; and knowes not why / To live, But that he thus may never leave to DY" (ll. 103–04). Similar verbal effects obtain in the transition into the third section of the poem:

> When These thy DEATHS, so numerous,
> Shall all at last dy into one,
> And melt thy Soul's sweet mansion;
> Like a soft lump of incense, hasted
> By too hott a fire, and wasted
> Into perfuming clouds, so fast
> Shalt thou exhale to Heavn at last
> In a resolving SIGH.
>
> [ll. 110–17]

Here the "SIGH" is captured in a sequence of hissing sibilants (these, DEATHS, numerous, last, incense, hasted, wasted, etc.), and the incantatory quality is maintained by the alliterative linking of the verses, especially through the letter *l*. Two aspects of the image in the above passage also merit notice. First, it bears a very marked resemblance to an image in Medinilla's "Canción" (quoted above, this chapter): "she exhales her Life into the Fire of its Author," which suggests a similar response on the part of each poet to the common inspiration in the life and work of Santa Teresa. Second, the sensuousness of the image is again mitigated by its ambiguity of reference. The primary meaning comes from human respiration, but "exhalation" in Crashaw's day also referred to the "breathing out" of a meteor from the heavenly sphere of fire. The poet, in effect, reverses the famous Shakespearian image: "I shall fall / Like a bright exhalation in the evening" (*Henry VIII*, III. iii. 225–26). Teresa's soul is like an "exhalation" soaring from earth up into the heavens.

Hence, the image is not calculated merely to create a lovely sensuous impression; indeed, the disintegration of a lump of incense, which cannot be brought into a precise relation with any bodily action, suggests only the vaguest sort of sensation. Moreover, additional significance emerges in these lines if they, too, are viewed with Santa Teresa's own writings as a background. The phrase "Thy Soul's sweet mansion," though it seems to imply the body (as dwelling place of the soul), most likely refers also to the structure of the soul itself; for it seems to derive from the fundamental metaphor of Teresa's *Moradas*, "which is to consider our soul as a castle all of diamond and very clear crystal, wherein there are many rooms, just as in heaven there are many mansions" (*Obras*, p. 365; cf. John 14:2). Just as the soul finds its true home in heaven, likewise God dwells within the soul.[20] Crashaw's figure of melting incense suggests that Santa Teresa's "numerous DEATHS," by subjecting her to purgatory on earth, gradually "resolve" her soul into a perfect image of God. Her flesh is so subdued, her spirit already so near to God, that final death—the separation of body and soul—is painless and gentle.[21] And therefore, in the last chapter of the *Vida*, Santa Teresa writes, "Lord, either to die or to suffer; I ask of you nothing else for me. It consoles me to hear the clock, because it seems to me I come a little nearer to seeing God, when I see another hour of life to have passed" (*Obras*, p. 188).

The fragrance implied by Crashaw's "perfuming clouds" (and by Medinilla's "Rosas" and "flores") also has a particular mystical significance in the writings of Santa Teresa. It is through the figure of a

garden that she usually introduces the image of fragrance, for the
garden, probably suggested by the Song of Songs, is always important
in her conception of the soul. The image of dissolving incense in
Crashaw's hymn seems to be anticipated in the epilogue of the
Moradas:

Although no more than seven mansions are dealt with [in her book], in each of
these are many, below and above and on the sides, with lovely gardens and
fountains and labyrinths, things so delightful that you will desire to dissolve
[lit., "unmake"] yourself in praises of the great God who created it in His
image and likeness. [*Obras,* p. 450]

The fragrance symbolizes the praises of God which issue from the soul
in which potential similarities to God—or virtues—are realized. In
Crashaw's image the soul, like incense, dissolves in the virtuous and
"perfuming" praises of God when it is "melted" by the "heat" of love.
In Teresa's most elaborate and famous use of the garden metaphor, in
the *Vida* (chapters 11–19), the soul is cultivated, as a garden, in four
progressive stages of "irrigation" or prayer. In the third stage, says
Santa Teresa, "Already, already the flowers open, already they begin
to yield fragrance."[22] As she then explains, the soul is enjoying God
and glorifying him, as in the psalms sung by David (*Obras,* p. 77).
Crashaw's image of the sweet clouds of incense is then, a means of
signifying the effects of mystical experience: the incense gives off
fragrance as it dissolves in the fire; the saint dissolves in joyous praises
of God, purifying, with great agony, her soul in the fire of divine
love—hence, "a sweet and subtle PAIN." Whether or not Crashaw's
personal experiences were comparable in depth and intensity to the
mystical ecstasies of Santa Teresa, or even of Henry Vaughan, remains
an unanswered question; in any case, it is not a question for literary
criticism. What the critic can see is that Crashaw has assimilated the
concepts and images of Teresa's own works in two poems, "A Hymn to
Sainte Teresa" and "The Flaming Heart," which are true to the form
and spirit of the saint's own expression of her experiences, and comparable to the poetic celebrations of her life written by her countrymen
in the seventeenth century.

II

In view of the care exercised by Crashaw in his treatment of
mysticism in the Teresa poems, it is reasonable to expect a similar care

in his allusions to mystical experience in other poems. At his best Crashaw lives up to our highest expectations, especially in poems which reflect the influence of Spain, where mysticism was a far more familiar concept to devotional poets and writers generally than in England. If there is a certain irresponsibility in his choice of images suggestive of mystical union in "Ode on a Prayer-book,"[23] there is, to the contrary, a brilliant enhancement and deepening of the Nativity poem, with its predominantly gay and popular quality, by a deft suggestion that the mystics' quest for union with the Godhead is directly related to the mystery celebrated at the Nativity. In this respect, Crashaw's "Hymn in the Holy Nativity" once more resembles Lope de Vega's treatment of this feast in *Pastores de Belén*.

Lope himself had at his disposal not only his country's well developed practice of poesía a lo divino, but also the example of a religious order, Teresa's Discalced Carmelites, which had become a model of intense contemplative devotion for an entire nation, thereby mediating between popular piety and the highest reaches of mystical aspiration. Crisógono de Jesús, biographer of San Juan de la Cruz, takes special notice of the emphasis this prince of mystics placed on the ceremonious, if humble, celebration of Christmas (e.g., *Vida y obras*, pp. 217, 282); and a famous anecdote regarding San Juan's celebration of this feast is taken by R. O. Jones as an indication of how sacred parody manifested the permeation of Spanish culture by Christian spirituality:

The *a lo divino* movement caught up the words of popular dances (including "indecent" dances like the saraband), and even games and pastimes were allegorized. . . . Nothing was thought inappropriate for transformation: in an age of faith there is no barrier between the profane and the divine: one can nourish the other. We are told in an illuminating anecdote that San Juan de la Cruz sang, as he danced holding in his arms an image of the infant Jesus snatched from a crib, the words of an old love song:

> Si amores me han de matar
>   agora tienen lugar.
> [If love must kill me let it happen now.]

In this ecstatic interfusion of the secular and divine he seems to embody the spirit of an age.[24]

This great mystic's childlike devotion to the Christmas feast and the child Jesus implies a continuity between popular and ecclesiastical worship and contemplative prayer; in each instance what is sought is

contact with God, and, for the Christian, the mediation of Christ
Jesus, the Incarnate Word, is always involved.

In the twenty-second chapter of her autobiography, Santa Teresa
insists upon the importance of the corporal humanity of Christ as a
worthy focus of mystic contemplation (*Obras,* pp. 99ff.) and elsewhere
adds that she never remembers "that our Lord spoke, if not in his
Humanity" (*Cuentas de conciencia,* no. 22, *Obras,* p. 480). San Juan de
la Cruz likewise elaborates the mystical significance of the Incarnation
in his commentary on the fifth stanza of his own *Cántico espiritual:*

> Mil gracias derramando
> pasó por estos sotos con presura
> y, yéndolos mirando,
> con sola su figura
> vestidos los dejó de hermosura.

[Scattering a thousand graces, he passed quickly through these groves and,
gazing in going, with only his look he left them garbed in beauty.]

The poet explains these verses by placing them in the context of the
essential goodness of God's creation (Genesis 1:31), which was made
through the Son, who is "the splendor of his glory and the figure of his
substance" (Hebrews 1:3). With the Incarnation of the Son, with his
embodiment in the realm of creatures, they were endowed with more
than natural standing:

And not only did He communicate natural being and graces to [natural crea-
tures] by gazing at them . . . , but also *with only this look* of his Son *he left them
garbed in beauty,* communicating supernatural being; which occurred when he
was made man, exalting him in the beauty of God and, as a result, all creatures
in Him, by having united himself with the nature of all of them in man. [*Vida
y obras,* p. 644]

San Juan proceeds to explain the importance of the glorification
not only of humanity, but of the creation generally, wrought by the
Incarnation, in his explication of the sixth stanza of the *Cántico espiritual.* In a passage reminiscent of the medieval Augustinian concept
of *vestigia Dei,* [25] the Spanish mystic sees in the supernatural glories,
which invest nature itself, the inspiration of the mystics' longing
quest:

And, therefore, the soul wounded by this track of creatures through which she
has become acquainted with the beauty of her Beloved, anxious to see that

invisible beauty which caused this visible beauty, she speaks the following stanza:

¡Ay! ¿quién podrá sanarme?
Acaba de entregarte ya de vero;
no quieras enviarme
de hoy más ya mensajero,
que no saben decirme lo que quiero.

[*Vida y obras,* p. 644]

[Alas! Who is able to heal me? Finish giving yourself to me now in earnest; will no longer to send me a messenger today, for they know not how to tell me what I desire.]

A beautiful paradox: the natural beauties that lead man beyond himself—that "wound" him with the love of the divine Spouse—are themselves incapable of satisfying the need they arouse, of "healing the wound." Hence the mystic finds God in nature only to lose him, only to desire infinitely more in the transcendent experience of contemplative union.

The treatment accorded the Nativity by both Lope de Vega and Richard Crashaw emerges as far more profound, as well as more intelligible, if it is considered in the context of San Juan's mystical vision of the relation between natural and supernatural orders. The Incarnation of the second person of the Trinity and his birth on earth mark a convergence of human and divine which parallels the union with divinity sought by the mystic. Crashaw's "Hymn in the Holy Nativity" therefore emphasizes the paradoxical implications of the Creator entering creation:

Tity. Poor World (said I,) what wilt thou doe
To entertain this starry STRANGER?
Is this the best thou canst bestow?
A cold, and not too cleanly manger?
Contend, ye powres of heav'n and earth.
To fitt a bed for this huge birthe.
. . . .
Thyr. Proud world, said I; cease your contest
And let the MIGHTY BABE alone.
The Phaenix builds the Phaenix' nest.
Love's architecture is his own.

The BABE whose birth embraves this morn,
Made his own bed e're he was born.

[ll. 37-42, 44-49]

In these lines Crashaw stresses that the birth of Christ transforms the meanest earthly setting, even as San Juan de la Cruz stresses that a mystical union with Christ transforms the beloved soul. Commenting on the twelfth stanza of his own *Cántico espiritual*, the Spanish mystic explains "the desired eyes that I keep engraved within" (*los ojos deseados / que tengo en mis entrañas dibujados*) in this fashion:

According to this similitude and transformation, we can say that her [the soul's] life and the life of Christ are all a single life through union of love. This will be effected perfectly in heaven in the divine life of all those who merit seeing themselves in God, because, transformed in God, they will live the life of God, and not their own life; although indeed their own life, because the life of God will be their life. [*Vida y obras*, p. 658]

"Love's architecture" makes a heaven, a "Phoenix' nest," wherever the "Phoenix" comes. As Louis Martz points out, the 1648 version of this line—"Love's architecture is all one"—works as well as the 1652 version quoted above: "Love's architecture is all one because all nature is God's own and thus all physical nature may be included properly within the poem's building."[26] The pattern is similar to San Juan's mysticism, which aims to incarnate Christ in the individual soul through a "union of love."

In images remarkably similar to Crashaw's, Lope de Vega likewise suggests that the power of the incarnate Christ to transform a physical setting is an indication of his power to transform souls into which he is received:

> El hombre mal pagador
> pagó como pobre en pajas,
> y este Fénix con ventajas
> les dió tan alto valor,
> que hasta la tierra humillado,
> donde está temblando al hielo,
> *unas pajas vuelve cielo*
> *y las enciende abrasado.*
>   Tanto en amarnos se extrema,
> que vuelve en pajas iguales

las aromas orientales
adonde el Fénix se quema.

[*Obras escogidas,* II, 1256]

[Man, a bad debtor, paid as a pauper with straw, and this Phoenix gave it a
higher value with interest, for humbled even to the earth, where he is trembling in the ice, *he turns some straw into heaven and kindles it into a blaze*. To such
extremes he goes in loving us, that he makes in straw the equal of the oriental
aromas where the Phoenix consumes himself in fire.]

In this passage from *Pastores de Belén,* as in Crashaw's Nativity poem,
the focus is on paradoxically bridging the abyss of incommensurability
between God and man. The emphasis of these poets on the transformation of man and the human milieu reflects the background of
Spanish mysticism. "One of the causes that most moves the soul to
desire to enter into this thicket of the knowledge of God," maintains
San Juan de la Cruz, "and to be acquainted deep within the beauty of
His divine Wisdom is . . . in order to come to unite his understanding
in God, in accordance with the news of the mysteries of the Incarnation, as the highest and most delightful of all His works" (*Vida y obras,*
p. 728).

The mystical resonance of Crashaw's and Lope's treatments of
the Christmas feast is further suggested by their adaptations of the
conventional figures of Renaissance erotic verse in the mode of poesía a
lo divino. It is, moreover, the suggestion of mysticism which justifies,
as well as accounts for, such figures in such a context. Crashaw's
depiction of the Blessed Virgin in his Nativity hymn is not unlike his
depiction of Mary Magdalen in "The Weeper." When he describes the
infant Jesus' "new-bloom'd CHEEK" lying in the "snow" of his
Mother's breasts (ll. 67–68), he deploys a lush visual image, associated
with Petrarchan love poetry, which simultaneously evokes intense,
passionate desire and also purity. George Williams observes that the
image "contrasts neatly the colors of white and red, reconciling their
differences in the Child and His Mother."[27] Sacred parody bestows on
the somewhat weary Petrarchan color symbolism a new vigor because
the conjunction of contrasted colors signifies a profoundly radical rap-
prochement of passion and purity. Lope de Vega makes the point in a
song from *Pastores de Belén,* dedicated to her "who has honored always
both chastity and nature":

. . . que sois nieve pura
sobre que deshojan
purpureos claveles
o encarnadas rosas.

[*Obras escogidas,* II, 1213]

[for you are pure snow over whom are cast the petals of purple carnations or
red roses.]

In this sensuous realization of the traditional theme of Virgin and
Child, effected through sacred parody, Lope and Crashaw imply that
the Blessed Virgin's unique status of supernatural union with the
Godhead makes her a model for mystical contemplation. Such an interpretation is consonant with Crashaw's work, which consistently
symbolizes mystical union through erotic imagery, as in the Teresa
poems and "Ode on a Prayer-book." This view of our Lady is endorsed
by San Juan de la Cruz who, in his *Subida del Monte Carmelo* (3, 2,
10), says that her "works and petitions" were "most glorious" since
she, "being from the beginning raised to this high state [of union with
God], never had imprinted in her soul the form of any creature, nor by
any was moved, but her motion was always by the Holy Spirit" (*Vida y
obras,* p. 480). Hence, we may infer a mystical import in the sensuous
imagery by which the Virgin is depicted by Crashaw and, perhaps, by
Lope. In the "Hymn in the Holy Nativity," the infant Christ stays
warm although he sleeps in the "snow" of Mary's breasts, which are
"Two sister-seas of Virgin Milk"; and she offers him "many a rarely
temper'd kisse/That breathes at once both MAID and MOTHER,/
Warmes in the one, cooles in the other" (ll. 87–90). Lope provides
numerous depictions of Mother and Child of similar import. In one
poem from *Pastores de Belén,* Christ hangs from Mary's "virgin
breasts" like "the cluster from a palm" (*Obras escogidas,* II, 1266–67),
and in another poem heat and cold are conjoined in a description of the
Christ child with breast frozen and soul aflame:

Niño satisfecho
de fuego y de hielo,
solo amor padeciera
tan grande tormento. [28]

[*Obras escogidas,* II, 1260]

[A Child content with fire and with ice, only love would suffer *such great
torment.*]

Christ brings into the world, above all, the fire of love which burns in
the soul despite the ice of nature or of man's sinful heart, and which is
yet not destructive of the cold purity of chastity. Such imagery recalls
San Juan's symbol of a fire that burns, but with gentleness and delicacy: "¡Oh llama de amor viva, / que tiernamente hieres / de mi alma en
el más profundo centro!" (*Vida y obras,* p. 288: "Oh living flame of
love, how tenderly you wound me in the deepest center of my soul!").

To mystical overtones of Crashaw's "Hymn in the Holy Nativity"
and of the poetry of Lope's *Pastores de Belén* lead beyond the concrete
fact of Christ's human birth: it is not sufficient for the Incarnation to
be realized thus; Christ must become incarnate in the soul of the
individual, and the latter must seek to lose himself in the love of
Christ. Crashaw makes this point by converting a lo divino another
Petrarchan cliché, as he bestows upon the Christ child the sunlike
eyes of the disdainful mistress. Here, however, the fire is not destructive scorn but holy passion:

> Each of us his lamb will bring
> Each his pair of sylver Doves;
> Till burnt at last in fire of Thy fair eyes,
> Ourselves become our own best SACRIFICE.
> [ll. 105–08]

Lope's shepherds likewise anticipate the self-surrender of divine rapture in which the self is consumed in union with Christ:

> Come este divino Halcón
> corazones solamente:
> dichoso el que le sustente
> de su mismo corazón.
> Tu llegues en ocasión
> que apenas puedes volar;
> mira que le has de llevar
> el corazón en la mano.
> *No corras, Gil, tan ufano*
> *a ver el Niño divino,*
> *piensa despacio el camino*
> *y lleva el alma en la mano.*
> [*Obras escogidas,* II, 1253]

[This divine Falcon only feeds on hearts: happy he who sustains Him with his
own heart. You arrive opportunely, for you are hardly able to fly; behold you

must bring your heart in your hand. *Don't run, Gil, so proudly to see the divine Child; consider the way slowly and bring your soul in your hand.*]

A subsequent poem ("Este Niño y Dios, Antón," p. 1269) reveals that Lope's shepherds, too, attribute the dazzling eyes of the Petrarchan lady to the Christ child, who "looks with little eyes that pierce the heart," eyes "so beautiful that the soul goes after them as to a natural center."[29]

Writing of Lope de Vega, E. Allison Peers remarks that "with very few exceptions, in his lyric verse as a whole, he was about as unmystical a religious poet as his age produced."[30] This proposition is undeniably true, and there is certainly no attempt to represent mystical experience as such in *Pastores de Belén.* Yet there could be no better indication of the pervasiveness of mystical influence in the siglo de oro than the hints of an aspiration to mystical union that surface in the lines quoted above. The close of Crashaw's Nativity hymn makes explicit the hints of mysticism in *Pastores de Belén* and in the earlier stanzas of his own poem: the birth of Christ requires the rebirth of man; his making of a stable into a heavenly dwelling challenges man to do likewise with his heart. If Christ will dwell *among* us, then we must dwell *in* him. In suggesting that the shepherds, who are the most ordinary sort of persons, are called to mystical union with Christ, Crashaw echoes the teaching of the fifth "mansion" of Santa Teresa's *Moradas*—that most exquisite work of "love's architecture":

Since there is such great benefit in entering it [the fifth mansion], it will be well that those to whom the Lord does not give such supernatural gifts not appear to be left without hope, for true union can be attained—with the favor of our Lord—if we exert ourselves to attempt it by having no will, except as tied to what is the will of God.[31]

[*Obras completas,* p. 399]

Crashaw's notion of burning in the eys of the Christ child, of becoming "our own best SACRIFICE," is herein anticipated by Santa Teresa's paradoxical idea that we must exert ourselves—an act of the will—to have no will. Thus divine union is open to anyone who seeks it, but only "with the favor of our Lord"! Or in Crashaw's phrasing, "Love's architecture is his own." In siglo de oro Spain a powerful current of mysticism with its springs in popular medieval devotion flooded every corner of the country's religious life, even the poetry of that most conventional of feasts, Christmas, by so "unmystical" a poet as Lope de Vega. Drawing on such a background, Crashaw's "Hymn in the Holy Nativity" encompasses an extraordinary tonal and thematic range, closing on a note of mysticism which looks forward to his Epiphany hymn.

III

Mysticism assumes a more exalted tone in two of Crashaw's hymns. Especially notable in the "Hymn to the Name of Jesus" is a neoplatonic quality, pointed out by Carol Maddison, in references to the soul as "winged," another to the soul's memory of its "Parent HEAVN," and the whole passage which invokes "Great NATURE" (ll. 29ff.).[32] A more explicit development of this strain of mysticism occurs in Crashaw's "Hymn in the Glorious Epiphanie"—his most elaborate treatment of mystical theology. It is an overemphasis on just this neoplatonic element, a failure to see how Crashaw integrates it with his characteristic vision, which has led to a general misapprehension of the Epiphany hymn. Curiously, the most striking facet of this poem, the reference to Dionysius the Areopagite and the mysticism of the *via negativa* ("negative way"), is seemingly digressive and has proven to be the poem's most puzzling feature. Earlier commentators, like Austin Warren and Ruth Wallerstein, regarded a poem marked by the austere doctrines of the Areopagite as an anomaly in the Crashaw canon, and the apparent digressiveness of the Dionysius passage could be taken to suggest a certain irresponsibility in Crashaw's handling of mystic themes.[33]

A helpful approach to this problem is to compare Crashaw's hymn to the formulations of the via negativa by a recognized mystic of his own era. The obvious choice is San Juan de la Cruz, the mystical doctor who originated the term, "dark night of the soul." It is this concept of the dark night which unifies, as central theme, Crashaw's Epiphany hymn with its seeming diffuseness and widely divergent elements. Indeed, one of Crashaw's major contributions to devotional literature is his unique meditation on the relation between mystical experience and the Church's celebration of Gospel events.[34]

Part of the uncertainty surrounding Crashaw's Epiphany hymn results from a perplexity in understanding mystics. Because the via

negativa is so forbiddingly severe, there has been a tendency to assume
that its exponents form a separate school, distinct from mystics who
favor affective imagery in their contemplation; and Crashaw would
obviously seem to fall in with the latter group.[35] San Juan de la Cruz
and the entire Carmelite tradition furnish a corrective to this
dichotomy. Emilio Orozco points out what we have noticed in preceding pages, that Spanish mystics in general were endowed with "a
tendency to plasticity of vision, to lively and concrete representation";
moreover, he demonstrates that San Juan himself was deeply influenced by the makers of literal images as devotional aids and showed a
definite familiarity with the craft of the *imaginero*.[36] Most significant,
of course, is the simple fact that the saint's four major treatises of
mysticism are commentaries on his own ravishing and sensuously
beautiful poems.

As his chosen religious name implies, San Juan de la Cruz was
particularly devoted to the Crucifixion of our Lord, and a principal
motive of his mystical prayer is "the living image that he seeks within
himself, which is Christ crucified" (*Vida y obras*, p. 525).[37] It is
precisely such an association between the Passion and Death of Christ
and the mystics' entrance into the dark night of the soul, the via
negativa, which accounts for Crashaw's introduction of the Areopagite
into his "Hymn in the Glorious Epiphanie." The conventional liturgical theme of the feast of the Epiphany, the "showing forth" of Christ
to the Gentiles, is thus transformed through internalization: it is an
"epiphany" of the Savior within the individual soul.

Crashaw's first step in broadening the scope of the feast is not
surprising: "The juxtaposition of the events of the Nativity and
Epiphany with those of the Passion," observes Rosemond Tuve, "of
the Word made manifest, with the Word rejected, is traditional and
ubiquitous."[38] Crashaw does, however, vary the approach of the medieval form, the soliloquy or "complaint" of Christ, imitated in George
Herbert's "Sacrifice": Crashaw begins with the Epiphany and looks
forward with exultation to the Passion, rather than looking backward
with bitterness and irony from the perspective of the Cross. In his
poem, the Passion is not so much an occasion of somber penitence as of
excited joy; for the Kings foresee not the sufferings of Christ (which
are never explicitly mentioned) but the eclipse of the sun which ac-
companies it: the obeisance of nature to its Maker. Whereas Herbert,

following the lead of the medieval sources cited by Tuve,[39] views the Crucifixion in terms of the evil inflicted by men upon the Judge of all men; Crashaw instead sees that event as the means of man's salvation.

The pervasive influence of mysticism on the general devotional literature of Golden Age Spain can be seen in a recurrent feature of the Christmastide poems of that era: the shepherd who, like Crashaw's Kings, looks forward to the Passion of Christ even as the babe lies in the manager. Three of the four extant villancicos by Santa Teresa herself include this element, and it occurs several times in a volume of religious verse compiled by López de Úbeda, *Cancionero general de la doctrina Christiana* (1579, 1585, 1586).[40] Lope de Vega's *Pastores de Belén,* which includes poetic celebrations of all the ecclesiastical feasts associated with the birth of Christ, is full of references to the coming Passion; and, like Crashaw, Lope usually chooses to concentrate on the joy and triumph of the work of salvation rather than on the sobering ironies of Christ's suffering. And as has been observed in Lope's sacred pastoral, some of the poems are positively lighthearted:

> Tenga yo salud,
> Niño Dios, en tu virtud,
> pues me vienes a salvar,
> *y ándese la gaita por el lugar.*
> . . . No haga yo al mundo el buz
> por sus gustos ni por él;
> después que naciste en él
> tienen mis tinieblas luz.
> Toma Tu por mí la cruz,
> y tómela yo por Tí;
> anda, Niño, para mí,
> desde la cuna al altar,
> *y ándese la gaita por el lugar.*
>
> [*Obras escogidas,* II, 1253]

[Let me have health, Infant God, in your virtue, since you come to save me, *and let the hurdy-gurdy go through the village.* . . . Let me not kiss the hand of the world for its pleasures nor for itself; since you have been born into it my darkness takes on light. Take you the cross for me, and let me take it for you; go, Infant, for me, from the cradle to the altar, *and let the hurdy-gurdy go through the village.*]

The Christ child comes as light into the darkness of the world, and even his death on the Cross—a moment of apparent darkness[41]—is identified with the Eucharist, the sacrifice of the altar. The imagery of Crashaw's Epiphany poem is quite different from these verses of Lope's, but the sense of deep excitement over the great change breaking over the world is quite similar:

> Time has a day in store
> When this so proudly poor
> And self-oppressed spark, that has so long
> By the love-sick world bin made
> Not so much their sun as SHADE,
> Weary of this Glorious wrong
> From them and from himself shall flee
> For shelter to the shadow of thy TREE;
> Proud to have gain'd this pretious losse
> And chang'd his false crown for thy CROSSE.
>
> [ll. 133–42]

The kind of wit Crashaw displays in referring to the sun as a "proudly poor and self-oppressed spark"[42] courted by the "love-sick world" (with the Passion of Christ in the background) recalls the impulse which prompts Lope's shepherd to celebrate the Nativity and Crucifixion simultaneously with the hurdy-gurdy and to promise not to "kiss the hand of the world." Both poets have thus chosen to regard the Crucifixion in its larger theological significance as Christ's triumph by which He wrought man's deliverance, rather than in its immediate tragic sense. Such is the purpose of the conjunction of the Cross with the joyful feasts of Christmastide. At the same time, both poets are also very much concerned with the meaning of the Cross for the individual soul.

One of Góngora's loveliest Nativity poems, a dialogue among shepherds reminiscent of Crashaw's "Hymn in the Holy Nativity," likewise anticipates the Epiphany poem by introducing an implicitly mystical element toward the close, in a shepherd's rapturous vision of the Passion:

> ¡Oh, qué ajeno
> me siento de mí y qué lleno

de otro! Tocad el rabel,
¿Qué diremos del clavel
  que nos da el heno?
Mucho hay que digamos dél,
  mucho y bueno.
Diremos que es blanco, y que
lo que tiene de encarnado,
será más disciplinado
que ningún otro lo fue;
que de las hojas al pie
huele a clavos, y que luego
que un leño se arrime al fuego
  de su amor
agua nos dará de olor
piadoso hierro cruel.

[*Obras completas,* pp. 366–67]

[Oh, how estranged I feel from myself and how full of another! Strike the rebeck, What shall we say of the carnation which straw has given us? We shall say that He is white, and that what He has of red will be more rigorously scourged than any other ever was; that from the leaves at his feet comes the scent of cloves, and at the time when a timber is joined to the fire of his love, water of merciful scent shall be given us by cruel iron.]

The key to this passage is a pun on *clavos,* which I have translated "cloves" (suggesting the Magi's gift of burial spices), but which could also be translated "nails" (suggesting the Crucifixion). The sense of transport in the shepherd's rapture and the reference to the "timber" joined to the "fire" of Christ's love suggest a mystical interpretation of the Cross, which Góngora could have breathed in with the air of Spain in the sixteenth and seventeenth centuries. Hence in Góngora's oblique allusions to the Magi, the Passion, and mysticism, in his Nativity dialogue of 1615, we find the major elements of Crashaw's Epiphany hymn. What is more, Góngora's poem furnishes an excellent example of the way in which the most esoteric and sublime aspects of mystical teaching were manifest in the work of essentially secular poets.

The most important model for Crashaw's treatment of the via negativa, however, is to be found in the poetry and commentaries of San Juan de la Cruz. When the lines from the first part of the Epiphany poem are contemplated from the mystical perspective of San

Juan de la Cruz, they gather additional symbolic import. The journey
of the three Kings, for example, takes on a deeper significance:

> We, who strangely went astray,
>   Lost in a bright
>   Meridian night,
> A Darkenes made of too much day
>   Becken'd from farr
>   By thy fair starr,
> Lo at last have found our way.
> To Thee, thou Day of night! thou east of west!
> Lo we at last have found the way.

[ll. 15–23]

Although the *Noche oscura* of San Juan de la Cruz is an utterly different kind of poem in tone, texture, and explicit content, it nevertheless provides a model of the soul's nocturnal journey whose symbolic
pattern is recalled by the journey of Crashaw's Kings from "a Dar-
kenes made of too much day" to "Day of night":

> 1. En una noche obscura,
>   con ansias en amores inflamada,
>   ¡oh dichosa ventura!
>   salí sin ser notada,
>   estando ya mi casa sosegada:
> 2. a escuras y segura
>   por la secreta escala, disfrazada,
>   ¡oh dichosa ventura!
>   a escuras y en celada,
>   estando ya mi casa sosegada;
> 3. En la noche dichosa,
>   en secreto, que nadie me veía
>   ni yo miraba cosa,
>   sin otra luz y guía
>   sino la que en el corazón ardía.
> 4. Aqueste me guiaba
>   más cierto que la luz del mediodía.

[*Vida y obras*, p. 363]

[1. In a dark night, with desires inflamed in love, oh happy venture! I went
out unnoticed, my house now being quiet. 2. In darkness and secure by the
secret stair, disguised, oh happy venture! in darkness and concealed, my house

now being quiet; 3. In the happy night, in secret, for no one saw me nor did I look upon a thing, with no other light and guide save that which burned in my heart. 4. That guided me more certain than the light of noon.]

On the surface there is little similarity between these two passages. An insistence upon reiterated phrases—Crashaw's variations on "lo we at last have found our way" and San Juan's "oh dichosa ventura"—gives each of the quotations a quality of excitement, even obsessiveness. But the real parallel lies in the basic symbolic structure of the poems: Crashaw's Kings, who have been lost in the light of noon ("a bright meridian night"), have found their way by means of a single divine star to the "DAY of night"; San Juan is guided in darkness by a light that burns within brighter than the light of noon. Crashaw's emphasis on the word "way," which is used as a rhyme word seven times in the Epiphany poem, indicates that it has a special significance; and since the poem's climax is the introduction of Dionysius the Areopagite, it would appear that the way the Kings have found may be related to the mystic way set forth by San Juan de la Cruz in the *Noche oscura*.

Once the poem's metaphorical variations upon the images of light and dark are seen in terms of mystical concepts, then certain lines which seem incidental, even gratuitous, acquire a profounder implica tion:

> Welcome, the world's sure Way!
> HEAVN's wholsom ray.
> Wellcome to us; and we
> (SWEET) to our selves in THEE.

> [ll. 60–63]

This theme of the divine Spouse within the human soul and the soul reciprocally in Him is a New Testament idea which was eagerly interpreted in mystical terms in sixteenth-century Spain. One of Santa Teresa's poems is based on the refrain, "Alma, buscarte has en Mí, / Y a Mí buscarme has en tí" (*Obras completas*, p. 500: "Soul you must seek yourself in Me, / And you must seek Me in yourself"); and this very phrase, which she "understood in prayer," was the subject of discussion and interpretation by several members of her order, including San Juan de la Cruz (Ibid., pp. 1134–36). The same theme finds expression in San Juan's *Noche oscura*:

5. ¡Oh noche que guiaste!
¡oh noche amable más que la alborada!
¡oh noche que juntaste
Amado con amada,
amada en el Amado transformada!

[*Vida y obras*, p. 363]

[Oh night that guided! oh night more dear than dawn! oh night that joined
Lover with beloved, beloved transformed in the Lover!]

Crashaw's phrase, "Heavn's wholsom ray," seems to be the counterpart of the light "burning in the heart" in San Juan's third stanza,
quoted earlier, and a mystical interpretation of this "ray" is reinforced
by the correspondence between the "welcome" of Crashaw's Kings and
San Juan's transformation in the Lover, or Christ, in this his fifth
stanza. The mystical overtones of the language in the first part of
Crashaw's poem indicate that the explicit mysticism of the passage
which deals with Dionysius grows directly out of the fabric of the
poem as a whole. The Kings anticipate a "transformation" of themselves, or a discovery, perhaps, of their true selves in the presence of
the Messiah; they also seek a permanent indwelling of Christ in their
souls. It is this expectation which gives their prophecy of the events of
the Passion and their exposition of its mystical significance, at the
climax of the poem, a cogency in the context of its total structure.

Further evidence of the unity of "Hymn in the Glorious
Epiphanie," of its consistent development in mystic terms, appears in
these lines:

His superficall Beames sun-burn't our skin;
    But left within
The night and winter still of death and sin.
Thy softer yet more certaine Darts
Spare our eyes, but peirce our Harts.

[ll. 75–79]

The dart image immediately recalls Santa Teresa's famous account of
her transverberation in her autobiography (*Obras completas*, p. 131),
but the concept of the spiritual wound is not exclusively hers. San
Juan de la Cruz finds the image appropriate to his own rendering of
the negative way in *Noche oscura*:

> 7. El aire del almena,
> cuando yo sus cabellos esparcía,
> con su mano serena
> en mi cuello hería,
> y todos mis sentidos suspendía.[43]
>
> [*Vida y obras*, p. 363]

[The breeze off the battlement, while I fluttered his hair, with his serene hand he wounded me in the neck, and suspended all my senses.]

The dart in Crashaw's hymn is "soft," and the wound in San Juan's poem is given by a "serene hand"; in each case, the action in some way circumvents the senses and has its effect within. Perhaps the most important point to be made by this parallel is that Crashaw's use of the word "dart" and other terms with mystical resonance is not merely in pursuit of adventitious, local effects; such imagery is consistent with the thematic development of the entire poem.[44]

Considered in conjunction with the sensuous and erotic quality of San Juan's *Noche oscura,* the meaning of the lengthy assault on heathen worship in Crashaw's Epiphany hymn becomes clear in relation to the poem's mystical conclusion. The pagan deities, "Those beauteous ravishers" who "opprest so sore / The too-hard-tempted nations," are depicted largely in terms of sexual license. Isis is a "wanton heyfer," and if Osiris, who must "See his horn'd face, and dy for shame," is in some sense cuckolded by Christ, then his relationship with humanity clearly has sexual overtones. The worship of the pagans is described generally as "the immodest lust of adulturous dust" (an idea common enough in the Old Testament), and classical myths of the relations between gods and men (of the kind so dear to Ovid) are stigmatized as "perverse loves" and "religious rapes." Against the lasciviousness of such beliefs and rites is set the virginity of Christ's "All-unblemish't mother." The three Kings thus declare that they will turn away from the impure and unnatural lust of paganism and seek a holy, spiritual marriage with Christ, spouse of both the Church and the individual believer: "Therefore with His proud persian spoiles / We court thy more concerning smiles. / Therefore with his Disgrace / We guild the humble cheek of this chast place" (ll. 80–83). The key words in this passage are "court" and "chast"; the one implies seeking the fulfillment of desire, the other that the desire is pure and its object holy. Man's capacity for passionate love is to be indulged to its full extent, but in the proper way. Likewise, in San Juan's *Noche oscura,* the soul must keep herself chaste for the wedding with the divine Spouse:

> 6. En mi pecho florido,
> que entero para él solo se guardaba,
> allí quedó dormido
> y yo le regalaba
> y el ventalle de cedros aire daba.
>
> [*Vida y obras,* p. 363]

[In my flowering breast, which pure for him alone I kept, there he remained sleeping and I delighted him and the breeze fanned through the cedars.]

Both poets then, Richard Crashaw and San Juan de la Cruz, on the subject of the forbidding austerity of the via negativa, similarly employ sensuous symbolism of the mystical marriage. Easy generalizations regarding distinctions between abstract, philosophical mysticism and visionary, imagistic mysticism evidently fail to account for the complexity of the subject.

Thus, in the climatic section of the Epiphany hymn (ll. 189–231), when Crashaw expands the darkness at the Passion into a symbol for the experience of the via negativa, the mystical import of the poem has already been well established by suggestive images and phrases. In the same poem, the meaning of the three Kings' prophetic utterance is in part clarified by referring to the close of his "Hymn in the Holy Nativity," in which the shepherds, characterized by innocence and unaffected simplicity, anticipate an experience analogous to mystical rapture in the physical presence of the Christ child: "Till burnt at last in fire of Thy fair eyes, / Our selves become our own best SACRIFICE" (ll. 107–08). Their innocence is such that a preceding reference to "Maja," a pagan deity, is natural and harmless. It is symbolically fitting that they should find Christ in their own village. The Kings, however, have had to make a long journey: intellectual and sophisticated, their complicity with the seeming-bright powers of darkness has been deeper and more perilous; they must utterly renounce the pagan gods. But they foresee a time when Christ is to be rejected: how, then, can man find and attain union with Christ once he has been denied? This is the question posed and answered in Crashaw's Epiphany poem: what is the "way" to salvation when a physical journey no longer suffices?

The answer traditionally given by the Church is, of course, faith. Crashaw's Kings look forward to the teachings of "the right-ey'd Areopagite," the "Great master of the mystick day," who will "teach obscure MANKIND a more close way / By the frugall negative light / Of a most wise and well-abused Night / To read more legible thine originall Ray, / And make our Darknes serve THY day" (ll. 191, 207–12). According to San Juan de la Cruz, the mystical via negativa (Crashaw's "frugall negative light") is simply faith in its most radical form; for faith, the Spanish saint argues, in the commentary on his own poem, is a "dark habit of the soul"

because it produces belief in truths revealed by God Himself, which are above human understanding incommensurably. Hence it is that this excessive light which is given by faith is dark *tenebrae,* because the greater dazes and conquers the lesser, just as the light of the sun interdicts any other lights in such manner that they seem not to be lights when it shines, and it conquers our visual faculty in such manner that it rather blinds and deprives it of the sight which is given, inasmuch as its light is very disproportional and excessive to the visual faculty; thus the light of faith, through its great excess, oppresses and conquers the understanding. [*Vida y obras,* p. 396]

It is the rejection of Christ's incarnate life on earth which forces man to seek his Savior in the darkness of faith. San Juan hints at the parallel between Christ's Passion and the mystic's dark night of the soul in the phrase I have rendered "dark *tenebrae,*" since *tenebrae* is the office of matins for the last three days of Holy Week.[45] Elsewhere the parallel is made quite explicit:

The soul feels itself being exhausted and consumed in the face and sight of its miseries with a cruel death of the spirit; just as if swallowed by a beast, it were to feel itself being digested in its dark belly, suffering this anguish like Jonah in the belly of that marine beast (Jon. 2, 1). For it is obliged to be in this sepulcher of dark death on account of the spiritual resurrection for which it hopes.[46] [*Vida y obras,* pp. 573–74]

Crashaw's association of the Passion with the "frugall negative light" of mystical purgation is, then, consistent with the pattern set forth by the Spanish saint. Since the world rejects Christ, the Christian must

reject the world and all that pertains to it. The via negativa of San
Juan de la Cruz involves an absolute "death" to the world of the senses
and reason. His purpose is to restore in the soul a perfect image of God
(as man was originally created) in order to attain union with him. For
Crashaw, such union is equivalent to the concrete historical experiences of the Nativity and Epiphany. Now that Christ is no longer in
the world in the flesh, the senses and reason are only impediments; we
"Now by abased liddes shall learn to be / Eagles; and shutt our eyes
that we may see" (ll. 231–32). In the words of San Juan, sense and
reason must be purged of their effects—"emptied" and laid to rest in
the blinding light of God:

And inasmuch as any creatures at all and their actions and habiliments neither
suit nor attain to what is God, therefore it is necessary to strip the soul of all
such creatures and their actions and habiliments, to wit: of its understanding,
pleasure and feeling, so that, when all which is dissimilar and incongruent to
God is emptied out, it comes to receive the likeness of God, since nothing
remains in it which is not the will of God; and thus it is transformed in God.
[Vida y obras, p. 401]

In the face of the uncompromising rigor of this doctrine (so utterly at
variance with typical twentieth-century attitudes) it is difficult, but
necessary, to keep in mind that the three preceding passages are
quoted from treatises, Subida del Monte Carmelo (Ascent of Mt. Carmel) and Noche oscura (dark night), which are simply San Juan's
extended commentaries on the first three stanzas of his own poem,
Noche oscura, which has also been quoted at length in this chapter.[47]
Hence it is again apparent that Crashaw's interest in and treatment of
the via negativa as a poetic theme is not as anomalous as is sometimes
suggested.

The ultimate paradox of San Juan de la Cruz is the way in which
he endows the forbidding doctrines of the via negativa with vitality,
intensity, and concreteness. The way is dark and harsh, but the
Spaniard enters it in a spirit of passionate excitement:

> Tras de un amoroso lance,
> y no de esperanza falto,
> volé tan alto, tan alto,
> que di a la caza alcance.
> . . . Cuando más alto subía

deslumbróseme la vista,
y la más fuerte conquista
en escuro se hacía;
mas, por ser de amor el lance,
di un ciego y oscuro salto,
y fui tan alto, tan alto,
que di a la caza alcance.

[*Vida y obras,* pp. 943-44]

[*Upon an amorous chase, and not wanting in hope, I flew so high, so high, that I overtook my prey.* . . . When I soared higher, my vision was dazzled, and the fiercest conquest was made in darkness; but, the chase being amorous, I made a blind and dark leap, and I went so high, so high, *that I overtook my prey.*]

In the "dark night of the soul," the mystic is technically passive; but the experience is recalled as intense activity and expressed in the language of fervent desire. San Juan thus furnishes a precedent, not only for the imagery, but also for the energetic tone and tempo of the climactic section of Crashaw's Epiphany poem:[48]

O prise of the rich SPIRIT! with what feirce chase
   Of his strong soul, shall he
   Leap at thy lofty FACE,
And seize the swift Flash, in rebound
From his obsequious cloud.

[ll. 196-200]

Crashaw makes good use of his irregular form, especially in the short, enjambed lines, in attaining an effect of powerful excitement. The break between "he" and its verb "leap," for example, is quite effective in evoking a sense of the action described. The English poet achieves, indeed, a surprising measure of the *vertigo de altura* ("dizziness from height") which grows out of the rapid unfolding of San Juan's *amoroso lance.*[49]

    The achievement of Crashaw's "Hymn in the Glorious Epiphanie" is to combine the qualities of a hymn—a poem of liturgical celebration—with an evocation of the mystic *via negativa.* The Epiphany poem, writes Anthony Low, "would be at its best performed in church with full chorus and orchestra."[50] But at the same time, as the numerous parallels to the verse and commentaries of San Juan de la Cruz suggest, the Epiphany poem is a skillful representation of mystical experience; for it was Crashaw's particular genius to express the ultimate harmony of the mystical vision with the ordinary worship of the Church calendar. Nowhere does his similarity to the literature of siglo de oro Spain emerge more forcefully than in this convergence of the public and popular with the sublime and exalted.

5

Celebrating Sacred Occasions:
Crashaw and the Liturgical Poem

RASHAW'S EARLIEST EXTANT POEMS, the Latin verse of *Epigrammata Sacrorum Liber* (1634), are based on the Sunday Scripture readings of the *Book of Common Prayer;*[1] and most of his sacred poetry discloses a liturgical orientation throughout his career.[2] As noted at the close of the preceding chapter, the Epiphany hymn, though a treatment of a deeply personal mysticism of the "dark night of the soul," is also precisely what its title proclaims it, a hymn—a song intended for the praise of God or his saints during public worship.[3] The most notable changes in the 1648 version of *Steps to the Temple*, compared to its predecessor of 1646, grow out of the increase in the number of hymns.[4] In these poems, which give the later volume (as well as its successor, *Carmen Deo Nostro*) its distinctive tone and which represent Crashaw's greatest poetic accomplishment, the emphasis on liturgical celebration unites his work to the literature of the Catholic Reformation in Spain as surely as his interest in mysticism. The very fact that siglo de oro Spain was a land of saints and mystics made mystical experience a more familiar phenomenon to the ordinary Spanish Christian than it could possibly have been in Protestant countries. In providing formally for the specifically religious life in the various orders, which had been rigorously reformed in the wake of the Council of Trent, Catholicism could assimilate the most extreme and intense manifestations of devotional ecstasy, while in mid-century England religious exaltation was a wholly exotic growth—the exclusive preoccupation of retired eccentrics like Vaughan and (later) Traherne, or of "enthusiastic" Ranters.[5]

Hymn singing, to be sure, has been frequently associated with Puritanism, but the Puritan idea of a hymn was quite different from that fostered by the liturgical tradition deriving from the Middle Ages. "The sermon was directed to men's understanding," writes Christopher Hill, "music and ritual to their emotions. Hence the dislike which many Puritans felt for anthems, polyphony, and organ music in church. Congregational singing of psalms, with music as merely an edifying accompaniment to the Word, was different."[6] Moreover, the intellectual emphasis of Puritan worship was practical, even utilitarian. As surely as they rejected the affective hymnody represented by the *Dies Irae* and the *Stabat Mater,* with their "tender and haunting melancholy" and "awesome and plaintive foreboding," even so the Puritans rejected the witty "metaphysical" hymns of St. Thomas Aquinas and Adam of St. Victor, associated by Walter J. Ong with a separate tradition in medieval hymnody.[7] Crashaw translates hymns from both medieval schools, adding a baroque complexity of wit to the former and a luxuriant elaboration of imagery to St. Thomas's eucharistic hymns, *Adoro Te* and *Lauda Sion,* and to the *Dies Irae* and *Stabat Mater* alike. As Anthony Low observes, Crashaw's interest in the hymn, manifest in these translations as well as in his own feast-day hymns, began while he was still an Anglican, deeply involved in the Laudian liturgical revival.[8] Already his conception of the hymn as part of a patterned, seasonal ritual of formal worship was utterly at variance with the Puritan view. For Crashaw, the Catholicism represented by Santa Teresa seems to have meant a mystical deepening of this liturgical devotion.

The third and final section of "A Hymn to Sainte Teresa" (ll. 118–82) furnishes a clear instance of how Crashaw was able to bind into a whole the faith of all Christians by placing Teresa's mystical raptures in the context of the transtemporal life in grace of the Communion of the saints to which the humblest member of the Church Militant is joined in prayer and sacrament. The poem's conclusion presents a vision of the saint's reception and glorification in heaven. Taken together, the three sections constitute an admirable poetic structure. The gay childlike quality of the first section of the hymn balances the ecstatic tone of the second section, reinforcing it by

[Celestial spirits, who in the dawn of your being acknowledged the rule in the humanity of Christ, sow with white lilies from the eternal gardens the three regions of the wind even to the field of the moon. Sister Inés rises to her Bridegroom; sing, lovely seraphim: for she who is so much like you, merits such sweet verses. You yourselves are witnesses of the burning zeal of her ardent charity; her fire is rising to its center.]

Like Crashaw's Teresa, Sor Inés climbs to heaven, to her spouse, in fire; and, also like Teresa, she is to be greeted by angels who have witnessed her divine love on earth.

The first of Santa Teresa's meritorious works mentioned by Crashaw are her purgatorial pains and sorrows; these are transfigured and turned "divine" (l. 148). Something like this is implied in the second quatrain (the first is quoted above, p. 116) of Lope's seventh sonnet to Teresa:

> Tanta solicitud, tanto camino,
>   y todo un monte, que en tus hombros pesa,
>   anticipan el premio de tu empresa,
>   y antes del tiempo a coronarte vino. [12]

[Such diligence, such a calling, and a whole mountain (i.e., Carmel), that weighs on your shoulders, anticipate the prize of your undertaking, and He came in advance to crown you.]

The crown mentioned in this sonnet is only a foretaste of the crown in heaven, but it is clearly in reward for the hardships she suffers in this world—the mountain on her shoulders.

Such an emphasis on Santa Teresa's reception in heaven and her coronation is not unique. The theme of the heavenly reward of the saints and the presentation of the crown of glory is commonplace during the period, especially in the graphic arts. Not surprisingly, depictions of this kind, of our Lady as pre-eminent among the saints, abound; and virtually every important Spanish painter from El Greco to Velázquez has left paintings both of her Assumption and Coronation. [13] The reception of a saint in heaven is a favorite theme portrayed in baroque churches, especially in Italy. Perhaps the most famous is Andres del Pozzo's vault of the Jesuit church of Sant'Ignazio in Rome, in which the celestial welcome of the order's founder is painted. [14] Still, the most compelling parallel to Crashaw's poem from the visual arts is El Greco's famous *Burial of Count Orgaz*. While the body of the

fourteenth-century nobleman is laid in the earth by the miraculous
apparitions of St. Augustine and St. Stephen, his soul, cradled in the
arms of an angel, rises to the waiting Christ and Mary. Helmut
Hatzfeld follows earlier commentators who see in this painting a picto-
rial version of Santa Teresa's contrast between "this farce of this life"
(*esta farsa de esta vida*) and the "true life" (*la vida verdadera*) of heaven.
Hatzfeld adds that El Greco's *Burial* also depicts Santa Teresa's idea of
a holy death, and he quotes a key passage from the thirty-eighth chapter
of the *Vida:* "Death seems to me quite an easy thing for him who
serves God, because in a moment his soul seems free of this prison and
placed in rest."[15] This sentence gives a concise summary of Crashaw's
view of Teresa's own death.

It is, however, for the last theme adduced by Crashaw, the effect
of Santa Teresa's books by which she, a virgin, bore "children," that a
notable parallel exists in Spanish literature.[16] It is also the theme
which most clearly evinces the liturgical orientation of the hymn by
revealing the manner in which the mystical adept influenced the
whole community of the faithful. We have seen already in Lope's "San
Hermenegildo," how Teresa is called "mother and maid" and is said to
be a "torch that illuminates the whole Church." These motifs occur
elsewhere in Lope's poetry: in the eighth of his sonnets on Teresa, he
celebrates her writings which were "dictated" by the Holy Ghost; and
in another poem, "El soldado vestido," Teresa is the "Virgin mother of
so many children."[17] In Sonnet LXXIV of his *Rimas sacras,* Lope
compares Santa Teresa to Abigail, who came down from Mt. Carmel
and placated David (I Sam. 25), because her good works plead for
God's mercy on sinful man: "Desenójase Dios por la piadosa / ofrenda
de los frutos que le ofrece, / hijos de su oración maravillosa"[18] (God is
appeased through the reverent oblation of the fruits which she offers
him, children of her wondrous prayer). The "children of her prayer"
are, of course, the nuns and friars of the Discalced Carmelite Order
which she reformed. At the close of his "Canción," Baltasar de
Medinilla likewise asks for Teresa's intercession, calling her "spiritual
Mother, Virgin fecund of Angels on earth."[19] But perhaps the nearest
parallel to Crashaw's poem comes in a work of prose, mentioned already in this study, Gerónimo de San Ioseph's *Historia del venerable
padre fr. Ivan de la Cruz.* This book is dedicated to "la Gloriosa Virgen y

Santa Madre Teresa de Iesus" and the dedication reads, in part, as follows:

It is incumbent on you, from your place in heaven, to shelter him to whom you gave a being almost celestial on earth. Those who reverberate in the mirror of this religious life [i.e., Teresa's *Vida*] are splendors of your beautiful light. One of the rays, and the brightest that this Sun awakened; one of the sparks, that, in order to burn in charity leaped into the world from this divine volcano of your breast, is the Venerable Fray IVAN DE LA CRUZ. It is just that as a true and zealous Mother, you seek that time not quench this spark, nor emulation darken this ray. If the wise son is a pleasure, and crown of his parents, what more pleasurable and rich for the flourishing immortality of your brow, than this in all ways most wise son?[20]

Geronimo commends Juan to Santa Teresa as the "crown" of her "brow," the most illustrious of her "children"; Crashaw applies the same figures to all the "sons of [her] vowes":

> Those rare WORKES where thou shalt leave writt
> Love's noble history, with witt
> Taught thee by none but him, while here
> They feed our soules, shall clothe THINE there.
> Each heavenly word by whose hid flame
> Our hard Hearts shall strike fire, the same
> Shall flourish on thy browes; and be
> Both fire to us and flame to thee;
> Whose light shall live bright in thy FACE
> By glory, in our hearts by grace.
>   Thou shalt look round about, and see
> Thousands of crown'd Soules throng to be
> Themselves thy crown. Sons of thy vowes,
> The virgin-births with which thy soveraign spouse
> Made fruitful thy fair soul.
>
>   [ll. 155–69]

These lines recall motifs from any number of the above-cited Spanish poems, but they center on the two basic images of Geronimo's "Dedication": Teresa is a flame that kindles fire or "sparks" in other souls, the children of her "virgin-births"; and these souls form her crown in heaven.

    The three sections of Crashaw's "Hymn to Sainte Teresa" pro-

vide perspectives on three different facets of that remarkable woman:
Teresa as a small girl gives way to Teresa in ecstasy and, at last, to
Teresa in glory. The poet manages several shifts of tone and manner in
order to incorporate the hymn's diverse materials, adapting the rhythm
of his verse and his style of discourse to fit each perspective from
which he views the subject. There are, in the Spanish poetry of the
seventeenth century, analogues to virtually every aspect of this hymn.
In assimilating the style and tone of the poems written in honor of
Santa Teresa in her native Spain, Crashaw also assimilates the pronounced emphasis on her role in the religious life of the Christian
community, which makes her a fit subject for public liturgical celebration. This aspect of the hymn helps to account for its artistic unity in
spite of its wide range of feeling and idea. Like the best of his Spanish
predecessors, Crashaw did not use incidents from Teresa's *Vida* su-
perficially, but rather worked within the spirit of her writings. The
three parts of the poem are thus held together by the dominant idea
stated at the poem's outset: "Love, thou art Absolute sole lord / Of LIFE
and DEATH"; that is, life must "die" in order to "live in death." Since
this idea is at the heart of both the New Testament and Catholic
worship, especially in Baptism and the Sacrament of the Altar,[21]
Crashaw's celebration of Santa Teresa's mystical life properly assumes
the form of a hymn intended for the liturgy of Teresa's feast.

II

   Apart from the inclusion of "The Office of the Holy Crosse" and
the translations of medieval hymns in the volume of 1648, the clearest
indication—and certainly the most important example—of Crashaw's
continuing interest in liturgical poetry is the group of four Christmastide hymns which first converge in Crashaw's last, posthumous book,
Carmen Deo Nostro: "To the Name of Jesus," "In the Holy Nativity,"
"For New Year's Day," and "In the Glorious Epiphanie." These
poems, as A. R. Cirillo observes, "form a sequence with a remarkable
structural and progressive unity of themes climaxed in the 'Epiphany
Hymn.'"[22] It is, however, to the first of these poems that I wish to call
attention.
   "Hymn to the Name of Jesus" is often regarded as Crashaw's most
characteristic work, as the full expression of his particular sensibility.

"This ode," says Austin Warren, "is Crashaw's chief achievement in the form toward which his talents inclined him."[23] Nevertheless, comment on this poem—in contrast to the "Hymn in the Glorious Epiphanie"—has been largely confined to matters of style. Most critics seem to have been so preoccupied with the remarkable display of technical virtuosity in the hymn that its total significance, which grows out of a complex of exegetical and devotional practice, in relation to a specific Christian feast, with roots in the Middle Ages, has been neglected.[24] The necessary theological and liturgical background material has lain unnoticed in certain works of the Spanish siglo de oro.

Once again there is an interesting counterpart to a poem of Crashaw's in *Pastores de Belén*. In the fourth book Lope, *in propria persona,* devotes a lengthy canción to the theme of the name of Jesus. The mood and tone of this poem are similar to Crashaw's, and Lope begins by assuming a comparable posture of humility: "I, then, most divine Name, although the most rustic of these shepherds and the one with the most discordant voice and habits, with your leave, sing thus with humble lyre" (*Obras escogidas*, II, 1284). An apparent similarity even exists between the two poems in prosodic form. True, Lope's stanza is a regular, if complex arrangement of seven- and eleven-syllable lines: abCabCcdeeDfF. In the early seventeenth-century edition of *Pastores de Belén* which I have seen,[25] as well as the edition of Sainz de Robles, however, some of the stanzas are arbitrarily run together, obscuring the regularity of the poem and giving it the look of an irregular or "mixed" ode, like Crashaw's poem.

The most important resemblances, however, are in the realm of imagery. In both poems the various classes of creatures are invoked to worship and praise the name of Jesus. Lope proceeds with this in a very orderly fashion, beginning with the angelic hierarchies, moving then to the stars and planets, next to the elements of the earth, and concluding with man. The first two stanzas show how he is intent upon establishing a mood of exaltation by means of an abundant flow of opulent images:

> Humíllense a tu Nombre,
> dulce Jesús, los cielos,
> y al eco del dulcísimo sonido
> del nombre de Dios Hombre,

de los talares velos
y del zafiro fúlgido ceñido,
el querubín vestido
de resplandor y ciencia
las rodillas incline,
y cuanto más empine
de su conocimiento, la excelencia,
más se postre y derribe,
y esté con más temor, cuanto más prive.
   Serafín abrasado,
al dulce nombre humilla
el vivo fuego que del pecho exhalas,
¡Oh trono levantado
en la tercera silla!
bate a su nombre las fenicias alas,
y tú, que luego igualas,
dominación hermosa,
tan alta jerarquía,
a la dulce armonía,
a la alta consonancia sonorosa
de cinco letras tales
derribe tus cabellos celestiales. [26]

[May the heavens bow down to your Name, sweet Jesus, and at the echo of the sweetest sounding of the name of God Man, girded in flowing veils and resplendent sapphire, may the Cherub, dressed in radiance and science, bend his knees, and the more he raise the excellence of his knowledge, may he the more humble and cast himself down, and may he be more fearful the more he enjoy favor.

    Blazing Seraph, bend to the sweet name the living fire that you exhale from your breast. Oh throne raised in the third place!, at his name beat your phoenix wings, and you, beautiful domination, who then equals such a lofty hierarchy, at the sweet harmony, at the high, sonorous consonance of five such letters cast down your celestial tresses.]

The association of the name with musical harmony, and the invocation of luminous beings of a higher order who dwell in the favor and protection of the name suggest several passages in Crashaw's hymn. In fact, the latter begins with a similar invocation of the blessed souls in heaven (cf. Rev. 3:4–5):

    Hearken, And Help, ye holy Doves!
    The high-born Brood of Day; you bright

Candidates of blisseful Light,
The HEIRS ELECT of Love; whose Names belong
Unto the everlasting life of Song;
All ye wise SOULES, who in the wealthy Brest
Of This unbounded NAME build your warm Nest.

[ll. 6–12]

There are, to be sure, numerous differences in detail between these two descriptions, but from the outset the poets share the obvious intention of evoking a sense of enchanting sound and dazzling light.

The same general similarity of poetic mood can be observed in the way in which both poets handle the effect of the name upon what may be loosely termed celestial phenomena. In *Pastores de Belén*, the sun and moon are called upon to pay homage:

¡Oh sol hermoso!, el arco,
centro, donde caminas,
traslada al escabelo de este Infante
de tu epiciclo y marco;
arroja las cortinas,
luna, a sus pies, por humildad menguante.

[*Obras escogidas*, II, 1284]

[Oh beautiful sun!, change your arc, your center, where you travel, your epicycle and limit, to the footstool of this Infant; cast down your curtains at his feet, moon, waning through humility.]

Somewhat analogously, the heavens are depicted in a state of humble expectation in "Hymn to the Name of Jesus":

O see, so many WORLDS of barren yeares
Melted and measur'd out in Seas of TEARES.
O see, the WEARY liddes of wakeful Hope
(LOVE's Eastern windowes) All wide ope
     With Curtains drawn,
To catch The Day-break of Thy DAWN.

[ll. 143–48]

The important point of comparison here is the vagueness of the imagery of both passages; vague, that is, if one tries to visualize what is being described. For indeed, in the lines quoted above and in others throughout both poems, effects of light and harmony and of vast cosmic spaces are created without any clear picture ever emerging. And this is as should be: the theme of each poem—the name of Jesus—is inherently beyond imagination and comprehension. The poets attempt to suggest the importance of the name by describing its impact on the whole of physical and spiritual creation. By not allowing these effects to assume an overly specific or literal form, the transcendence of the theme is preserved.

Another similarity in the two poems is the attempt to indicate the awful powers of the name; it is terrible as well as beautiful, and it elicits dread as well as love. Lope stresses this aspect by invoking appropriate cataclysms in the earth:

> La tierra sus montañas,
> y sus gigantes pinos
> las sierras, que más presto alcanzan nieve,
> como débiles cañas
> de arroyos cristalinos,
> estén al nombre que los cielos mueven.
>
> [*Obras escogidas,* II, 1284]

[Let the mountains of the earth, and the gigantic pines of the highlands that are soonest covered with snow, be like weak reeds in the crystalline streams before the name that moves the heavens.]

And a grim warning is added:

> La blasfemia enmudezca,
> la fiera tiranía,
> la ira, la soberbia y la envidiosa
> calumnia desfallezca,
> y cuanto la osadía
> derribó de la sierpe venenosa
> de aquella luz hermosa,
> y en la cadena fiera
> eternamente herrados,
> a tu Nombre postrados,
> ciegos del sol de tu divina esfera,
> conozcan que no tienen
> fuerza y poder donde tus letras vienen.
>
> [Ibid., 1284–85]

[Let blasphemy be silent; cruel tyranny, anger, pride, and envious calumny fade away; and all those whom the audacity of the venemous serpent cast out of

that beautiful light and in the cruel chain eternally fettered, prostrated to your
Name, blind from the sun of your divine sphere; let them know they have no
strength and power where your letters come.]

The principal motifs of each of the above passages are combined in the
conclusion of Crashaw's hymn, an anticipation of the Judgment Day
(cf. Rev. 16:17–21); the mountains of the earth give way, and evil is
discomfited and made aware of its folly:

> For sure there is no Knee
> That knowes not THEE.
> Or if there be such sonns of shame,
> Alas what will they doe
> When stubborn Rocks shall bow
> And Hills hang down their Heavn-saluting Heads
> To seek for humble Beds
> Of Dust, where in the Bashful shades of night
> Next to their own low NOTHING they may ly,
> And couch before the dazeling light of thy dread majesty.
> They that by Love's mild Dictate now
> Will not adore thee,
> Shall Then with Just Confusion, bow
> And break before thee.
>
> [ll. 226–39]

Perhaps the closest parallel between the celebrations of the name
by Lope and Crashaw comes in images of the bliss it offers to the
devout. Here is a part of this image found in Lope:

> Las virtudes te alaben,
> que encierra, Jesús mío,
> ese divino título, que se baña
> los labios, que saben
> de celestial rocío,
> de panales de miel, que desengaña
> cuanto el veneno daña
> de nuestro vil deseo.
>
> [*Obras escogidas,* II, 1285]

[May the virtues, my Jesus, praise you, who contain that divine title, which
bathes their lips, for they know about celestial dew, about honeycombs, which
undeceive our vile desire as much as venom harms it.]

Crashaw's vision of celestial joy is remarkably similar:

> Lo, where Aloft it comes! It comes, Among
> The Conduct of Adoring SPIRITS, that throng
> Like diligent Bees, And swarm about it,
>   O They are wise;
> And know what SWEETES are suck't from out it.
>   It is the Hive.
>   By which they thrive,
> Where All their Hoard of Hony lyes.
> . . . O fill our senses, and take from us
> All force of so Prophane a Fallacy
> To think ought sweet but that which smells of Thee.
>
> [ll. 151–58, 170–72]

There are a number of possible common sources for Lope and
Crashaw, most notably Dante's description of the angels flying in and
out of the white rose of Paradise: "sì come schiera d'ape che
s'infiora/una fiata e una si ritorna/là dove suo laboro s'inspora"
(*Paradiso*, XXXI, 7–9: like a crowd of bees that inflower themselves
for a while and then return to where their labor is made sweet). In
addition, Crashaw had earlier translated another imitation of Dante's
image in the third stanza of Marino's *Sospetto d'Herode*. But the resemblance between the lines of Crashaw and Lope is closer, each
including the hive (or honeycomb) and the dew, neither of which
appears in the stanza from Marino, though Crashaw adds them to his
translation.[27] Moreover, there is a striking fact that both poets use the
images in virtually identical contexts: Lope's angels, or "virtues,"
bathe their lips in the celestial dew or honeycomb of the name;
Crashaw's "Adoring SPIRITS" suck honey from the name, or "Hive."
In both poems there is a special kind of wisdom involved in the knowledge of the name's sweetness. Finally, the two poems share an
additional noteworthy characteristic: the joy available to the devout in
the name of Jesus is depicted in metaphors of sensuous pleasure, in
that way the name is explicitly set in opposition to worldly or fleshly
temptations—Lope's "vile desire" (*vil deseo*), Crashaw's "Prophane
Fallacy." A divine mystery is celebrated in terms of sensuous delight,
but sensuous things are themselves lifted onto a higher plane and are
reinterpreted as aspects of the one essential reality, Jesus' name. In
this respect, both poems are reminiscent of the love poetry influenced

by Renaissance neoplatonism in which a beautiful woman is a rung on the ladder leading up to the idea of Beauty. Also a neoplatonic association is the suggestion that what appeals to the senses is ultimately illusory. This concept is quite obvious in the quotation from Crashaw, in which the senses are inundated in order to be transcended, and at least implicit in Lope's reference to the "disillusion" (*desengaño*), which the true sweetness of the name Jesus brings to our "vile desire."

There are, then, clear resemblances between the poems in the passages examined above, and in the overall mood and tone of each poet's work. But the most notable parallel is the generally similar poetic treatment of a rather unusual theme. Jesus' name is celebrated as an entity per se, something of enormous force and profound significance in its own right; and the meaning of both poems is involved with the meaning of the name. The conclusion of Crashaw's poem indicates an important scriptural clue to this meaning, Phil. 2:9–11: "Wherefore, God also hath highly exalted him, and given him a name which is above every name, That at the name of Jesus every knee should bow, of things in heaven, and things in earth, and things under the earth, And that every tongue should confess that Jesus Christ is Lord, to the glory of God the Father." Nevertheless, the problem remains of knowing how Crashaw, or Lope, would have understood this text, and with what meaning they might have invested the name. A possible answer may be found in a second source, from Spanish literature, in all probability known to both poets.

Fray Luis de León was one of the most remarkable and attractive figures of the Spanish Renaissance: Augustinian friar, professor of theology at the University of Salamanca, Hebrew scholar, humanist, translator of Virgil and Horace, and a poet in his own right. It is incontrovertible that Lope de Vega was acquainted with and admired the work of Fray Luis; although the poetry of the latter remained in manuscript until published by Quevedo in 1631, he is accorded a place of honor in Lope's poetic pantheon, *Laurel del Apolo* (1630), and had probably been familiar to Lope for years.[28] In addition, there are traces of the influence of his massive prose work, *Los nombres de Cristo* (1583, 1585, 1587, and numerous subsequent editions) in *Pastores de Belén*, especially in the canción on the name of Jesus. In the section of his work devoted to the explication of the name Jesus, Fray Luis says that "the original [in Hebrew] of his name *Jesus*, that is *Iehosuah*

. . . has all the letters of which is composed the name of God, that they call of *four letters*." This is, of course, the *tetragrammaton*, the ineffable name of God, difficult to pronounce, Fray Luis speculates, because of the disposition of its letters; and as a result of the difficulty, mysterious and forbidden. But, he continues, the name Jesus contains all the letters of the name of God and may be pronounced:

Therefore, in the same manner, in the person of Christ divinity is joined with the soul and with the flesh of man; and the divine *word*, that was not read, together with these two letters is read, and the hidden, made visible and speakable, emerges into the light; and Christ is a *Jesus*, that is, a conjoining of the divine and the human, of that which is not pronounced and of that which may be pronounced, and it is the cause that what is joined with it is pronounced.[29]

Closely parallel to this passage is the following from *Pastores de Belén*, from a speech by Aminadab which anticipates the birth of Christ:

But now we who are worthy of seeing such happy days with a certain beautiful harmony of the voice, that which they [their forefathers] with dark sense, and hardly intelligible, pronounce in the *Tetragrammaton*, we shall say in this most sweet name of Jesus, composed of those same four letters, the real and true name of God, never before known to the world, until his most holy Son came into it, and now known and hoped for by many, since the angel spoke to this most divine Maiden, to whom the sky, the earth and hell bow down. [*Obras escogidas*, II, 1244]

Finally, this same motif appears in Lope's poem on the name:

> Tú solo, que derribas
> de aquellas letras vivas
> del gran Jehovah, que inexplicable tanto
> con miedo de su mengua
> osaba apenas pronunciar la lengua.
>
> [Ibid., 1285]

[You alone, for you subdue those living letters of the great Jehovah, that so inexplicable, the tongue with fear of its own unworthiness dared hardly to pronounce.]

Because the name Jesus, by making the tetragrammaton speakable, matches the nature of Christ who combines the divine and the human, making deity incarnate and visible, Fray Luis maintains that Jesus is the "proper name" of Christ as a man (*Dabar*, "Word," is his proper name in his divine aspect). This concept, too, is echoed in Lope's celebration of the name:

> De tu naturaleza,
> y no del hombre puesto
> tienes, Jesús, tan agradable Nombre.
>
> [Ibid.]

[Of your nature, and not given by man, you have, Jesus, such an agreeable Name.]

In these quotations from Lope's poem and in their evident source in *Los nombres de Cristo,* the underlying motive for Crashaw's "Hymn in the Name of Jesus" is manifest. For Fray Luis, and subsequently for Lope and Crashaw, the name itself is significant, as Karl Vossler points out:

We are accustomed to distinguish rigorously between things and words and between the substantial, permanent being of things and their fluctuating denominations.

But in these dialogues, the names of God-Man do not appear as arbitrary images of the human fantasy, but rather are accepted in a devout and believing manner, as sublime watchwords of divinity which descend like rays, like revelations of the Holy Spirit, into our sad valley of tears.[30]

As Vossler indicates, *Los nombres de Cristo* is composed of dialogues after the manner of Plato; moreover, the imagery and terminology of the book are shot through with the influence of Renaissance neo-platonism (while remaining perfectly orthodox). Fray Luis gives, for instance, a thoroughly Platonized version of the significance of Jesus' name:

I mean that [God] is present and joined with our being, but very far from our sight and from the clear knowledge for which our understanding hungers. Therefore, it was convenient, or rather it was necessary, that *while we walk pilgrims from Him* in these lands of tears, seeing as how His face is not visible to us nor joined with our soul, we have, in place of that, some word or name in our mouth, and in our understanding some figure of Him, howbeit imperfect and dark, and, as St. Paul calls it, *enigmatic.* Because, when it flies from this prison of earth, in which now our captive soul labors and yearns, as placed in darkness, and emerges into the brilliance and purity of that light, He himself, who is joined with our being now, shall join himself with our understanding then.[31] [*Obras completas castellanas,* I, 422–23]

This vision of a soul flying up to a heaven of light where the understanding will be glorified has a flavor similar to the general ambience of
Crashaw's "Hymn to the Name of Jesus" with its "architects of Intellectual Noise," its abundant light imagery, and its injunction to the
soul to be "All Wing."

A careful examination of *Los nombres de Cristo,* especially in the
treatment of the name Jesus, reveals still more specific and detailed
parallels with Crashaw's hymn. In view of the fact that Crashaw's
poem is a good deal more complex than Lope's (and also better), these
deeper parallels may be attributable to a firsthand knowledge of *Los
nombres de Cristo* on the part of Crashaw. That he knew about Fray
Luis can hardly be doubted: the first edition of Santa Teresa's *Obras*
was edited and introduced by him; this was the text used by Sir Toby
Mathew in his translation of the saint's *Vida* into the English of *The
Flaming Hart,* and in the preface to this work he identifies the original
editor as "Lewis of Leon" (incorrectly calling him a Dominican) and
quotes him for some eleven pages.[32] That Crashaw was acquainted
with this translation, which is dedicated to his own protectoress,
Queen Henrietta-Maria, is sufficiently demonstrated by his use of the
same title, "The Flaming Heart," for one of his Teresa poems. It is
unlikely that Crashaw would not take pains to find out more about
Fray Luis, who played such a prominent role in the publication of
Santa Teresa's "dear bookes", and whose *Los nombres de Cristo* was
among the most popular and available Spanish works.[33]

A comparison with certain passages of *Los nombres de Cristo* helps
to clarify and deepen our understanding of "Hymn to the Name of
Jesus" as a poem whose purpose is to illuminate the spiritual significance of a liturgical feast. Let us begin by recalling that Fray Luis
asserts that Jesus is the "proper name" of Christ; to the explanation of
this idea quoted above, he adds the following discussion of the meaning
of the name:

Jesus, then means *salvation* or *health,*[34] for thus the angel said it. Therefore if
Christ is called *health,* certain it must be that he is, and if he is, that he is
such for us; because for himself he has no need of *health,* he who in himself
suffers no lack nor has any fear of suffering it. And if Christ is *Jesus* and *health*
for us, clearly it is understood that we are sick, for whose remedy is ordained
the *health* of Jesus. [*Obras completas castellanas,* I, 775–76]

Further, Jesus is correctly taken as Christ's "proper name" because all the others (e.g., "Branch," "Way," "Prince of Peace") are comprehended in it:

And he is properly named by it [Jesus] because the sickness is in so many cavities and spread out through so many branches, that all the rest of Christ's offices and names are thereby like parts that are ordained for this *health;* and the name of *Jesus* is the *all,* thus everything that the other *names* mean, either is part of this *health,* which is Christ, and which Christ makes in us, or is ordained for it or follows from it necessarily. [Ibid., 776–77]

If the name of Jesus is identified with *salud*—with "health," "salvation," "state of grace"—then the basis for Crashaw's rapturous celebration gathers rational force. The very name itself, by including the letters of the tetragrammaton, brings God into the world by incorporating the divine mystery. In addition, the meaning of the name represents Christ's redemptive work; it is the naming of Christ with this "Name above every name" that marks him with the title of man's Savior, indeed of his very salvation. If we see in "Jesus" the ineffable name of God made speakable and also the summation of all the other names of Christ (that is, the fulfillment of the Messianic prophecies), then the opening lines of Crashaw's poem strike a far deeper chord:

> I Sing the NAME which Nonc can say
> But touch't with An interior RAY:
> The Name of our New PEACE; our Good:
> Our Blisse: and Supernatural Blood:
> The Name of All our Lives and Loves.
>
> [ll. 1–5]

These lines may be read as more than a random collection of high-sounding but arbitrary attributes; they may be read as titles. The extra emphasis on "NAME" in the first line is probably more than a chance decision by the printer, for it suggests the primacy of the name "Jesus," which expresses Christ's union with, and the ineffable Name of God. "RAY" in the following line is likewise reminiscent of Christ in another aspect, discussed by Fray Luis: "*Sun of justice* that in our souls, now free through Him, being born in them, spreads through all parts of them his shining rays in order to make them clear and beautiful" (*Obras,* I, 778). The various names listed in the succeeding lines suggest the various offices and facets of Christ of which "Jesus," is the culmination. The names of "Good," "Blisse," and "Lives" are all related to "health"; and "Supernatural Blood" refers to Christ's office of uniting manhood with divinity. "Our New Peace" and "Loves" seem to correspond to two other names treated by Fray Luis, "Príncipe de la Paz" and "Amado." Obviously, there is nothing unusual about such a description of Christ by way of Old Testament typology, but Crashaw's insistence upon the terms of description as names discloses a design of both celebrating and expounding the feast of the Holy Name in terms of such a theological scheme as that of *Los nombres de Cristo*.

Several important details of imagery in Crashaw's poem also bear a strong resemblance to passages in *Los nombres de Cristo*. Perhaps the most striking aspect of the imagery of the hymn is the emphasis on music, especially the celestial harmony or music of the spheres. In his hymn of praise, the poet first calls for help from the blessed souls in heaven, "whose Names belong/ Unto the everlasting life of Song"[35] (ll. 9–10); then he seeks to convoke the entire Creation:

>   Goe and request
> Great NATURE for the KEY of her huge Chest
> Of Heavns, the self involving Sett of Sphears
> (Which dull mortality more Feeles then heares)
>   Then rouse the nest
> Of nimble Art, and traverse round
> The Aiery Shop of soul-appeasing Sound.
>
>   . . . .
>   Wake; In the Name
> Of HIM who never sleeps, All Things that Are,
>   Or, what's the same,
>   Are Musicall;
>   Answer my Call
>   And come along;
> Help me to meditate mine Immortal Song.
>   . . . .
>   . . . Bring All the Powres of Praise
> Your Provinces of well-united Worlds can raise;
> Bring All your LUTES and HARPS of HEAVN and EARTH;
> What e're cooperates to The common mirthe
>   Vessells of vocall Joyes,

> Or You, more noble Architects of Intellectual Noise,
> Cymballs of Heav'n, or Human sphears,
> Solliciters of SOULES or EARES.
>
> [ll. 28–34, 55–61, 72–79]

It hardly need be pointed out that Crashaw is trading in familiar goods; the idea of the celestial harmony goes back to Pythagoras, gets into Christianity by way of St. Augustine, and is a commonplace during the Renaissance.[36] But we need not assume that Crashaw is using the concept merely because it was a popular source of colorful imagery. The repeated emphasis on harmony suggests that it has a special significance here, a significance explained by *Los nombres de Cristo:*

Health is a good which consists in proportion and in harmony of different things, and is like concerted music that the humors of the body make among themselves; and the same is the office which Christ performs, which is another cause whereby He is called *Jesus.* Because not only, by virtue of his divinity, is He the harmony and proportion of all things, but also, by virtue of his humanity, He is the music and good correspondence of all parts of the world . . . therefore He is the peace of all that is different, and the knot that binds in himself the visible with what is not seen, and that which concerts in reason and sense; and He is the harmonized and sweet melody above all manner, at whose holy sound all that is disturbed is quieted and composed. And thus is He truly Jesus. [*Obras completas castellanas,* I, 783]

Given this passage as background, the stress placed upon music in Crashaw's hymn seems quite fitting. The topos of *musica mundana* acquires a specific significance in this context. The poet invokes the harmony of the universe in praise of the name of Jesus because the name is the principle underlying all harmony. As the Second Person of the Trinity, the creating Word, Christ is "the harmony and proportion of all things"; but incarnate, as "the knot that binds in himself the visible with what is not seen," Christ unites heaven and earth, calling forth a united hymn of praise from man and angel, earth and heavenly sphere. It is the unifying office of Jesus which explains the poet's emphasis on his own place, the place of redeemed humanity, in the heavenly praise of the Redeemer:

> Chear thee my HEART!
> For Thou too hast thy Part

And Place in the Great Throng
Of This unbounded All-imbracing SONG.

. . . .

May it be no wrong
Blest Heavns, to you, and your Superior song,
That we, dark Sons of Dust and Sorrow,
A while Dare borrow
The Name of Your Delights and our Desires,
And fitt it to so farr inferior LYRES.

[ll. 88–91, 97–102]

The liturgical bent of Crashaw's poetry is never more apparent; the celebration of the feast of the Holy Name furnishes an opportunity to establish the general grounds of corporate worship in the union of Church Triumphant with Church Militant, in prayer and praise. The participation of the latter in the life of "SONG" is a participation in the life of blessedness—the life of angels and saints in divine harmony.

Crashaw had a pattern for this image not only in *Los nombres de Cristo,* but also in the poetry of Fray Luis. Indeed, that the "dark Sons of Dust and Sorrow" might for a while join the universal chorus of Creation in the "everlasting Song" of praise to the Creator is a favorite theme of the Spanish friar. His most notable expression of this theme is in an ode, "To Francisco Salinas."[37] The opening stanzas seem to be echoed by the beginning of "Hymn to the Name of Jesus," in which Crashaw seeks, in song, a memory of his soul's "parent HEAVN":

El aire se serena
y viste de hermosura y luz no usada,
Salinas, cuando suena
la música extremada
por vuestra sabia mano gobernada.
A cuyo son divino
el alma, que en olvido está sumida,
torna a cobrar el tino
y memoria perdida,
de su origen primera esclarecida.

[*Obras completas castellanas,* II, 746–47]

[The air grows calm and dresses in an unusual beauty and light, Salinas, when the consummate music sounds, governed by your wise hand; at whose divine sound my soul, that is submerged in oblivion, recovers the touch and lost memory of its first noble origin.]

Forgetting gold, "which the vile mob adores," and "fragile, deceptive beauty," the soul rises on the wings of music to the "highest sphere" and "hears another mode of imperishable music, that is of all the first." Figured in music is nothing less than a vision of God:

> Ve cómo el gran maestro,
> a aquesta inmensa cítara aplicado,
> con movimiento diestro
> produce el son sagrado
> con que este eterno templo es sustentado.
>
> [*Obras completas castellanas*, II, 747]

[It sees how the great master, bent over that immense harp, with skillful stroke produces the sacred sound with which this eternal temple is sustained.]

In effect, the entire Creation is the continuously produced music of God; Crashaw suggests roughly the same conception: "All Things that Are, / Or, what's the same, / Are Musicall." Likewise in Crashaw, the blessed enjoy "The everlasting life of Song," and the poet seeks a role in "This unbounded All-imbracing SONG." In "Hymn to the Name of Jesus," this musical ecstasy is finally elaborated into a complete rapture of the senses:

> O thou compacted
> Body of Blessings: spirit of Soules extracted!
> O dissipate thy spicy Powres
> (Clowd of condensed sweets) and break upon us
> In balmy showrs;
> O fill our senses, And take from us
> All force of so Prophane a Fallacy
> To think ought sweet but that which smells of Thee.
>
> [ll. 165–72]

The following stanzas from "To Francisco Salinas" are somewhat more restrained—after all, Fray Luis was a great admirer of Horace; nevertheless, the vision of utter, rapturous joy is similar to Crashaw's rapture:

> Aquí el alma navega
> por un mar de dulzura, y, finalmente,
> en él ansí se anega,
> que ningún accidente
> extraño y peregrino oye o siente.

¡Oh, desmayo dichoso!
¡Oh, muerte que das vida! ¡Oh dulce olvido!
¡Durase en tu reposo
sin ser restuido
jamás a aqueste bajo y vil sentido!

[*Obras completas castellanas,* II, 748]

[Here the soul sails through a sea of sweetness, and finally, is annihilated in it, so that it neither hears nor feels anything accidental, foreign and alien. Oh happy swoon! Oh, death that gives life! Oh, sweet oblivion! Let me stay in your repose not ever to be returned to those base, vile senses!]

Fray Luis and Crashaw alike make use of music's dual nature: as an art with close relationships to mathematics, it is an excellent symbol for the principle of divine order and harmony; yet, it is also a powerfully affective art. As Ruth Wallerstein points out, Crashaw's "verse music" is an essential means by which "the sensuous emotional ecstasy" with which he invests the theme of music is realized; and Anthony Low observes, "much of the effect of this hymn depends on the skillful building of musical effects over a large number of lines."[38] Thus the English poet embodies the idea of musical ecstasy in a concrete, quasi-musical poetic structure. In both poems, however, the personal devotional rapture is implanted in the concept of public worship: by Fray Luis in the liturgical music of Salinas, and by Crashaw in the Church feast.

Dovetailing with mystical and liturgical aspects is a second important motif in "Hymn to the Name of Jesus"; that is, light—especially the light associated with the dawning of a new and special day. The elect whom Crashaw invokes are "bright/Candidates of blisseful Light," and he finds himself unequal to "this GREAT mornings mighty Busynes" (ll. 9, 23). He seeks to convene all parts of the Creation "to wait at the love-crowned Doores of/This Illustrious DAY," to participate in "the worke of LOVE this morning (ll. 42–43, 54). Moreover, the name itself is to come from a realm of light, and its coming will bring a dawn of dazzling splendor to earth and mankind:

> Come, lovely NAME! Appeare from forth the Bright
>   Regions of peaceful Light
> Look from thine own Illustrious Home,
> Fair KING of NAMES, and come.

Leave All thy native Glories in their Gorgeous Nest,
And give thy Self a while The gracious Guest
Of humble Soules, that seek to find
                The hidden Sweets
                Which man's heart meets
When Thou art Master of the Mind.
Come, lovely Name; life of our hope!
Lo we hold our HEARTS wide ope!
Unlock thy Cabinet of DAY
Dearest Sweet, and come away.
            . . . .
O see, The WEARY liddes of wakeful Hope
(LOVE's Eastern windowes) All wide ope
                With Curtains drawn,
To catch the Day-break of Thy DAWN.
O dawn, at last, long look't for Day!
            . . . .
WELCOME to our dark world, Thou
                Womb of Day!
Unfold thy fair Conceptions; And display
The Birth of our Bright Joyes.
                    [ll. 115–28, 145–49, 161–64]

"Christ," Fray Luis observes, "wished to take as his proper name *health*, that is *Jesus*, because health is not a single blessing, but rather a universality of innumerable blessings." He lists some of these blessings and then adds a comment which markedly anticipates Crashaw's "womb" image in the lines quoted above:

So then, *health* is a pregnancy of all blessings, and thus, because Christ is truly this pregnancy, thereby this *name* is the one which suits Him best. Therefore Christ, just as in his divinity He is the idea and the treasure and the fountain of all blessings . . . with respect to his humanity, He has all cures and all medicines and all healths that are necessary for all. [*Obras completas castellanas*, I, 780–81]

Luis de León interprets the Messianic Psalm 109 (KJV 110) as a prophetic vision of the universal "health" brought by Christ as "Jesus." In the third verse of this psalm is the origin for the "pregnancy" and "womb" imagery in both Fray Luis and Crashaw: "The people shall be willing in the day of power; in the beauties of holiness from the womb

of morning, thou hast the dew of thy youth." Fray Luis then comments
on this verse:

Therefore he says that *in the day* that will dawn, when the night of this most
dark world is finished, for that is truly *day,* because it does not proceed toward
the night; and *day,* because the truth shall shine in it; and thus it will be *the
day of holy splendors,* because the splendor of the just, that is now hidden in
their breast, shall emerge then to light and be discovered in public and shall
shine through the eyes and through the face and through all the senses of the
body; for in that day, which is *day, all the people of Christ will be nobles.* [*Obras
completas castellanas,* I, 781–82]

Crashaw's hymn and Fray Luis' comment on the psalm share the idea
of an especially significant day that dawns with surpassing brightness
and glory. Evidently both writers are thinking of the same day which is
associated with the name of Jesus.

At this point we must take up a question posed by Louis Martz:
"But what is this 'great morning,' this 'illustrious day?' " The problem
is that the feast of the Holy Name did not become a feast of the
universal Church until 1721. This fact led Martz to speculate that
Crashaw's poem referred to the Franciscan celebration of the Holy
Name on January 14, a practice begun in the sixteenth century: "The
occasion of the poem may have been Crashaw's first participation in
this relatively new devotion." Martz has, however, subsequently
changed his mind. Taking note of the close association between the
naming of our Lord and his circumcision in Scripture, he suggests that
the occasion of the poem is the feast of the Circumcision itself, whose
Gospel reading includes this verse: "When the eighth day arrived for
his circumcision, the name Jesus was given the child, the name the
angel had given him before he was conceived" (Luke 2:21).[39] But
there is further evidence. In *The Golden Legend,* Jacobus de Voragine
associates the feast of the Circumcision with both "the conferring of a
new name upon the Lord, for our salvation," and with "the first
shedding of Christ's blood for men."[40] This joining of the two seems to
have continued in siglo de oro Spain. In the poem on the name of Jesus
in *Pastores de Belén,* examined above, Lope involves himself in the
shepherds' celebration of the circumcision of the infant Christ. Lope
may well have derived an example from *Los nombres de Cristo,* for Fray
Luis quotes a lengthy passage from St. Bernard's *In Circumcisione
Domini, sermo 2,* which deals with "the name that is above all names,

the name of Jesus, to whom all knees are bowed" (*Obras*, I, 778–79); and Fray Luis himself refers to the verse from Luke quoted above.[41] This association between the Circumcision and the Holy Name was by no means confined to the erudite in seventeenth-century Spain: besides Lope's pastoral a lo divino, José de Valdivielso (1560–1638), who wrote poems of a distinctly popular flavor, composed a "Ballad on the Circumcision and Name of Jesus" (*Romance á la Circuncisión y Nombre de Jesús*). Certain motifs in the poem are reminiscent of *Los nombres de Cristo* and also seem to anticipate Crashaw's hymn:

> Jesús os llaman, amores,
> ¡Oh qué lindo nombre, os dan!
> Con ser Dios el que le toma
> Su sangre le ha de costar;
> Que vale sangre de Dios,
> Niño, el nombre que tomáis.
> Jesús, dice, Dios y Hombre,
> Que en Jesús juntas están,
> Hombre que pueda morir,
> Y Dios que pueda salvar.
>
> . . . .
>
> Es el maná de los cielos,
> Y bien le llamo maná,
> Pues tras que del cielo vino,
> En Él los gustos están.[42]

[They call you Jesus, Love, Oh what a fine name they give you! Since he who takes it is God, it has to cost him his blood; for it is worth the blood of God, Child, the name that you are taking. Jesus, it says, God and Man, for in Jesus they are joined, Man that he be able to die and God that he be able to save. . . . It is the manna of heaven, and well I call it manna, for since it came from the sky, pleasures are in it.]

If we assume that the occasion is the Circumcision, then the structure and significance of Crashaw's poem become clearer. When Crashaw calls upon the name as "thou/Womb of Day" to "unfold thy fair Conceptions; And display/The Birth of our Bright Joyes" (ll. 162–64, quoted above), he reminds us that the Virgin Mary presents the "fair Conception" of her womb for circumcision in the temple in an act which foreshadows the grand action of the poem and ratifies Christ's acceptance of humanity in conjunction with his divinity, signified by his name, "Jesus." More important, an apparent digression

on the early Christian martyrs at the close of the poem is seen to be
integral to the poem's meaning. The infant Christ sheds blood—an
anticipation of his Passion—and is given "a Name above every name";
that is, "Jesus": "health" or "salvation." The sufferings of the martyrs
are then the repeated "dawnings" of this "day" of Jesus' circumcision
and naming:

> Little, alas thought They
> Who tore the Fair Brests of thy Friends,
>   Their Fury but made way
> For thee;
>
>   . . . .
>
> What did their Weapons but sett wide the Doores
> For Thee: Fair, purple Doores, of love's devising
> The Ruby windowes which inrich't the EAST
> Of Thy so oft repeated Rising.
> Each wound of Theirs was Thy new Morning;
> And reinthroned thee in thy Rosy Nest,
> With blush of *thine own Blood thy day adorning.*
>
>   [ll. 207–10, 216–22]

I have added the emphasis in the last line to highlight the parallel
between this passage and one of Fray Luis, already quoted above: "and
thus, it will be *the day of holy splendors,* because the splendor of the
just, that is now hidden in their breasts, shall emerge then to light and
be discovered in public and shall shine through the eyes and through
the face and through all the senses of the body." Also worth pointing
out is the similarity between the imagery of blood and sunrise in
Crashaw's lines on the martyrs in "Hymn to the Name of Jesus," and
on the Circumcision in "Hymn for New Year's Day":

> Rise, thou best and brightest morning!
> Rosy with a double Red;
> With thine own blush thy cheeks adorning
> And the dear drops this day were shed.
>
>   [ll. 1–4]

The passage on martyrdom is, therefore, related to the principle
theme of the poem: the name of Jesus. For in addition to praising the
name, Crashaw exhorts it to descend and dwell among men; since the
infant Christ received the name "Jesus" with his circumcision, with
the shedding of blood, the name is manifest again whenever men shed

blood "for His Name's sake." In this vein the poet recalls, perhaps, a verse from Psalm 115, part of the office of vespers for the feast of the Holy Name: "Precious in the eyes of the Lord is the death of his saints." Crashaw's injunction to Jesus, "give thy Self a while The gracious Guest / Of humble Soules," finds an answer in the description of "thy old Friends of Fire, All full of Thee" who, in fact, did carry the name into the world:

> On their Bold Brests about the world they bore thee,
> And to the Teeth of Hell stood up to teach thee,
> In Center of their inmost Soules they wore thee,
> Where Rackes and Torments striv'd, in vain, to reach thee.
>
> [ll. 203–06]

In its conclusion, however, "Hymn to the Name of Jesus" looks forward to the Judgment Day, the day when the name will be visible not in the blood of suffering martyrs, which is one kind of "dawn," but in the full noon of "the dazeling light of thy dread majesty." This apocalyptic closing passage seems also to answer earlier lines in the poem, which in retrospect are somewhat ironic:

> Lo how the thirsty Lands
> Gasp for thy Golden Showres! with long stretch'd Hands
> Lo how the laboring Earth
> That hopes to be
> All Heaven by Thee,
> Leapes at thy Birth.
>
> [ll. 129–34]

On the last day the earth shall "leape" indeed! The image of the thirsty lands, as George Williams in *The Complete Poetry* notes, echoes the *Book of Common Prayer*, Ps. 143:6; but it is also similar to a passage in *Los nombres de Cristo,* where Fray Luis quotes Psalm 102:10–11 (KJV 103) and adds: "They [who fear the Lord] are base earth, but your mercy is like the heaven. They hope like dry earth for its blessing, and it rains blessings upon them" (*Obras completas castellanas,* I, 800). This observation follows from his discussion of Psalm 109 (KJV 110) which looks forward to the "day of the Lord" when "I make thine enemies thy footstool." The whole creation, not only men, he says, shall recognize that Christ is its health, its "Jesus," "for his cross embraces everything and his clean blood makes it bright, and his holy humanity purifies it, and through Him the elements and the heavens shall have a new estate and better qualities than now they have, and *Jesus* is in all and for all" (Ibid, I, 797). The discussion of "Jesus" in *Los nombres de Cristo* ends with a metrical translation of Psalm 102 (KJV 103) which, as the first verse indicates, provides a fine summary of the principal theme of "Hymn to the Name of Jesus": "Bless the LORD, O my soul, and all that is within me, bless his holy name."

III

By comparing Crashaw's poem to the work of Fray Luis and Lope de Vega, one can see that "Hymn to the Name of Jesus" possesses a thematic unity and clear relationship between image and meaning; the poem is not merely a vague, if impressive, sequence of melodious sounds and sensuous images. By identifying the day for which the hymn was written as the feast of the Circumcision, and seeing the concluding passage on the blood of the martyrs and the Judgment with reference to the first blood shed by Christ, the import of devotion to the Holy Name of Jesus and of the hymn's relationship to the other Christmastide hymns are both made clearer. In *Carmen Deo Nostro,* the Nativity hymn, the "Hymn for New Year's Day," and the "Hymn in the Glorious Epiphanie" stand in proper calendrical order as they had in the volume of 1648. The first and last celebrate, respectively, the manifestation of Christ to the Jews and Gentiles; the New Year's Day hymn, which commemorates Christ's fulfillment of the Law, concentrates on the event of the circumcision in temporal terms. "Hymn to the Name of Jesus," with the removal of two early Psalm translations which intervene in the 1648 edition, stands at the head of the Christmas group, and it justifies this positioning by treating the theme of the Incarnation in the widest possible sense. In contrast to the New Year's Day hymn, the hymn to the Holy Name considers the Circumcision and the naming of Jesus *sub specie aeternitatis* as the act which elevated human nature in Christ into the divine realm and won the salvation of the world. The recognition of the Spanish background of the poem reveals how successful Crashaw is, as a liturgical poet, in illuminating the meaning of a rite of public worship and, at the same time, investing it with intense personal devotion and an ardent sense of mystery.

6

The Eloquence of Love:
Crashaw and Gongorism

Es *la agudeza pasto del alma*, writes Baltasar Gracián: "Wit is food for the soul." And a few sentences later he adds, "subtlety is nourishment for the spirit." The point is further emphasized by yet another comparison: "What beauty is for the eyes, and harmony for the ears, that for the understanding is the conceit."[1] Thus the leading Spanish theorist of baroque poetics formulates the motive for the style of witty elaboration and startling imagery—at once sparkling and obscure—that we have encountered so often in preceding chapters, in the poetry of Lope and Góngora and their imitators. Given Gracián's epigrammatic equivalences for wit and the poetry of conceit which is its product, understanding Crashaw's attraction to the style is not difficult. The Spanish critic is not, to be sure, referring here to devotional poetry, but his view of the poetic enterprise furnishes an admirable foundation for the devotional poet. Crashaw's poems aspire to be "food for the soul" and "nourishment for the spirit," and a vision of the universe as a pattern of hidden correspondences provides an inexhaustible metaphorical quarry of material, from which Crashaw carves out images of the miracles of our Lord and of the saints' lives of wondrous grace. Gracián defines the conceit as "an act of understanding, which expresses the correspondence that is found among objects," and J. A. Mazzeo has termed the theories of Gracián and his Italian contemporaries a "Poetics of correspondences."[2] If we allow Góngora the pre-eminence conceded by his contemporaries, the later development of Crashaw's style, "towards a freer verse and a more complex metaphorical utterance,"[3] a development "away from Marinism,"[4] may well be conceived as a movement towards Gongorism.

Góngora's *Soledades* ("Solitudes") and *Fábula de Polifemo y Galatea* (based on a tale from Ovid's *Metamorphoses*, XIII) constitute the most extreme manifestation of certain tendencies of baroque poetry. Two principal directions in style are usually distinguished in the Spanish poetry of the baroque period: *conceptismo* and *culteranismo* (or *cultismo*). The former is largely a matter of verbal and intellectual ingenuity: pun, paradox, antithesis, conceit, and sharp, terse phrasing are the hallmarks of this style; the chief ingredient is *agudeza,* or "wit" as this term was understood in Donne's time. The latter, basically another name for Gongorism, is an intensification or exaggeration of style in the direction of a refined and artificial beauty: it stresses cultivation of intricate Latin rhetorical devices, exotic imagery and diction, erudite allusions, and a general abundance of brilliant and sensuous imagery. Often it involves obscurity deriving not from complexity of thought, but from elaborate syntax and cryptic mythological references. It has been suggested that conceptismo appeals primarily to the mind, culteranismo to the senses.[5]

These remarks may remind students of English literature of the distinction often drawn between the Metaphysical school of Donne and the Spenserians. Just as the attempt to create an absolute dichotomy out of this distinction has been challenged among scholars of English poetry,[6] so the older view among Spanish critics, in which conceptismo is set in direct opposition to culteranismo, has been called into question in recent decades. Many of Góngora's numerous rivals and antagonists—most notably Lope de Vega and Francisco de Quevedo (1580–1645)—are found to have indulged frequently in culteranismos. Dámaso Alonso maintains, for example, that a significant portion of Lope's lyric poetry imitates Góngora's style;[7] however, he also points out the underlying conceptismo in Góngora's own poetry: "With frequency in Góngora . . . beneath the brilliant coloring there is a wittiness, a conceptual complication, not essentially distinct from that of a Quevedo."[8] Andrée Collard argues that conceptismo should not be regarded as a separate school at all, but rather as a basic component of virtually all Spanish poetry in the siglo de oro: "The wit necessary to conceive metaphors, plays on words, and subtleties of thought in general was considered a privilege of the Spanish nation. From Juan de Valdés [d. 1545] until Gracián [1601–58] theoretical writings are sown with comments on the adaptability of the Castilian tongue for puns and on the Spanish propensity for wittiness."[9] Góngora's enemies accused him of corrupting his Spanish heritage with foreign affectations; it was not that he wrote in a new style, but that he seemed to be interested in style for its own sake.[10]

In simple terms, Gongorism consists of a brilliant superstructure of culteranismo erected upon a foundation of conceptismo, or Metaphysical wit. The example of Góngora serves, then, to illuminate one of the problems which troubles critics of Crashaw; the latter has always been included among the Metaphysical poets, but many commentators have been uncomfortable with this classification.[11] Perhaps Crashaw's style, at least the style of the later hymns, may be explained as a variety of Góngorism: a combination of Metaphysical wit and a tendency toward the richly sensuous and ornate. Crashaw shares, to some extent, the sharp wit of a poet like Donne; but the wit is turned away from complex argumentation toward equally complex development of sensuous imagery; and the drama, the sense of immediate conversation characteristic of Donne, is replaced by a sense of remote rapturous song. It is true that Crashaw never approaches the verbal obscurity often found in Góngora's verse; in this respect the latter has much in common with Donne, or even Chapman. Nevertheless, the blend of wit and sensuous beauty is nowhere better exemplified than in Góngora, and a comparison between the Soledades or the Fábula de Polifemo y Galatea, and Crashaw's poetry reveals a striking similarity of style, both in regard to imagery and metaphor, and prosody. In fact, Góngora's Soledades may well be the key to the origins of Crashaw's irregular ode.

With only a general description of Góngora's imagery, parallels to Crashaw begin to emerge. Dámaso Alonso points out that the habitual imagery of Góngora seeks "to evoke an atmosphere of brilliant or dense beauty." Moreover, this "atmosphere and the very expression of the poet tend toward the excessive: all is hyperbolized." Nevertheless, for all the radiant, shimmering beauty to be found in the poetic world created by Góngora, the element of the grotesque and shocking is ever-present; and the poet is able to move from one to the other rapidly, producing sudden, startling contrasts: "How we pass, at an imperceptible flick of the master's hand, from light to shadow, from harsh rusticity to ordered beauty!"[12] For the purpose of creating this poetic world, Góngora devises, in effect, his own "poetic language" in which the "real term" (i.e., "tenor") of a metaphor is customarily— almost systematically—omitted. Teeth and hair, for example, rarely appear in his culterano poems: in their place are pearls and gold.[13] Thus Alonso writes of "nature aesthetically deformed" in Góngora's poetry, and asserts that he employs a "poetic diction in which the designative metaphors are constantly placing an unreal barrier between the mind and the object itself."[14]

It is not difficult to see how a technique for creating an atmosphere of pervasive beauty would be of interest to Crashaw: an impulse toward aesthetic harmony in Góngora is matched by Crashaw's yearning for supernatural glory. In addition, even as Góngora's baroque sense of the flux of all things admits the dreadful, even the ugly, into his aesthetic paradise;[15] so the way to God in Crashaw's poetry is through penitential tears, sacrifice, mystic death, the agony and horror of martyrdom. It is evident that the immediate poetic effect sought by Crashaw in his sacred verse is, in some sense, parallel to that evoked in Góngora's culterano poems, however different the thematic intention of the two. It is not surprising, then, to find numerous similarities in technique. Austin Warren observes that Crashaw's imagery is "more than pageant . . . rather, it is a vocabulary of recurrent motifs." This characteristic of Crashaw's poetry seems to correspond to Góngora's "poetic diction" consisting of metaphorical vehicles repeated continually without their tenors. The effect of Góngora's metaphors—the creation of an unreal, aesthetic realm—is likewise found in the work of the English poet: "Crashaw's *concetti*," says Warren, "by their infidelity to nature, claim allegiance to the supernatural; his baroque imagery, engaging the sense, intimates a world which transcends them."[16]

If we consult the respective descriptions of the work of each poet, given by his leading commentator, it becomes apparent that the similarities between Góngora and Crashaw may be pursued in still greater detail. Warren notes that Crashaw's "palette" is limited, generally confined to primary colors; that he relies on contrast, on the "bold antithesis of black and white."[17] Alonso says that Góngora's "palette is not very extensive"; in colors, as in all else, he tends "to simplify the natural toward the beautiful"; his colors are generally "pure" and "absolute."[18] Another similarity lies in the use made by both Góngora and Crashaw of various kinds of traditional material. As Austin Warren suggests, the flora of Crashaw's poetry "soon turn to symbols," and the fauna "have never owed genuine allegiance to the world of Nature," coming rather from bestiary or Christian tradition.[19] In the poetry of Góngora, Dámaso Alonso finds a similar attraction to fabulous natural history. (It would be difficult to judge whether Crashaw or Góngora has more of a liking for the Phoenix.) Generally, Alonso continues, Góngora is quite aware of the falsity of this ancient lore, yet "it serves, nevertheless, like mythology or popular science, as a point of reference, an immutable fixture for shifting reality, or it has the relative truth of an established beauty."[20]

The mention of mythology in this quotation suggests yet another parallel between the stylistic habits of Góngora and Crashaw, but one for which the support of Warren is lacking, who asserts that Crashaw divests his sacred poetry of the usual Renaissance machinery of classical myth.[21] Although there are, indeed, fewer explicit references to mythical figures than one might expect, they are not altogether wanting: for example, Hyperion enters into the last line of the Epiphany poem;[22] there is a hint of Jove and Danae in the "Golden Showres" of "Hymn to the Name of Jesus" (l. 130);[23] the blind "love" of "Charitas Nimia" clearly refers to Cupid (ll. 5ff.); and there are the river nymphs in "Letter to the Countess of Denbigh" (ll. 20ff.). More important than clear allusions to specific myths is the mythic aura of much of Crashaw's imagery, the mythic way in which he orders his vision of the world. In this he again resembles Góngora, of whom Alonso says, "His brain is filled with the representative weight of the ancient fables. He takes refuge in this world. Automatically, he tends to root any of the forms of life in the fixed heaven of mythical representation."[24]

Crashaw's use of mythology needs clarification not only because it conflicts with Warren's view, but also because of the inherent complexity of the issue. Where Góngora builds his own mythical structures out of the shining rubble of pagan literary temples, Crashaw—in a highly sophisticated variation of sacred parody—employs some of the same blocks of Ovidian marble in constructing the poetic equivalent of baroque churches. A passage from the "letter to the Countess of Denbigh" shows how the pagan apprehension of the universe is assimi-

lated to the larger Christian vision. The issue at hand is the lady's
hesitancy to enter the Roman Catholic Church; her luke-warmness
which may turn into an "enduring chill":

> So when the Year takes cold we see
> Poor waters their own Prisoners be:
> Fetter'd and lock'd up fast they lie
> In a cold self-captivity,
> Th' astonish'd Nymphs their Floud's strange Fate deplore,
> To find themselves their own severer Shoar.
>
> [ll. 21-26]

A moral and psychological state is first compared to a concrete, natural
phenomenon: the Countess' continuing hesitation is likened to a river
freezing over. But then the concrete term of the comparison is assimilated to a universal category which has, despite its abstractness, more
emotional gravity: the river is personified, identified with the nymphs
of classical antiquity. By superimposing a mythical association,
Crashaw infuses a sense of regret, of anguished loss, into his simple,
physical comparison. The figure is effective because Crashaw blends
the natural image of the freezing river and the allusion to the
nymphs—woefully transformed like so many of their mythical
sisters—with no sense of strain. The nymphs introduce an element of
beauty but not of mere decoration, for their presence in the image is an
essential aspect of Crashaw's vision because they represent, to a
woman who is resisting the call of her Redeemer, the bitter (if
graceful) hopelessness of the entire pagan world in its lack of grace.

Góngora uses mythical imagery in a parallel, although non–
Christian, manner to enrich and complicate his image of a river in the
first *Soledad*:

> un río. . . que—luciente
> de aquellos montes hijo—
> con torcido discurso, aunque prolijo,
> tiraniza los campos útilmente;
> orleadas sus orillas de frutales,
> quiere la Copia que su cuerno sea;
> si al animal armaron de Amaltea
> diáfanos cristales.
>
> [ll. 198-205]

[a river . . . which—shining son of those mountains—with a tortuous discourse, although prolix, tyrannizes usefully the fields; its banks bordered with
fruit trees, Plenty wishes that it might be her horn; if diaphanous crystals
armed the animal of Amalthea.]

Góngora begins by abstracting the river into a "son of the mountains"
whose twisting course is a tedious "discourse" commanding the fields
to be fruitful; but the abundance along the river's curving banks
suggests the Horn of Plenty, and the poet immediately seizes upon the
mythic origin of this commonplace. Zeus, suckled as an infant by the
goat Amalthea, broke off one of the animal's horns and, endowing it
with the property of being filled with whatever its owner desired, gave
it to the women who had cared for him. [25] By incorporating the myth
into his image of the river, Góngora adds deeper overtones to his poem.
The witty observation of the fertility of the river valley is transformed
by a hint of the mysterious and primitive: the valley is not merely
fertile, it is blessed. Again the mythical element in the image is not
mere decoration, but helps to develop Góngora's vision of an earthly
paradise, which is at the heart of the *Soledades*. [26] This stylistic procedure is similar to Crashaw's because both poets employ myth to inten-
sify the emotional power of their verse and to amplify its significance,
and the similarity remains, despite important differences. The very
nature of Góngora's principal theme, the poetic recovery of the pagan
Golden Age, lends itself more readily to the mythological imagination;
hence Crashaw's myth-making is necessarily more oblique. Yet a certain
parallel of approach between the two poets is virtually inevitable, since
Góngora and Crashaw alike labor under the need to amplify their *materia
poetica,* in order to create the image of a transcendental realm and to
suggest that something lies behind the surface of reality which is
deeper and more important than our everyday experience would lead
us to expect.

Simple personification is another frequent recourse of the two
poets, and their use of this device often serves the same rhetorical
intention. In "Hymn to the Name of Jesus," Crashaw employs personification to demonstrate the awesome power and significance of the
Holy Name. What will become of those who refuse to kneel to the
name, the poet muses, on Judgment Day (cf. Rev. 8:8; Isa. 24:20;
etc.):

> When stubborn Rocks shall bow
> And Hills hang down their Heavn-saluting Heads
> To seek for humble Beds
> Of Dust, where in the Bashful shades of night
> Next to their own low NOTHING they may ly,
> And couch before the dazeling light of thy dread majesty.
>
> [ll. 230–35]

The personification here has a twofold effect: on the one hand, the power of the name is emphasized by the "personal" response of presumably inanimate objects, rocks and hills; on the other hand, attribution of a conscious purpose to natural phenomena suggests that nature itself is full of moral and spiritual significance. Man and nature are unified as parts of one divine creation; the supernatural permeates every corner of the universe. The figurative presentation of the rocks and hills thus magnifies Crashaw's principal theme, the name as Word, or sustaining principle of all things, and adds a deeper resonance to the mood of the poem as a whole.

In a passage in which the tone is different, Góngora makes a similar twofold use of personification. In the *Soledad* I, a group of country girls on their way to a wedding sing so beautifully that the sound might affect even the trees, and the birds gather to listen,

> mientras el arroyuelo para oílla
> hace de blanca espuma
> tantas orejas cuantas guijas lava.
>
> [ll. 558–60]

[while the brook in order to hear it (the song) makes as many ears of white foam as it washes stones.]

Góngora fancies that the frothy ripples formed in the stream as it sweeps over its pebbly bed are ears intentionally pricked up to listen to the singing of the girls. Besides stressing the captivating quality of the song (even the inanimate tree and brook, even the birds—themselves "feathered zithers"—listen), the personification, through which the natural phenomena are endowed with conscious purpose, suggests the harmony of man and nature. Even as this image of harmony is an appropriate element in Crashaw's heavenly vision, so it is likewise in Góngora's total vision of a world of beauty fashioned by poetry.

It is this need to elevate his subject, to lift the individual persons and objects in his poems onto a transcendental plane, which induces Góngora to "deform nature" through involutions of imagery and syntax. Hence the heroine of the *Fábula de Polifemo y Galatea* is more than a lovely nymph, she is a manifestation of beauty itself:

> Ninfa, de Doris hija, la más bella,
> adora, que vio el reino de la espuma.
> Galatea es su nombre, y dulce en ella
> el terno Venus de sus gracias suma.
> Son una y otra luminosa estrella
> lucientes ojos de su blanca pluma:
> si roca de cristal no es de Neptuno,
> pavón de Venus es, cisne de Juno.
>
> [ll. 97–104]

[He (Polifemo) adores, daughter of Doris, the most beautiful nymph seen by the realm of foam. Galatea is her name, and Venus sweetly sums in her the triad of her graces. One and another luminous star are the shining eyes of her white plumage: if she is not the crystalline rock of Neptuno, she is the peacock of Venus, the swan of Juno.]

The chiasmus of the closing couplet is encountered frequently in Crashaw.[27] The figure achieves its pointedness by crossing qualities of the two terms of a comparison. Galatea's eyes are like those in the tail of a peacock (Juno's bird), her skin as white as the feathers of a swan (Venus' bird); hence, she is Venus' peacock, Juno's swan. "The complication of the passage," observes Dámaso Alonso of the stanza as a whole, "establishes intertwined associations among these elements: a woman's beautiful body is now in the imagination of the reader a swarming of precious, radiant material, a cosmos of dazzling brilliance."[28] Again it is to be noted that ornate imagery is not necessarily *mere* decoration; Góngora's lavish description of Galatea serves the thematic intention of the poem by intimating a relationship between individual and universal beauty; a "cosmos of dazzling brilliance" in herself, Galatea is also a symbol of the greater cosmos, or at least of one aspect of it.

Obviously Góngora's way of elaborating symbols, of magnifying the individual into a manifestation of the transcendental, can become

available for sacred poetry; Crashaw's "Hymn in the Assumption"
furnishes an example:

> A peice of heav'nly earth; Purer and brighter
> Then the chast starres, whose choise lamps come to light her
> While through the crystal orbes, clearer then they
> She climbes; and makes a farre more milkey way.
>
> [ll. 3–6]

Since the feast of the Assumption celebrates the bodily rapture of the
Virgin Mary into heaven, Crashaw's emphasis on her physical beauty
is not inappropriate. To be sure, the moral theme is overt: the stars she
vanquishes in brightness are "chast," and she is also "purer" than they;
but the total impression is one of radiant beauty. The Virgin, invested
with the hyperbolic imagery typical of the Petrarchan love poetry of
the Renaissance, has a body of surpassing whiteness and crystalline
transparence. Crashaw, however, manipulates this imagery in the
manner of Góngora: the actual physical object of the imagery, the
immaculate body of our Lady, dissolves (as Galatea) into a brilliant
haze of figuration which cannot be visualized as a specific, concrete
entity.

A discussion of the idealizing facet of the imagery of Góngora and
Crashaw must not omit another important characteristic which the
two poets share: an intense sensuousness which often merges with the
apparently sensual or with the grotesque and shocking. The sensibility
of each poet includes a predilection for images of tactile sensation that
seem almost palpable. Let us consider again in this perspective a passage from "Hymn to the Name of Jesus" quoted above in chapter 5:

> Lo, where Aloft it comes! It comes, Among
> The Conduct of Adoring SPIRITS, that throng
> Like diligent Bees, And swarm about it.
>   O they are wise;
> And know what SWEETES are suck't from out it.
>   It is the Hive,
>   By which they thrive,
> Where All their Hoard of Hony lyes.
>
> [ll. 151–58]

Note the parallels in the "chorus" from the wedding hymn in *Soledad* I:

> Ven, Himeneo, y plumas no vulgares
> al aire los hijuelos den alados
> de las que el bosque bellas ninfas cela:
> de sus carcajes, estos, argentados,
> flechen mosquetas, [29] nieven azahares;
> vigilantes aquellos, la aldehuela
> rediman de el que más o tarde vuela,
> o infausto gime, pájaro nocturno;
> mudos coronen otros por su turno
> el dulce lecho conyugal, en cuanto
> lasciva abeja al virginal acanto
>   néctar le chupa hibleo.
> Ven, Himeneo, ven; ven, Himeneo.

[ll. 793–805]

[Come, Hymen, and let the little winged children of the lovely nymphs hidden in the woods, not the vulgar ones, give their feathers to the air; let these from their silver quivers shoot white musk roses, a snowfall of orange blossoms; let those, vigilant, guard the little village from the nocturnal bird that flies late or moans accursed; mute, let others surround in their turn the sweet conjugal bed while the sportive bee in the virgin acanthus sucks the hyblaean nectar. Come, Hymen, come; come, Hymen.]

In each of the preceding passages the poet rouses the expectation of the reader, builds excitement and suspense which culminate in the sensual "suck" (or *chupa*). In each case the center of intense excitement, whether the name of Jesus or the new bride, is reduced to an object of simple, gustatory desire: "a Hoard of Hony," a flower full of sweet nectar. The religious experience of the Christian in the contemplation of the name and the erotic experience of the groom in the enjoyment of his bride are by no means equivalent, but the images are parallel insofar as, in each, a profound and complex emotional state is reduced to a simple sensation in the interest of poetic intensity. The imaginations of Góngora and Crashaw are working along similar lines; they are handling their material in much the same way. Given the explicitly devotional context of the English poem, an ironic tension is inevitably generated between the terms of the comparison; however, both poets have additional means at their disposal for complicating tone.

The sensuality in Góngora and in Crashaw—and many of the

latter's critics have commented on this—is frequently mingled with a
certain grotesqueness or violence. Hence, *Soledad* I closes with an
image of the wedding night as "battles of love in a field of plumage" (l.
1091); and in "The Flaming Heart" Crashaw writes, "in love's field
was never found/A nobler weapon then a WOUND" (ll. 71–72). In
such images, love—human and divine—is pictured in terms of battle;
the suggestion of violence, like the strain of sensuality, leads to an
intensification of the sense of passion and thereby of poetic impact.
The sensual and the grotesquely violent are similarly blended in the
depiction of Santa Teresa's mystical rapture in Crashaw's hymn in her
honor:

> How kindly will thy gentle HEART
> Kisse the sweetly-killing DART!
> And close in his embraces keep
> Those delicious Wounds that weep
> Balsam to heal themselves with.
>
> [ll. 105–09]

Having considered these lines previously in chapter 4, as a representation of mystical experience parallel to similar passages in Spanish
devotional poets like Medinilla, we are now able to see how the style is
part of a wider baroque mode of poetic realization which stresses, by
means of sensual excitement in surprising contexts, the mysterious
power latent in virtually everything. Góngora's pre-eminence in this
mode emerges clearly in the way he enlivens so routine an effort as his
dedication of the *Soledades* to the duke of Bejar:

> arrima a un frexno el frexno—cuyo acero,
> sangre sudando, en tiempo hará breve
> purpurear la nieve—
> y, en cuanto da el solícito montero
> al duro robre, al pino levantado
> —émulos vividores de las peñas—
> las formidable señas
> del oso que aun besaba, atravesado,
>
> la asta de tu luciente jabalina.
>
> [ll. 13–21]

[rest against an ash (tree) your ash—whose steel, sweating blood, shall in a
brief time make the snow turn crimson—and, while the prudent mountaineer

gives to the hard oak, to the towering pine—living rivals to the boulders—the formidable signs of the bear that kissed, even transfixed, the shaft of your shining spear.]

Crashaw writes in honor of a saint, Góngora of a duke; both poets surpass our usual expectations of laudatory verse by means of boldly graphic imagery: an element of fierce sensuality gives a vivid impression of the saint's passionate devotion to God, or of the nobleman's masculine prowess. Given this particular comparison, it seems pertinent to remark here that if Góngora is undeniably the greater literary figure—more fertile and original and broader in the scope of his canon—still Crashaw found a more vital use of the style which the Spaniard perfected.

Crashaw is commonly depreciated for just the kind of imagery we have been discussing; but when he and Góngora are writing at their best, the inherent conflict between the tendency toward transcendent beauty and the opposing tendency toward the sensuous and graphically shocking is held in control and plays an important role in the total effect of their poetry. A final comparison between Crashaw's use of figurative language and Góngora's plainly indicates both the purpose of such imagery and also the way in which Crashaw avails himself of the tonal and textural qualities of Gongorism, of its way of imagining the world, while pointing to a different ultimate reality beyond it. As we observed in a discussion of these lines in the preceding chapter (p. 140), martyrdom is related to the central theme of "Hymn to the Name of Jesus," the manifestation of the Word:

> What did their Weapons but sett wide the Doores
> For Thee: Fair, purple Doores, of love's devising;
> The Ruby windowes which inrich't the EAST
> Of Thy so oft repeated Rising.
> Each wound of Theirs was Thy new Morning;
> And reinthron'd thee in thy Rosy Nest,
> With blush of thine own Blood thy day adorning.
> It was the witt of love o'reflow'd the Bounds
> Of WRATH, and made thee way through All those WOUNDS.
>   [ll. 216–24]

Crashaw never treats a theme more grotesque and dreadful than this depiction of the agonies of the martyrs of the early Church, but the imagery is both highly ornate and witty, with the wounds metaphorically transformed first into "Doores," then into sunrises. Encompassed in these lines are brutal violence, colorful and sensuous ornament, and the idea of "overflowing" love. And not only is the theme of martyrdom appropriately raised in a poem which celebrates the saving force of Jesus' name, this particular style of treatment is effective precisely because it succeeds in binding together both the celebration and the horror, both the sensuous beauty and the keen wit, with its unblinking gaze at every facet of reality. The closing stanzas of Góngora's *Fábula de Polifemo y Galatea* shows the pervasiveness of this double view in baroque literature, for it is a comparable attempt to harmonize a complex of discordant elements in a pagan secular context:

> Con violencia desgajó, infinita,
> la mayor punta de la excelsa roca
> que al[30] joven, sobre quien la precipita
> urna es mucha, pirámide no poca.
> Con lágrimas la Ninfa solicita
> las Deidades de el mar, que Acis invoca:
> concurren todas, y el peñasco duro,
> la sangre que exprimió, cristal fue puro.
>
> Sus miembros lastimosamente opresos
> del escollo fatal fueron apenas,
> que los pies de los árboles más gruesos
> calzó el líquido aljófar de sus venas.
> Corriendo plata al fin de sus blancos huesos,
> lamiendo flores y argentando arenas,
> a Doris llega, que con llanto pío,
> yerno le saludó, le aclamó río.

[ll. 489–504]

[He (Polifemo) dislodged, with infinite violence, the greatest peak of a towering rock that to the youth, on whom he casts it, is much for an urn, not small for a pyramid. With tears the Nymph implores the divinities of the sea whom Acis invokes: they all are attentive, and the blood pressed out by the harsh boulder was pure crystal.

His limbs were hardly oppressed grievously by the fatal crag when the liquid pearl of his veins shod the feet of the thickest trees. Running silver at last his white bones, licking flowers and silvering the sands, he reaches Doris, who, with pious lament, saluted him as her son-in-law, acclaimed him as a river.]

Upon first consideration, what could be more unlike than Crashaw's extended allusion to the martyred saints and Góngora's recasting of an Ovidian fable? Nevertheless, the poets handle analogous situations in much the same way. In each poem the quoted passage is preceded by a description of intense passion: Crashaw introduces the reference to martyrdom immediately after a long, rapturously sensuous account of the pleasures to be enjoyed by the devout soul in the name of Jesus; in Góngora's poem the jealous cyclops has interrupted the love-making of Acis and Galatea. Thus both poets follow a depiction of delight, rendered in sensual terms, with a depiction of gory death. However, both poems transform the grotesque and horrible through images of loveliness and witty metaphor. In Crashaw wounds become doors of dawns; Góngora parallels this ingenuity with a fatal crag which is too large to be a funeral urn but not too small to be a pyramid. Then the bloody wounds of Crashaw's martyrs, emblems of pain and suffering, are marvelously changed into "Ruby windowes," beautiful because the sun (Christ) "rises" in them; or they are a "Rosy Nest" wherein Christ is "enthroned." Likewise, the blood of Acis' mangled flesh and his crushed bones become a crystalline stream, licking the flowers and silvering the sand.

This similar pattern of imagery in the work of Crashaw and of Góngora indicates a similarity of imaginative engagement of reality. Of course, the intention of their poems at a conceptual level is quite different: Góngora distorts nature in order that it might be perfected aesthetically; Crashaw distorts nature that he might transcend it. The structure of image and figure in their poems, however, reveals that both are baroque poets, for it is in the selection and disposition of poetic elements that a style is defined. Citing Góngora's *Fábula de Polifemo y Galatea* as "the most representative work of the European Baroque," Dámaso Alonso maintains that baroque art "is the head-on clash of age-old tradition and unrestrained new daring, of the theme of languid beauty [e.g., Galatea] and of monstrous impulses [e.g., Polifemo]."[31] In Crashaw we also find the creation of an atmosphere of lush, rich beauty, but it is not the pagan paradise of Renaissance humanism; rather it is a representation of the joy of the presence of God, of heaven. The monstrous impulses are also present in Satan and in man's sinful, fallen nature. That Crashaw is aware of the temptations of the flesh and the world is evident from his admonitions to Mrs.

M. R. and to the Countess of Denbigh. It is rare that Crashaw dwells upon an overtly penitential theme, but he knows that the flesh and the spirit are in conflict: this is the source of the images of pain which are present almost invariably in his celebrations of spiritual pleasure. The "head-on clash" in his poems results, as we have noted in chapter 4, from the paradox that the joys of devotion and of mysticism can only be attained by renouncing the joy of the world, by taking the way of Christ's suffering, of mortification and martyrdom, or of "a death more mystical and high." Hence the imagery of Crashaw and of Góngora is similar because both are attracted by the beauty of man's natural world, yet both are aware of its deficiencies and evils. Góngora, in his major culterano poems, tries to harmonize the lovely and the grotesque, irreconcilable in reality, in an artificial, poetic realm. "For Crashaw," observes Austin Warren, "the world of the sense was evidently enticing; yet it was a world of appearances only—shifting, restless appearances. By temperament and conviction, he was a believer in the miraculous; and his aesthetic method may be interpreted as a genuine equivalent of his belief, as its translation into a rhetoric of metamorphosis."[32] It is in this "rhetoric of metamorphosis"—in the creation of images which distort and transform the common world of human experience—that Crashaw is most like Góngora.

II

Moreover, Góngora's very specialized version of the baroque style, with its culterano elaboration of a lavish and exotic poetic texture and deliberate obscurity, became immediately available for religious verse in Spain. We have noted in earlier chapters the culteranismo in much of Góngora's own devotional verse, as well as in that of his great rival, Lope de Vega; and the example of Baltasar de Medinilla indicates the influence of Góngora's style on a minor poet. The point is fully established by the poetry of Góngora's friend, Pedro Espinosa, who directly echoes the *Soledades* in poems which adapt the solitude theme to the purposes of Christian devotion. In a depiction of a garden which allegorizes the bleeding body of Christ, Espinosa recalls from *Soledad* I the striking evocation of Juno's peacocks as "flying piebalds which... draw the haughty goddess" (ll. 806–08: *volantes pías / que... / conduzcan alta* diosa):

Convierte ya la vista codiciosa,
en tiernas tibias lágrimas desecho
a esta tabla de flores, que es hermosa;
a las pías de Juno ha contrahecho.
Mira marchita la cerviz de rosa
y, entre claveles, blanqueando el pecho
de un mancebo que yace al aire frío,
bellísimo a mis ojos, Cristo mío.
Mira cárdeno lirio el rostro santo,
y el tirio carmesí del lado abierto. [33]

[Turn now the greedy gaze, melted in warm tender tears, upon this bed of flowers, which is beautiful; it has counterfeited the piebald mares of Juno. Behold the withered nape of the rose and, among pink carnations, the whitening breast of a youth who lies in the cold air, most beautiful to my eyes, my Christ.

Behold the livid lily, the holy face, the Tyrian crimson of the open side.]

Without the association of Góngora's "flying piebalds" (*volantes pías*), Espinosa's "piebald mares of Juno" (*pías de Juno*) is hardly intelligible; this phrase is but a particularly notable instance of the imitation of Góngora's culteranismos in Espinosa's sacred verse. His clear intention is to assimilate the methods of the occult symbolism of Góngora's vision of aesthetic solitude to his own devotion to the sacrificial Christ, and the result of a Spanish sacred poet imitating Gongorism is a poetry very much like Crashaw's.

A hundred lines further on in the same poem, Espinosa recurs to the garden/Christ imagery in still another sample of Spanish poetry that strikingly resembles the lush imagery of "Hymn to the Name of Jesus":

Abeja hiblia, en vagos desvaríos,
mordaz tomillo, azules romerales
cala, primero que a la Aurora el río
lave el pie azafranado en sus cristales,
tal, de las tirias rosas el rocío
de Cristo, dulce humor de mis panales,
solicito, y le ofrece mi porfía
cuanto pulsare y respirare el día. [34]

[The Hyblaean bee, in wandering caprice, tries pungent thyme, blue patches of rosemary, before the saffron-tinted river bathes Aurora's foot in his crystals,

so do I seek the dew of the Tyrian roses of Christ, sweet liquid of my hives,
and my persistence offers him as much as the day might throb and pant.]

Immediately we are reminded of Crashaw's figure of the angels as bees
and the name as a "Hive" or "Hoard of Hony," and also of an earlier
passage in "Hymn to the Name of Jesus":

> Leave All thy native Glories in their Gorgeous Nest,
> And give thy Self a while the gracious Guest
> Of humble Soules, that seek to find
> The hidden Sweets
> Which man's heart meets
> When Thou art Master of the Mind.
>
> [ll. 119–24]

The poems by Espinosa and Crashaw are similar not only in their
imagery, but also in their loose, rambling syntax, that piles phrase
upon clause, modifier upon appositive, to create a profuse surge of
figure and image which overwhelm the senses.

It is perhaps in this element of syntax that the Spanish culterano
style, of which Góngora is the leading exponent, is most easily distinguished from the style of the baroque neo-Latinists, who have often
been regarded as a principal influence on Crashaw. The following
verses by his contemporary, the German Jesuit Jacob Balde (1604–68),
from a poem in which one "Sabinus Fuscus" is "invited to the contemplation of heavenly things," furnish a representation of devotional
ecstasy which, though similar in intention, is equally different from
Crashaw and from Spaniards like Góngora, Lope, and Espinosa:

> Quaecunque, certe non inamabilis
> Insania haec est. cum sonitu poli
> Vertuntur. audis instrepentum
> Agmina luxuriare uocum?
> Et uero cantant! omnia sunt chorus;
> Stellaeque Musae, dum rota uoluitur,
> Et scena picturata transit,
> Aetherias modulantur odas.
> Quis iste Cygnus gutture diuidit
> Alisque lessum? flamina quae Lyrae?
> Orphea Testudo canorum
> Mille rapit thyasos in orbem. [35]

[Whatever it is, certainly this is not a displeasing madness. With the sound the heavens are whirled around. Do you hear the hosts of resounding voices swell? And truly they sing! All things are a chorus; and the Stars are Muses, while the wheel is turned, and the painted scene is passing, they measure out ethereal odes. Who is this Swan who divides between throat and wings his lamentation? Of what Lyre these breezes! The Orphean Lute ravishes a thousand bacchantes into its harmonious orb.]

The use of the music of the spheres as a poetic vehicle for religious ecstasy is an instantly recognizable parallel both to Crashaw's "Hymn to the Name of Jesus" and to Luis de León's "To Francisco Salinas"; however, with its predominance of short sentences and clipped phrases fitted tightly into Horatian alcaics, Balde does not even approach the extravagant rush of rapturous language which characterizes Crashaw, Góngora, Espinosa, and the others. Even Fray Luis, though he, too, is a frequent imitator of Horace, produces a more vibrantly ecstatic poem. In part, this may be due to a certain ironic diffidence of tone which Balde has picked up from the Horatian model for the first stanza quoted above:

> auditis, an me ludit amabilis
> insania? audire et videor pios
>   errare per lucos, amoenae
>   quos et aquae subeunt et aurae. [36]
>
> [*Carmina*, 3, 4, 5–8]

[Do you hear? Or am I tricked by delightful madness? I seem to hear and to wander among sacred groves through which run pleasant waters and breezes.]

Balde's *non inamabilis insania* is an obvious reminiscence of Horace's questioning *insania amabilis,* and the entire poem by the Jesuit is lightly touched by the wit that imitates the pagan poet with the aim of reinforcing the contrast between his doubtful poetic rapture and the certainty of Christian devotion. But a more important factor is the rigor of the Latin language and the classical poetic style. The complex constructions of the Roman Augustans produce a poetry in which each word seems to be fitted into a predestined niche—chiseled into the marble of their highly inflected Latin; and efforts to imitate them among the Jesuit Latinists of the seventeenth century result in a similar effect of tight linguistic control, regardless of the poems' themes. [37] But when the culterano poets of the Golden Age emulate

Latin linguistic techniques in a considerably less inflected Spanish, the effect is the verbal phantasmagoria examined in the poems of Crashaw and Góngora. It is obvious that Crashaw's style in his later hymns is much closer to Góngora than to contemporary Latin poets; the very nature of the languages involved makes this inevitable. Crashaw's pursuit of a poetic voice that would realize the effect of rapturous song leads to a prosodic development in which the similarity of Crashaw and Góngora becomes unmistakable.

III

Many critics have noticed the unusual character of Crashaw's versification, but none (with whom I am acquainted) has satisfactorily accounted for the origin of the eccentric verse form, now commonly called the "irregular ode," which is used extensively in the later hymns.[38] Ruth Wallerstein seems to maintain that the key to Crashaw's metrical irregularities lies in music: "Anyone who will read aloud, for example, the hymns *To the Name Above Every Name,* and *In the Glorious Epiphany,* will feel that each is as much a single and organic musical design as is a movement of a symphony."[39] This musical feeling, however, must be embodied in words if it is to become part of a poem; Wallerstein's speculations, interesting as they are, serve to restate the problem rather than to answer it. Austin Warren discusses with great acuity the development of Crashaw's versification "from the couplet to the ode," and his analysis of the relationship between style and meaning in Crashaw is quite persuasive.[40] But his suggestion that "the incipient change in poetic style" in the later poems "may be due ... not to some 'literary' influence but to an attempted change in the character of the poet's religious life,"[41] drives a destructive wedge between literature and religion (or style and content). A literary influence is not necessarily incompatible with other factors, conceptual or spiritual, in causing a stylistic change. There is no reason why an explanation for the unusual characteristics of Crashaw's poetry must be sought in his religious life to the exclusion of the influence of other poets.

Irregular verse forms are not unheard of in English poetry before Crashaw, but for various reasons none of the earlier examples seems very similar to his work. Although there is only a handful of such poems,[42] they cannot all receive individual treatment here. It is interesting, however, to compare with Crashaw's verse those irregular poems which it is safe to assume that he knew before be began to write his own. For example, among Donne's poems, which Crashaw must have read, we find "The Dissolution." But it must be scrutinized with care before one realizes that it is not just another complicated but regular stanza, like so many that Donne devised for the *Songs and Sonets*. It certainly does not seem to wander all over the page after the fashion of "Hymn in the Glorious Epiphanie." Donne uses the freedom of the irregular verse differently from Crashaw: rather than rapturous song there is a tortuous argument. Perhaps a more likely influence on Crashaw, a poem with which he was undoubtedly familiar, is Herbert's "The Collar." Here is poetry with a religious theme by a man whom Crashaw obviously admired (see *"On Mr. G. Herberts booke, The Temple"*). But in fact, Herbert uses the irregular or dithyrambic form to achieve almost the opposite effect from Crashaw:

> I struck the board, and cry'd, No more.
> I will abroad.
> What? shall I ever sigh and pine?
> My lines and life are free; free as the rode,
> Loose as the winde, as large as store.
> Shall I be still in suit?[43]

The short, abrupt periods and sequence of abrasive consonants (*struck; board; cry'd; abroad*) capture, much in Donne's manner, a discordant sense of inner turmoil: both of Crashaw's predecessors use the irregular style to gain a dissonant, almost antimusical effect. That Crashaw's poetry is musical is a judgment too common to require restatement.

Probably the most obvious potential source for Crashaw's irregular verse is the experimentation with it by Milton. This would include "Upon the Circumcision," "On Time," and "At a Solemn Music"; but these poems were not published until 1645, after Crashaw had gone to France. Although it is not impossible that Crashaw saw them in manuscript while still at Cambridge, we are on safer ground with "Lycidas," which was available in the printed volume, *Justa Edouardo King naufrago* (1638).[44] However, any consideration of Milton's influence in the matter of Crashaw's irregular verse raises, perforce, the possibility of Italian influence; for Milton's models, both in the shorter irregular lyrics and in "Lycidas," are Italian. F. T. Prince argues that the most likely sources of inspiration for the versification of "Lycidas" are to be found in some of the choruses and in "the partially rhymed semi-lyrical passages of dialogue" in the *Aminta* of Torquato Tasso and in Guarini's *Il Pastor Fido*. In Prince's opinion Milton's prosodic accomplishments in "Lycidas" are a direct development, indeed, the culmination, of certain trends in Italian poetry: "Two technical experiments—the attempt to evolve a poetic diction equivalent to that of Virgil, and the attempt to combine the tradition of the canzone with that of the classical eclogue—marked Italian pastoral verse in the sixteenth century. In England both these experiments bore fruit in *Lycidas*." There is no reason why Crashaw could not have known Milton's models as well as Milton's own work, but in fact, it is to be doubted whether either provides the key we are seeking. For if the influence of Milton and Italians like Tasso and Guarini cannot be altogether discounted, the quotation from Prince indicates that their work is still quite unlike Crashaw's: in his sacred verse there is little that could be described as "Virgilian" or "classical." Moreover, Milton and the Italians he followed only wrote "irregular" verse in a rather limited sense. Prince's formal analysis of "Lycidas" shows that Milton, while dropping the external specifications of the canzone, maintains the important structural features: the rare six-syllable lines, for example, always rhyme with a preceding ten-syllable line, creating thereby a sense of the division of the traditional two-part canzone stanza; and the closing ottava rima "stanza" seems to correspond to the *commiato* of the canzone.[45] In Crashaw's odes, or hymns, the length of lines and disposition of rhymes seem to owe nothing to prosodic rule; hence, when the several stanzaic divisions in the 1646 versions of "Ode on a Prayer-book" and "Hymn in the Assumption" are abandoned in subsequent editions, there is no appreciable loss in structural sense. From a prosodic standpoint these poems and the other hymns are altogether irregular in a way that Milton's verse never approaches.

To the possible sources of Crashaw's versification considered thus far, Carol Maddison adds the seventeenth-century practice of "neo-Latin mixed odes and dithyrambs." "Dr. Johnson," she observes, "blamed Cowley for the horror of the irregular *Latin* ode, but now it seems more probable that school exercises in Latin verse were responsible for the irregular English ode"; and she points out that Crashaw

himself was the author of several Latin dithyrambs.[46] But it is doubtful whether such apprentice work was of great importance in
Crashaw's later poems; the fact that they were "school exercises"[47] is
an argument to the contrary. Many years and a great shift in his
vernacular style intervened between the composition of these Latin
pieces and the English hymns. Compared with a poem like "Hymn to
the Name of Jesus," the following passage from one of these exercises,
"In Apollinem depereuntem Daphnen," is rigid: the periods are abrupt
and the alliteration, rather than establishing a progression from one
line to the next, merely stresses the paradoxical phrases; there is, in
short, nothing songlike here:

> Stulte Cupido,
> Quid tua flamma parat?
> Annon sole sub ipso
> Accensae pereunt faces?
> Sed fax nostra potentior istis,
> Flammas inflammare potest, ipse uritur ignis,
> Ecce Flammarum potens
> Majore sub flamma gemit.
>
> [ll. 1–8]

[Foolish Cupid, what is your flame preparing? Or don't kindled torches fade
under the sun alone? But my torch is more powerful than those, it is able to
inflame flames, fire itself is consumed, behold one powerful over flames beneath a greater flame moans.]

"In this one poem," writes Maddison, "Crashaw has all but exhausted
the metrical resources of Horace."[48] Obviously the "irregularity" of
this piece is the product of ingenious artifice alone, rather than of the
pressure of complex, expanding images. It is not surprising that such
contrivance lacks the essential feel of the later work.

Turning at last to the poetry of seventeenth-century Spain, one
comes upon a verse form, in common use, which matches in numerous
details the irregular verse of Crashaw: this is the *silva,* an irregular
combination of hendecasyllabic and heptasyllabic lines without a fixed
pattern of rhymes or stanzas. Some lines may be altogether unrhymed;
stanzaic breaks may conform to lengthy syntactical periods, or the
verse may proceed with no breaks at all. The silva, like so many of the
poetic forms employed during the siglo de oro, seems to have an Italian

origin; but Tomás Navarro, to whom the preceding description of the form is owing, names only one, not very prominent practitioner of it in sixteenth-century Italy, Anton Francesco Grazzini (Il Lasca, 1503–84). In fact, by the latter half of the seventeenth century, a reverse influence had occurred: silvas were being written in Italy which plainly imitated the manner of the Spanish poets of the earlier part of the century, especially Góngora.[49]

Many other Spanish baroque poets, including Lope de Vega and Quevedo, also wrote silvas, but Góngora is of the greatest interest for this study; for the *Soledades,* the best known and most controversial poem written in Spain during the seventeenth century, is composed in silvas. The rhetorical effect of this verse as Góngora uses it, the verbal arrangement it achieves, and even its appearance on a page are similar to the corresponding features of Crashaw's hymns. These similarities are doubly significant in light of the parallels to Crashaw's imagery in the *Soledades.* Dámaso Alonso argues that the *Soledades* are "the center of Gongorism"; one of the reasons he gives for this assertion is that for this work Góngora "chose a form whose stanzas, expansible or reducible at will, permitted the greatest syntactical daring and complication."[50] Moreover, the unrestrained form of the silva was necessary for a full development of Góngora's complex metaphorical utterance. The poetic impulse behind the Spaniard's use of the silva is readily comparable to that which brought Crashaw to write irregular verse.

A single, brief comparison between passages from the *Soledad* I and "Hymn to the Name of Jesus" suggests the similarity of stylistic intention which led each poet to employ irregular prosodic forms. In the following passage, Crashaw uses the limitless variations of irregular verse to expand through a series of musical images what is essentially a single idea: the name of Jesus (the Word) is the underlying principle of all created harmony, earthly and celestial; therefore, harmony as such is a hymn of praise to its Creator, a hymn which man must join. The "expansible" poetic form is thus the vehicle for an expanding image, a hyperbolic image of harmony and abundance:

> Bring All the Powres of Praise
> Your Provinces of well-united WORLDS can raise;
> Bring All your LUTES and HARPS of HEAVN and EARTH:
> What e're cooperates to The common mirthe
> Vessells of vocal Joyes,

> Or You, more noble Architects of Intellectual Noise,
> Cymballs of Heav'n, or Humane sphears,
> Solliciters of SOULES or Eares;
> And when you'are come, with All
> That you can bring or we can call;
> O may you fix
> For ever here, and mix
> Your selves into the long
> And everlasting series of a deathless SONG.
>
> [ll. 72–85]

Evident in these lines are the "sequences" of alliteration, pointed out by Warren, which "are not conceived of in terms of line-units but rather as ligatures between successive lines."[51] Notable here are such sequences as Powres, Praise, Provinces; Cymballs, sphears, Solliciters, SOULES; and come, can, can, call. This line-to-line linkage, a predominance of open vowels, and rambling, appositional syntax combine with the visual effect of the alternating line lengths to create a sense of undulating flow. The verse, then, corresponds aptly with the ornate and highly elaborate imagery, and is another factor in the exotic atmosphere of Crashaw's hymns.

Similar in prosodic technique is Góngora's description of a group of highlanders (*serranos*) on their way to the wedding celebrated in *Soledad* I. The Spanish poet, too, uses the expansible, irregular verse to elaborate a single idea through a series of images:

> Pasaron todos pues, y regulados
> cual en los equinocios surcar vemos
> los piélagos de el aire libre algunas
> volantes no galeras
> sino grullas veleras,
> tal vez creciendo, tal menguando lunas
> sus distantes extremos,
> caracteres tal vez formando alados
> en el papel diáfano del cielo
> las plumas de su vuelo.
> Ellas en tanto en bóvedas de sombras
> pintadas siempre al fresco,
> cubren las que [en] Sidón, telar turquesco
> no ha sabido imitar, verdes alfombras.
>
> [ll. 602–15]

[They all passed then, and arranged, as in the equinoxes we see cutting the high seas of the open air, not flying galleys, but rather swift-sailing cranes, their distant tips at times growing, at times shrinking moons, at times forming with the plumages of their flight winged letters on the diaphanous paper of the sky. Meanwhile, the girls, in vaults of shadows painted as frescos, cover green carpets that [in] Sidon the Turkish loom has not known how to imitate.]

The verse of this passage resembles Crashaw's in that the lines are linked by patterns of repeated initial consonants in accented syllables: regu*l*ados, *l*ibre, vo*l*antes, ga*l*eras, ve*l*eras, *l*unas; a*l*gunas, grullas, menguando; *t*al, *t*al, dis*t*antes, ex*t*remos, carac*t*eres, *t*al; *v*ez, *v*ez, *v*uelo. Both poets are also fond of the same details, such as transverse alliterative patterns: "*C*ymballs of *H*eav'n, or *H*umane *s*phears"; "*v*olantes no ga*l*eras / sino grullas *v*eleras." Most evident, however, is the similar use of long and short lines to pursue a single idea or to unfold a single scene through a series of images—unrestricted by a fixed prosodic form—which seem to tumble forth one on top of another. Metaphorical profusion is thus matched visually by an eccentric disposition of lines, and phonetically by patterns of alliterative echoes.

The irregular versification and extravagant imagery of Crashaw's later poems may reasonably be termed a manifestation of Gongorism. Whether a direct acquaintance with Góngora's poetry may have influenced Crashaw is impossible to determine. Crashaw would probably have moved, in any case, in the direction his work finally took— toward prosodic irregularity and superabundant imagery; and the style of Góngora, like various features of Spanish devotional writing surveyed in earlier chapters, establishes a religious and poetic context against which to measure Crashaw's achievement. Still, there is no doubt that a knowledge of Góngora's culterano poetry would have encouraged and inspired Crashaw, and such a knowledge could explain the very rapid development of his technique which seems to have been accomplished during his sojourn on the continent. At that time a man of Crashaw's interest would most probably have become aware of Góngora during a sojourn in France or the Netherlands. One cannot overemphasize the fame and influence of Góngora during his own lifetime and for several decades following his death. In Spain his poetry was attacked, defended, and explicated at extraordinary length, and five fairly complete editions of his work had been issued by the

time of Crashaw's death in 1649.[52] In Paris, Jean Chapelain refers
with apparent familiarity to a host of sixteenth- and seventeenth-
century Spanish writers, including the "fameux Góngora," in several
letters written between 1659 and 1662. "Il y a quarente ans," he
avers, "que je suis eclairci que cette brave nation [Spain] generalement
parlant n'a pas le goust des belles lettres."[53] Góngora, a great offender
in Chapelain's neoclassical eyes, had attained notoriety in France by
the mid-seventeenth century.

IV

The airy dismissal of Góngora by Chapelain serves as a fitting
note on which to round out this consideration of Richard Crashaw who
has suffered much the same fate as his great Spanish predecessor.
Indeed, the English poet's reputation lapsed into a far deeper obscurity
and a far more pronounced obloquy. Although Góngora, and
Crashaw's English contemporaries, Donne, Herbert, and Vaughan
have reached prominence, the same has not held true for Crashaw.
Given what I take to be the undeniable fact of Crashaw's talent—a
talent evinced by the persistent, if often puzzled, interest in his
work—I have sought to accomplish his rehabilitation by setting him in
the context of the Spanish baroque rather than in the context of the
English "Metaphysical" mode. This Spanish context provides a model
and, insofar as it provides a rationally defensible attitude toward the
faith, a vindication for Crashaw's bold use of the poetry of profane love
in his devotional pieces. The Spanish experience of the Counter Reformation, and the literature which Spanish culture produced in response to this religious experience, renders comprehensible and, in my
judgment, proves admirable both Crashaw's joyous gaiety and severe
passion of tone, both the profundity of his mystical aspiration and the
popularity of his liturgical forms. Perhaps the final key lies in the
realm of style. The aesthetic refashioning of reality in the verse of
Góngora is, like the transcendent contemplation of the mystics, an
expression of a loss of confidence in this world. If Crashaw drew on
the vision of mystics to shape his own ascent beyond the reach of
secular and sectarian strife, it is a poetic style like Góngora's that he
fashions. But the style, even in its most secular and pagan form, owes
something to the vision of the mystics. Donne expostulates with the

world, and Jonson reproves it; Herbert endures it, and Vaughan deplores it; Milton sets out to conquer it. From Santa Teresa, San Juan de la Cruz, and Fray Luis de León, even such giddy sensualists as Lope de Vega and Góngora learned, in their best moments, simply to turn away from the world. Crashaw learned the lesson too, and there was no literature outside Spain where it was as accessible. He acknowledges his debt in these beautiful lines addressed to Santa Teresa in his "Apologie for the Fore-going Hymne":

> . . . tis to thy wrong
> I know, that in my weak and worthlesse song
> Thou here art sett to shine where thy full day
> Scarse dawnes. O pardon if I dare to say
> Thine own dear bookes are guilty. For from thence
> I learn't to know that love is eloquence.

Notes

CHAPTER 1

1 "A Note on Richard Crashaw," *For Lancelot Andrewes* (Garden City, NY: Doubleday, Doran, 1929), p. 137.

2 Apologists for Crashaw have often developed elaborate and, in my view, fanciful interpretations of this poem which depend on abstruse "hidden meanings." See Stephen Manning, "The Meaning of 'The Weeper,'" *ELH*, 22 (1955), 34–47; Leland Chambers, "In Defense of 'The Weeper,'" *PLL*, 3 (1967), 111–21; Marc Bertonasco, "A New Look at 'The Weeper,'" *TSLL*, 10 (1968), 177–88, and again in *Crashaw and the Baroque* (University: Univ. of Alabama Press, 1971), pp. 94–117; and Lee A. Jacobus, "Richard Crashaw as Mannerist," *Bu R*, 18 (1970), 79–88. On the other hand, John Peter, "Crashaw and 'The Weeper,'" *Scrutiny*, 19 (1953), 258–73, takes "The Weeper" as a typical example of Crashaw's poetry and condemns him for a disproportionate weight of imagery in comparison to theme, indicative of a deficiency in technique and "integrity." I maintain that Crashaw cannot be generally condemned on the basis of this one poem, and that there is likewise no need to salvage it in order to defend his other work; although the poem is, in the sense of containing every cliché of the baroque religious style, "typical of the age," it is not typical of Crashaw's best work, secular or sacred.

3 "The Weeper," XIX (1652 version). Unless otherwise indicated, all quotations of Crashaw's poems are from the latest versions according to the text of *The Complete Poetry of Richard Crashaw*, ed. George Walton Williams (Garden City, NY: Doubleday, 1970).

4 *The Divine Poems of John Donne*, ed. Helen Gardner (Oxford: Clarendon,

1952), p. 15 (Holy Sonnet XVIII in the traditional Grierson arrangement).

5   "Dulnesse," in *The Works of George Herbert*, ed. F. E. Hutchinson (Oxford: Clarendon, 1941), p. 115. This particular example was suggested by Robert Ellrodt, *L'Inspiration personnelle et l'esprit du temps chez les poètes métaphysiques anglais* (Paris: José Corti, 1960), I, 396. See also Hamish Swanston, "The Second 'Temple,'" *Durham University Journal*, 56 (1963), 14–22.

6   *The Poetry of Meditation*, rev. ed. (New Haven: Yale Univ. Press, 1962), p. 167.

7   This identification is made by W. P. Mustard, ed., *The Eclogues of Antonio Geraldini* (Baltimore: Johns Hopkins Press, 1924), p. 59. Geraldini is quoted from this edition.

8   Here is the Latin text of the entire passage which I have quoted and paraphrased in bits and pieces; note the use of "Minerva" as a symbol for wisdom: "Id uulgus uanaeque solent seruare puellae, / Et pueri quibus est damnosi cura fritilli, / Tempora quos pingui mos est onerare Lyaeo. / Nos alios operum ludos decet edere; nostra / Quin age dudum aliquid dignum meditare Minerua. / Frontis honos, studii grauitas aetasque uirilis / Nil fluidum, nil turpe sinunt uel inane uel excors" (ll. 15–21).

9   For a good account of the neo-Latin Nativity eclogue, see W. Leonard Grant, *Neo-Latin Literature and the Pastoral* (Chapel Hill: Univ. of North Carolina Press, 1965), pp. 258–89.

10 John Milton, *Complete Shorter Poems*, ed. John Carey (London: Longman, 1968), p. 112.

11 Exodus, 34:29 (Vulgate): "Cumque descenderet Moyses de monte Sinai, tenebat duas tabulas testimonii, et ignorabat quod cornuta esset facies sua ex consortio sermonis Domini."

12 Mustard, p. 14, and the notes to the eclogue, pp. 59–61.

13 In addition to *The Poetry of Meditation*, see Helen Gardner, ed., *The Divine Poems of John Donne*, pp. l–lv.

14 Cf. Joseph H. Summers, *George Herbert: His Religion and Art* (Cambridge: Harvard Univ. Press, 1954), pp. 140–42; and William Halewood, *The Poetry of Grace* (New Haven: Yale Univ. Press, 1970), pp. 88ff.

15 *Works of Herbert*, p. 81.

16 That Beaumont was generally the borrower, Crashaw the lender, is the opinion both of Beaumont's editor, Eloise Robinson, *The Minor Poems of Joseph Beaumont* (London: Constable, 1914), pp. xxxvii–xl; and Austin Warren, *Richard Crashaw: A Study in Baroque Sensibility* (1939; rpt. Ann Arbor: Univ. of Michigan Press, 1957), p. 45. Apart from the fact that Crashaw was four years Beaumont's senior, is the highly derivative

character of all the verse of the latter, who in Robinson's words, owes specific debts of "word and phrase and thought... to almost all of his contemporaries and predecessors" (pp. xxxiii–xxxiv). Robinson then proceeds to detail parallels to Milton, Herbert, and Donne as well as Crashaw, and mentions additional borrowings from Raleigh, Wotton, and Southwell.

17 Robinson, pp. 16–17. I have expanded various seventeenth-century abbreviations.

18 An obvious exception is the "Hymn to the Name of Jesus," but even here Crashaw ties a fundamentally abstract subject to the very concrete notion of martyrdom, ll. 197–224. See chapter 5, below.

19 This is the speculation of Warren, pp. 112, 220, n. 43.

20 *The Metaphysical Mode from Donne to Cowley* (Princeton: Princeton Univ. Press, 1969), p. x. But cf. Ellrodt, I, 377: "Le poète de *Musicks Duell*, l'auteur des divers *hymnes* est le plus grande poète lyrique du XVIIᵉ siècle, mais son lyrisme tend à l'impersonalité. La raison est simple. Donne cherchait à se trouver; Crashaw n'aspire qu'á se perdre."

21 Miner, p. 55, who approaches Crashaw as "private" and dramatic" in the same sense as Donne and Herbert.

22 Cf. Louis L. Martz, *The Paradise Within* (New Haven: Yale Univ. Press, 1964), pp. 3–4. As Martz points out, with respect to "the power of liturgical and eucharistic symbols," Crashaw has much in common with Donne and Herbert in a way that Vaughan, Traherne, and Milton (and I would add Marvell) do not. Nevertheless, though Donne and Herbert write in terms of Church ritual and symbolism, their focus is still individual; Crashaw's is corporate.

23 *The School of Donne* (New York: Random House, 1961), p. 100.

24 Ibid., p. 99.

25 Mario Praz, "Crashaw and the Baroque Style," in *The Flaming Heart* (1958; rpt. Gloucester, MA: Peter Smith, 1966), pp. 204–63; L. C. Martin, ed., *The Poems English, Latin and Greek of Richard Crashaw*, 2nd ed. (Oxford: Clarendon, 1957); and Williams, ed., *Complete Poetry*.

26 *Poems English, Latin and Greek*, pp. xci–xcii.

27 *The Flaming Heart*, pp. 233, 248, 252–53. See also Ruth Wallerstein, *Richard Crashaw: A Study in Style and Poetic Development*, University of Wisconsin Studies in Language and Literature #37 (Madison: Univ. of Wisconsin Press, 1935), pp. 35, 53; and Warren, *Richard Crashaw: A Study*, p. 158.

28 *The Poet of the Marvelous: Giambattista Marino* (New York: Columbia Univ. Press, 1963), pp. 250–51. Mirollo also points out that "in his relations with Iberian literature Marino was more the borrower than the

lender" (p. 265; see also pp. 252–54). Marino's "borrowings" from Lope de Vega were first detailed (as Mirollo acknowledges) by Dámaso Alonso, "Lope despojado por Marino," *Revista de filología española,* 33 (1949), 110–43. For differing angles on Marino's relation to Crashaw, see Laura L. Petoello, "A Current Misconception Concerning the Influence of Marino's Poetry on Crashaw's," *MLR,* 52 (1957), 321–28; and Louis R. Barbato, "Marino, Crashaw, and *Sospetto d'Herode,*" *PQ,* 54 (1975), 522–27.

29 *English Literature in the Earlier Seventeenth Century, 1600–60,* 2nd ed. (Oxford: Clarendon, 1962), p. 147.

30 Cf. Helmut Hatzfeld, "El predominio del espíritu español en la literatura europea del siglo XVII," *Revista de filología hispánica,* 3 (1941), 9–23. Hatzfeld undoubtedly overstates his case; nevertheless, he is correct in claiming a far greater importance for Spanish literary influence during the baroque period than is commonly recognized.

31 *Richard Crashaw: Style and Poetic Development,* p. 35.

32 For the literary impact of the Jesuit spiritual exercises in England, see Gardner and Martz as in nn. 4 and 6 above.

33 Cf. Robert T. Petersson, *The Art of Ecstasy* (New York: Atheneum, 1970), pp. 4–6; and R. O. Jones, *A Literary History of Spain,* vol. II, *The Golden Age: Prose and Poetry* (London: Ernest Benn and New York: Barnes & Noble, 1971), p. 76. It is interesting to note that even the rabidly anti-Catholic J. A. Froude has grudging words of praise for the Spanish bishops at the Council: see *Lectures on the Council of Trent* (New York: Scribner's, 1896), pp. 181–83, 209, 214–25, 228–29.

34 *Poesía española: ensayo de métodos y límites estilísticos,* 5th ed. (Madrid: Editorial Gredos, 1971), p. 133. See also Jones, *Golden Age,* p. 5; Ramón Menéndez-Pidal, *El lenguaje de Cristóbal Colón* (Buenos Aires: Espasa-Calpe, 1942), p. 140; E. R. Curtius, *European Literature and the Latin Middle Ages,* trans. Willard R. Trask (New York: Harper & Row, 1953), pp. 541–43; and Leo Spitzer, *Classical and Christian Ideas of World Harmony,* ed. Anna Granville-Hatcher, preface René Wellek (Baltimore: Johns Hopkins Press, 1963), p. 111.

35 Dámaso Alonso and José Manuel Blecua, ed., *Antología de la poesía española: poesía de tipo tradicional* (Madrid: Editorial Gredos, 1956), p. xvii.

36 "Spanish and English Religious Poetry of Seventeenth Century," *Journal of Ecclesiastical History,* 9 (1958), 47. It is well known that Donne's motto on a youthful portrait is in Spanish, and Izaak Walton, *Lives,* ed. George Saintsbury (London: World's Classics, 1927), p. 26, affirms that Donne did not return from the Cádiz expedition "till he had staid some years first

in *Italy,* and then in *Spain,* where he made many useful observations of those Countreys, their Laws and manner of Government, and returned perfect in their Languages." J. B. Leishman, *The Monarch of Wit,* 6th ed. (London: Hutchinson University Library, 1962), p. 30, suggests an earlier time for the sojourn, but agrees that it took place. Itrat-Husain, *The Mystical Element in the Metaphysical Poets of the Seventeenth Century* (London: Oliver & Boyd, 1948), pp. 181–82, quotes a certain Dr. Lloyd to the effect that Crashaw knew Spanish and points out that Nicholas Ferrar, with whose Little Gidding community Crashaw was on such intimate terms, knew Spanish and had probably brought back Spanish devotional literature from his continental travels.

37 *The Poet of the Marvelous,* pp. 252–54.

38 Alphonse Vermeylen, *Sainte Thérese en France au XVIIe Siècle* (Louvain: Université de Louvain, 1958), pp. 15–18. The remark by Cervantes, originally from *Persiles y Segismonda* (1617), is quoted by Vermeylen, p. 16.

39 "Some Light on Richard Crashaw's Final Years in Rome," *MLR,* 66 (1971), 494.

40 *Richard Crashaw: A Study,* pp. 46–52.

41 Publication data regarding Santa Teresa, San Juan, and Lope are taken from *Obras completas de Santa Teresa de Jesús,* ed. Efren de la Madre de Dios and Otger Steggink, 2nd ed. (Madrid: Biblioteca de Autores Cristianos, 1967), I, 46ff.; *San Juan de la Cruz: Obras,* ed. José M. Gallegos Rocafull (Mexico: Editorial Seneca, 1942), pp. 38–41; and *Obras escogidas de Lope de Vega,* ed. Féderico Carlos Sainz de Robles, 4th ed. (Madrid: Aguilar, 1964), II, 1174. See also Vermeylen, p. 12.

42 Vermeylen, p. 46 and passim.

43 Martin, p. xcii.

44 René Wellek and Austin Warren, *Theory of Literature,* 3rd ed. (New York: Harcourt, Brace, Jovanovich, 1962), p. 258.

45 Ibid.

46 Ibid.

47 *Poetical Works,* ed. Herbert J. C. Grierson (London: Oxford Univ. Press, 1929), p. 14.

48 *Works of Herbert,* ed. Hutchinson, p. 102.

49 Bennett, p. 102. Cf. Herbert Grierson, *Cross Currents in English Literature of the Seventeenth Century* (London: Chatto & Windus, 1929), pp. 174–76, and Bush, pp. 147–50, for similar instances of blank incomprehension erected into dogma.

50 Cf. E. I. Watkin, "William Crashaw's Influence on his Son," in *Poets*

and Mystics (London: Sheed & Ward, 1953), pp. 179–80; and R. V. Young, Jr., "Truth with Precision: Crashaw's Revisions of *A Letter . . . ,*" *Faith & Reason,* 4, No. 3 (1978), 3–17.

CHAPTER 2

1   *Historia de la poesía lírica a lo divino en la Cristiandad occidental* (Madrid: Revista de Occidente, 1958), p. 68. This book is the only systematic treatment of the subject, which received its first important notice among Spanish scholars studying the poetry of San Juan de la Cruz. See also José María de Cossío, "Rasgos renacentistas y populares en el 'Cántico espiritual' de San Juan de la Cruz," *Escorial,* 9 (1942), 205–28; Dámaso Alonso, *La poesía de San Juan de la Cruz,* 4th ed. (Madrid: Aguilar, 1966), pp. 24–112; and Alonso, *Poesía española,* pp. 220–68. For the concept of sacred parody, or *poesía a lo divino,* set forth in this chapter, I am very much in debt to these authors.

2   Alonso, *Poesía española,* p. 222.

3   Ibid.; Cf. Wardropper, p. 9.

4   *The Harley Lyrics,* ed. G. L. Brook, 3rd ed. (Manchester: Manchester Univ. Press, 1964), p. 16. The poems are nos. 31 and 32. See also *Medieval English Lyrics,* ed. R. T. Davies (Evanston, IL: Northwestern Univ. Press, 1964), pp. 23–24.

5   Davies, pp. 23–24; cf. Wardropper, chaps. 6–10.

6   Wardropper, pp. 255ff., 266–71, 272, 280ff. The work has appeared in a modern edition by Glen R. Gale (Madrid: Castalia, 1971).

7   For a description of the extent and impact of the divinization movement, especially in Spain, see Alonso, *Poesía española,* pp. 222ff.

8   Ibid., pp. 242–51.

9   Ibid., pp. 256–68. See also Alonso, *Poesía de San Juan,* pp. 24–77; and Cossío, pp. 211, 220.

10 Cf. Wardropper, pp. 50–51.

11 *The Poetry of Meditation,* p. 183.

12 *Poesía española,* pp. 296–99.

13 Despite his acquaintance with Spanish books, it is unlikely that Donne was influenced by any of the major Spanish poets, although there are a number of resemblances between his poetry and theirs, especially that of Lope and Quevedo. Donne's love poetry is quite similar in style and tone to some of the poetry in Lope's *Rimas,* but this book was not published until 1602. Likewise there are remarkable parallels between the "Holy Sonnets" and some of the sonnets of *Rimas sacras* (1614), but if Helen Gardner's dating of the former is correct (*Divine Poems,* pp. xxxvii ff.),

then Lope's collection was published too late to have affected Donne. None of Quevedo's poetry was published till 1605, and the vast bulk of it remained in manuscript till 1648, three years after his death. Donne has sometimes been compared to San Juan de la Cruz and Góngora, but the parallels are few and rather general; in any case, none of the saint's works was published till 1618, and the latter's works remained unpublished till 1627. George Herbert, however, is another matter. It has been pointed out by Mirollo that his brother Edward, Lord Herbert of Cherbury, while in France, became acquainted with and borrowed from Lope's poetry (*Poet of the Marvelous*, pp. 252–54); hence it is not inconceivable that George Herbert was familiar with Lope's poetry. Edward Wilson ("Spanish and English Devotional Poetry," p. 51) has pointed out a similarity of sensibility in Herbert and Lope, and I should call attention to parallels of metaphoric conception and tone which obtain between Herbert's "The Priesthood": "When God vouchsafeth to become our fare, / Their hands convey him, who conveys their hands. / . . . Wherefore I dare not, I, put forth my hand . . ." (Hutchinson, p. 161); and a sonnet of Lope: "When in my hands I behold you, eternal King, / and I elevate the shining white host, / I am fearful of my bold unworthiness, / and I wonder at the mercy of your breast" (*Obras escogidas*, II, 183).

14 *Five Metaphysical Poets*, p. 94. Cf. Grierson, pp. 174–76.
15 "Taste and Bad Taste in Metaphysical Poetry: Richard Crashaw and Dylan Thomas," in *Seventeenth Century English Poetry*, ed. W. R. Keast (New York: Oxford Univ. Press, 1962), p. 271. Adams's view of this poem and of Crashaw's work as a whole was anticipated by William Empson, *Seven Types of Ambiguity*, 3rd ed. (New York: Meridian, 1955), pp. 249–50. For a cogent reply to this psychoanalytic approach, see the headnote to this epigram in Williams's edition, p. 14; and also Russell M. Goldfarb, "Crashaw's SUPPOSE HE HAD BEEN TABLED AT THY TEATES," *Explicator*, 6 (1961), item 35. Marc Bertonasco, "Crashaw and the Emblem," *English Studies*, 49 (1968), 530–34, has found sources in the emblem books for many of Crashaw's more shocking images, including the one in this epigram; and Hamish Swanston (as cited chap. 1, n. 5) shows that most of Crashaw's "grotesqueries" can be equalled in Herbert. None of this makes the epigram a good poem, but it does relieve Crashaw of the onus of psychological abnormality. Finally, Rosemond Tuve, *A Reading of George Herbert* (Chicago: Univ. of Chicago Press, 1952), esp. part 1, "'The Sacrifice' and Modern Criticism," presents a withering critique of the general method of treating seventeenth-century poetry exemplified by Empson and Adams.
16 Cf. Helen C. White, *The Metaphysical Poets* (New York: Collier-

Macmillan, 1962), pp. 233-34: "The Puritan is too much aware of the
dangers of certain confusions, of the perils of certain parallels. The
Freudian can never entirely remember that sex was known before Freud,
and that its implications for the life of the whole man did not await
twentieth-century discovery. And the last thing that neither will ap-
preciate is the matter-of-factness with which certain allusions were handled by a generation as yet unaware of the self-consciousness of both." In
addition, an especially shrewd and.pointed discussion of this issue, as it
relates to the classic Spanish mystics, may be consulted in Denis de
Rougement, *Love in the Western World,* trans. Montgomery Belgion, rev.
ed. (New York: Pantheon, 1956), pp. 168-75. Finally, for an intriguing
account of the revaluation of the term and concept *passio* under the
impact of Christianity and the Passion of Christ, see Erich Auerbach,
Literary Language and its Public in the Latin Middle Ages, trans. Ralph
Mannheim (New York: Harper & Row, 1965), pp. 75-81.

17 *Forms of Discovery* (n.p.: Alan Swallow, 1967), pp. 91-92.
18 Cf. Evelyn Underhill, *Mysticism* (New York: World, 1955), p. 449: "Yet
    of course this transcendence, this amazing inward journey, was closely
    linked, first and last, with the process of human life. It sprang from that
    life, as man springs from the sod."
19 St. Augustine, *On Christian Doctrine,* I, xxii, 21, trans. D. W.
    Robertson, Jr. (Indianapolis: Bobbs-Merrill, 1958), p. 19.
20 Ibid., I, vi, 6, p. 11. Cf. Wardropper, pp. 31-34, who sees in Augustine's
    discussion of the phrase *spoliare Aegyptios,* in the same work (II, xl, 60),
    theological justification for sacred parody.
21 *Forms of Discovery,* p. 92. Winters's attitude toward the issue is highlighted
    by his insistent use of the definite article: "*the* mystical experience,"
    "*the* religious experience," etc.
22 C. S. Lewis and E. M. W. Tillyard, *The Personal Heresy* (London: Ox-
    ford Univ. Press, 1939), p. 97.
23 "Sacred Parody of Love Poetry and Herbert," in *Essays by Rosemond Tuve:
    Spenser, Herbert, Milton,* ed. Thomas P. Roche, Jr. (Princeton: Princeton
    Univ. Press, 1970), pp. 210-12, 216, 217, 231.
24 Ibid., pp. 211, 231.
25 By A. F. Allison, "Some Influences in Crashaw's Poem 'On a Prayer
    Booke Sent to Mrs. M. R.,'" *RES,* 23 (1947), 40-42. See Also Allison's
    "Crashaw and St. François de Sales," *RES,* 24 (1948), 295-302.
26 *Obras completas de Santa Teresa de Jesús,* ed. Efren de la Madre de Dios,
    and Otger Steggink, 2nd ed. (Madrid: Biblioteca de Autores Cristianos,
    1967), p. 499. All quotations of Teresa's works are taken from this one-
    volume version of the BAC edition.
27 *Vida y obras de San Juan de la Cruz,* ed. Lucinio de SS. Sacramento, and

Matías del Niño Jesús, 5th ed. (Madrid: BAC, 1964), p. 363. All quotations of San Juan are from this edition.

28   *Obras escogidas,* II, 1001.

29   Cf. Helmut Hatzfeld, "Los elementos constitutivos de la poesía mística (San Juan de la Cruz)," in *Estudios literarios sobre mística española,* 3rd ed. (Madrid: Editorial Gredos, 1976), p. 389: "In order to prevent this exalted symbolism from descending to the level of profane love, it is involved in a network of paradoxical obstacles. Thanks to this the concrete cannot move freely, but can escape only toward the spiritual, and the spiritual only toward the concrete." This comment indicates just where Crashaw's "Ode on a Prayer-book" goes wrong. The concrete aspects of carnal love have an independent existence in the poem, not essentially related to the devotional purpose, which seems merely superimposed. In other poems, Crashaw, too, succeeds in limiting these concrete elements so that they can only refer to a spiritual plane.

30   Jerónimo de San José, *Historia del venerable padre fr. Iuan de la Cruz* . . . (Madrid, 1641), p. 262.

31   "Some Influences in Crashaw's Poem . . . ," pp. 40–42.

32   Cf. "Love" (I & II), *Works of Herbert,* p. 54; and "Holy Sonnets," 10, *The Divine Poems of John Donne,* p. 11. The Herbert poems are simply a plea for sacred parody, and his poems which express a close relation to God are generally filial or friendly (e.g., the end of "Jordan" (II): "But while I bustled, I might heare a *friend /* Whisper" (p. 103, emphasis added). In the Donne poem, the famous closing figure," for I / Except you'enthrall mee, never shall be free, / Nor ever chaste, except you ravish mee," appeals largely to the intellect as a paradox. It does not in the manner of Crashaw, attempt to describe how the presence of God *feels* by means of sexual analogy.

33   *The Enclosed Garden: The Tradition and the Image in Seventeenth Century Poetry* (Madison: Univ. of Wisconsin Press, 1966), esp. pp. 25–27. Stewart treats Crashaw briefly (pp. 24–29, 79, 90–91), but his whole study is aimed at the explication of Marvell's "Garden." Even if his interpretation of the Marvell poem is correct—and, for my part, "The Garden" is a profoundly secular treatment of scriptural themes—it demonstrates conclusively that Crashaw was working in a very different tradition; for, despite their use of similar rhetorical devices, nothing could be further from Crashaw's opulent devotion than Marvell's cool irony.

34   Sermon LXXXIV, on Canticles, 1, in *Late Medieval Mysticism,* ed. Ray C. Petry, vol. 13 of *Library of Christian Classics,* ed. John Baillie, John T. McNeill, and Henry P. Van Dusen (Philadelphia: Westminster, 1957), p. 74.

35   Warren, *Richard Crashaw: A Study,* p. 4, puts this discovery in 1638 on the

basis of a Latin oration by Crashaw's Peterhouse colleague, Joseph Beaumont.

36 *Obras completas castellanas,* ed. Félix García, 4th ed. (Madrid: BAC, 1957), I, 72. All quotations of Fray Luis de León are taken from this edition.

37 Égloga II, 1-9, *Obras de Garcilaso de la Vega,* ed. T. Navarro Tomás, Clásicos castellanos no. 3 (Madrid: Espasa-Calpe, 1924), pp. 27-28. See also ll. 74ff., ll. 910ff., and the comments by Alonso, *Poesía de San Juan de la Cruz,* pp. 32-34.

38 Ángel del Río, *Historia de la literatura española,* rev. ed. (New York: Holt, Rinehart & Winston, 1963), I, 170. The Spanish popular tradition is considered in more detail in chapter 3 of the present study.

39 *Poesía española,* pp. 227-35.

40 *Obras completas,* ed. Juan and Isabel Millé y Giménez, 6th ed. (Madrid: Aguilar, 1967), pp. 188, 222. In the first of the two quoted passages I have corrected an obvious misprint in the seventh line, *carrera,* to *cerrera.* Cf. *Obras poéticas de Luis de Góngora,* ed. R. Foulché-Delbosc (New York: Hispanic Society of America, 1921), II, 122; and the facsimile of the edition of 1627, *Obras en verso del Homero español,* intro. Dámaso Alonso (Madrid: Clásicos hispánicos, 1963), p. 84. Notwithstanding its obvious shortcomings, Millé y Giménez is the most convenient complete edition, and Góngora is quoted from this text throughout the present study.

41 Cf. Robert Jammes, *Études sur L'Oeuvre Poétique de . . . Góngora* (Bordeaux: l'Université de Bordeaux, 1967), p. 455.

42 Cf. Francisco Pacheco, *El Arte de la Pintura* (Sevilla, 1649), on the conventions of painting the Immaculate Conception, excerpted in *Italy & Spain, 1600-1750: Sources and Documents in Art History,* ed. Robert Engass and Jonathan Brown (Englewood Cliffs, NJ: Prentice-Hall, 1970), p. 166: "She [the Blessed Virgin] should be painted wearing a white tunic and blue mantle. . . . She is surrounded by the sun, an oval sun of white and ochre, which sweetly blends into the sky. Rays of light emanate from her head around which is a ring of twelve stars. An imperial crown adorns her head without, however, hiding the stars. Under her feet is the moon. Although it is a solid globe, I take the liberty of making it transparent so that the landscape shows through. The upper part is darkened to form a crescent moon with the points turned downward." Anyone familiar with the renderings of this mystery by such seventeenth-century Spanish painters as Murillo and Zurbarán will immediately recognize these details, which are also reminiscent of the depiction of Our Lady in Crashaw's Assumption hymn.

43 Alonso, *Poesía española,* pp. 233-34.

44 Cf. Yvor Winters, *In Defense of Reason* (New York: Alan Swallow, 1947), pp. 84, 131–33. Winters, so far as I know, was the first critic to notice the influence of the song-books in Crashaw's verse, and the pages he devotes to Crashaw in this volume are sympathetic and perceptive. He does not specifically refer to the Assumption poem; this connection is first made by Louis L. Martz, "The Action of the Self: Devotional Poetry in the Seventeenth Century," in *Metaphysical Poetry*, ed. Malcolm Bradbury and D. J. Palmer (Bloomington: Indiana Univ. Press, 1970), pp. 118–20.

45 *England's Helicon*, ed. Hugh MacDonald (Cambridge: Harvard Univ. Press, 1962), p. 164. The song first appeared in Dowland's *First Book of Songs and Ayres* (1597 and several subsequent printings). See *English Madrigal Verse, 1588–1633*, ed. E. H. Fellowes, rev. Frederick W. Sternfeld, and David Greer, 3rd ed. (Oxford: Clarendon, 1967), p. 460.

46 Lib. IV, Ode 21. The odes were first published, with great international acclaim, in 1625 and 1628. A selection with verse translations by G. Hils was published in London in 1646. A facsimile of this edition, *The Odes of Casimire*, intro. Maren-Sofie Roestvig, Augustan Reprint Society no. 44 (Los Angeles, 1953), pp. 82, 84, has served as my text with minor corrections from *Horatius Sarmaticus* sive R. P. Mathiae Casimiri Sarbievii . . . *Lyricorum Libri* IV (Colonae Agrippinae, 1721). The Hils translations are neither graceful nor particularly accurate and, as the date indicates, could have had no influence on Crashaw, so I have ignored them.

47 *Odes of Casimire*, p. ii.

48 Ibid.

49 Here the verse is the first Archilochian as in Horace, *Odes*, IV, 7.

50 In many respects, the late poem "A Letter to the Countess of Denbigh" is similar to "Ode on a Prayer-book" in theme and approach. In the former, however, the occasion of the "letter" is not a personal gift, so the speaker is not so intimately involved; the purpose of the admonition—salvation through conversion to Catholicism—is far clearer, and the imagery tends to be less rapturous and mystical (especially in the apparently later pamphlet version) and is therefore more in keeping with the situations both of poet and Countess. On this last point, see Young, "Truth with Precision," p. 9 (cited above, chap. 1, n. 50).

51 "Crashaw's 'Death More Mysticall and High,'" *JEGP*, 55 (1956), 379.

52 *Estudios literarios sobre mística española*, 3rd ed. (Madrid: Editorial Gredos, 1976), p. 14.

53 Image and Symbol in the Sacred Poetry of Richard Crashaw (Columbia: Univ. of South Carolina Press, 1963), p. 65.

54 Cf. *Vida y obras de San Juan*, pp. 929–30. The complications arising from

the similarity of the poems by Santa Teresa and San Juan and various other textual problems do not affect the issue under discussion here. For a treatment of the problem, see Hatzfeld, *Mística española*, pp. 169–211.

55 Cf. Eleanor McCann, "Oxymora in Spanish Mystics and English Metaphysical Writers," *CL*, 13 (1961), 18–19.

56 *Poesía española*, pp. 23–38.

57 "Love" I, *Works*, p. 54. See above, n. 32.

CHAPTER 3

1 Cf. Crashaw's hymn (ll. 35–36): "We saw thee; and we blest the sight/ We saw thee by thine own sweet light."

2 *Obras escogidas*, II, 1174.

3 *Obras escogidas*, II, 1178. All subsequent quotations of Lope's *Pastores de Belén* are taken from this edition.

4 The *justa poética* ("poetic joust" or "tournament") or *certamen* ("contest") was quite common in the Spain of Lope's day. Such events were frequently held in honor of religious heroes. The practice is discussed in more detail below in this chapter.

5 *Cristo en la poesía de Lope de Vega* (Madrid: Ediciones Cultura Hispánica, 1967), p. 56. See Lope's "Al Nacimiento de nuestro Señor," *Rimas humanas y divinas*, in *Obras escogidas*, II, 230ff.

6 *Homo Ludens: A Study of the Play Element in Culture* (Boston: Beacon, 1950), pp. 18, 19, 26–27, 58–63, 139–40, 158–59. Josef Pieper, *Leisure: The Basis of Culture*, trans. Alexander Dru, intro. T. S. Eliot (New York: Pantheon, 1952), pp. 71–81.

7 *Homo Ludens*, p. 180.

8 *Religion and the Rise of Capitalism* (1926; rpt. New York: Mentor, 1947), pp. 165, 166.

9 *The Autobiography of Richard Baxter*, abr. J. M. Lloyd Thomas, ed. N. H. Keeble (rev. ed., London: J. M. Dent, 1974), p. 22; see also p. 35.

10 See Daniel Neal, *The History of the Puritans* . . . (London, 1822; rpt. Westmead, Farnborough, Hants., England: Gregg, 1970), III, for the 1644 Parliamentary declaration mandating that the day "which heretofore was usually called the feast of the nativity of our Saviour" should be kept as the usual fast of the last Wednesday of each month, "and that this day in particular is to be kept with the more solemn humiliation, because it may call to remembrance our sins, and the sins of our forefathers, who have turned this feast, pretending the memory of Christ, into an extreme forgetfulness of him, by giving liberty to carnal and sensual delights." Cf. William Haller, *The Rise of Puritanism* (New York: Columbia Univ. Press, 1938), p. 151; Leah Sinanoglou Marcus, "Herrick's *Noble Numbers*

and the Politics of Playfulness," *ELR*, 7 (1976), 115-16; and Frederick D. Wilhelmsen, "Christmas in Christendom," in *Citizen of Rome* (LaSalle, IL: Sherwood Sugden, 1980), pp. 330-32.

11 *Cristo en la poesía*, pp. 37-38.

12 While the traditional songs of fourteenth- and fifteenth-century Spain were (despite a degree of humanist scorn for all things medieval) a vital source of inspiration for Lope and his contemporaries, their English counterparts were generally the object of, at best, a rather condescending nostalgia. Cf. Sidney's *Apology* in *Elizabethan Critical Essays*, ed. G. G. Smith (Oxford: Clarendon, 1904), I, 178: "Certainly I must confesse my own barbarousness: I neuer heard the olde song of Percy and Duglas that I found not my heart mooued more then with a Trumpet; and yet it is sung but by some blind Crouder, with no rougher voyce then rude style; which being so euill apparrelled in the dust and cobwebbes of that un-ciuill age, what would it worke trymmed in the gorgeous eloquence of *Pindar?*" Even the most "medieval" of English Renaissance poets, Spenser, was engaged largely in a task of artificial reconstruction of language and literary forms but dimly remembered and understood. No doubt the crucial factor here is the great change in the English language during the fifteenth century: it is probably no more difficult for a modern, educated Spaniard to read the *Poema del Cid* (twelfth century) than it was for a sixteenth-century Englishman to read Chaucer.

13 José F. Montesinos, ed., "Introducción," to *Lope de Vega: Poesías líricas* (Madrid: Espasa-Calpe, 1925), I, xxxiv.

14 The *villancico* is explained above in the text. The *romance* is loosely parallel to the English ballad, and the *letrilla* usually refers to the words of a short popular song composed around an *estribillo* (refrain or burden) and is probably best rendered into English as "song." The *glosa*, cognate with "gloss," is a form unique to Iberian literature. To write a glosa the poet takes another piece of poetry (often anonymous and usually very short, e.g., a four-line estribillo) as a text, using each of its lines, in order, as the last line of each of his own stanzas (most commonly *decimas:* ababacdcdc). During the sixteenth and seventeenth centuries the glosa was a great favorite for the display of poetic virtuosity and the variations on the basic idea were countless. For a thorough discussion of the subject, see Hans Janner, "La glosa española," *Revista de filología española*, 27 (1943), 181-232.

15 *Cristo en la poesía*, p. 100.

16 "Structure and Symbol in Crashaw's *Hymn in the Nativity*," *PMLA*, 73 (1948), 108. Neill provides a fine account of the development of the poem through its three editions: 1646, 1648, 1652.

17 *Image and Symbol*, p. 54, n. 110.

18 "Al Nacimiento de nuestro Señor," Égloga primera, 1. 11, in *Rimas humanas y divinas del licenciado Tomé de Burgillos* (Madrid, 1634), in *Obras escogidas*, II, 230. The entire volume is reprinted in *Lope de Vega: Obras poéticas*, ed. José Manuel Blecua (Barcelona: Editorial Planeta, 1969), I, 1327–1554.

19 "Structure and Symbol," p. 111.

20 See, for example, John Bucke, *Instructions for the Use of the Beades* (Louvain, 1589), in *A Critical Anthology of English Recusant Devotional Prose*, ed. John R. Roberts, Duquesne Studies, Philological Series no. 7 (Pittsburgh: Duquesne Univ. Press, 1966), p. 300, on the third joyful mystery, the Nativity: "cōsider in what poor estate the lorde of all the worlde wolde be borne and brought in to this worlde: and here learne to cōtemne al worldlie pompe and vainglorious curiositie." See also Gaspar Loarte, *Instructions and Advertisements, How to Meditate the Misteries of the Rosarie* . . . , [trans. John Fen] (n.p.: [1579?]), in Roberts, pp. 294–96.

21 E.g. Virgil, *Georgics*, II, 458ff.: "O fortunatos nimium, sua si bona norint, / agricolas! . . ."; and Horace, *Epodes*, II: "Beatus ille, qui procul negotiis, / ut prisca gens mortalium, / paterna rura bobus exercet suis." Cf. Maren-Sofie Roestvig, *The Happy Man: Studies in the Metamorphosis of a Classical Idea*, Oslo Studies in English no. 2, 2nd ed. (Oslo: Norwegian Univ. Press, 1962), I, passim, for a thorough discussion of the general influence of the theme in seventeenth-century English poetry.

22 The four poems are "A Christmas Carol . . . ," "The New-yeeres Gift, or Circumcision Song," "Another New-yeeres Gift . . . ," and "The Star-Song." They were first published in *His Noble Numbers* in 1648 (though dated 1647), two years after the first edition of *Steps to the Temple*. Herrick's poems are slighter and less ambitious by far than Crashaw's Nativity poem.

23 "Herrick's Noble Numbers and the Politcs of Playfulness," *ELR*, 7 (1976), 115. See also Marcus, "Herrick's *Hesperides* and the 'Proclamation made for May,'" *SP*, 76 (1979), 49–74; and Robert H. Deming, *Ceremony and Art: Robert Herrick's Poetry* (Mouton: The Hague, 1974), pp. 10, 21, 48, 57, 85–89, 141–57.

24 "Another New-yeeres Gift, or Song for the Circumcision," ll. 25–30, in *The Complete Poetry of Robert Herrick*, ed. J. Max Patrick (New York: Norton, 1968), p. 484. Patrick also sees a compliment to Charles and the Queen in "The Star-Song," p. 486.

25 "'Eliza, Queene of shepheardes,' and the Pastoral of Power," *ELR*, 10 (1980), 163.

26 Ibid., p. 182.

27 "Herrick's Noble Numbers," p. 126.

28 Williams, ed., *Complete Poems*, p. 217. See also Martin, *Poems*, p. xci;
    Warren, *Richard Crashaw: A Study*, p. 119; and Praz, "Crashaw and the
    Baroque Style," p. 231.

29 *Marino and Crashaw: Sospetto d'Herode: A Commentary*, Lund Studies in
    English no. 39 (Lund: C. W. K. Gleerup, 1971), pp. 135–36.

30 In the appendix to his *Devotional Poetry in France, c. 1570–1613* (Cam-
    bridge: Cambridge Univ. Press, 1969), pp. 321–24, Terence Cave has
    printed another possible model, the *Cantique premier* of César de Nos-
    tredame's *Divers cantiques, à la sacrée nativité du sauveur du monde* (1607),
    which likewise shares the familiar Nativity motifs of angels, shepherds,
    and supernatural light, and even includes a particularly Crashavian
    touch: the ox and ass warming the Christ child with their "sweet breath"
    (*haleine douce*). But Nostredame carries the Petrarchan portrayal to
    excess—stanzas nine and ten are a long blazon—and, as Cave notes (pp.
    266–69), there is a stiff artificiality, largely the result of Nostredame's
    painter's insistence on detailed yet formal visual evocation, which sup-
    presses the sense of pastoral innocence notable in Crashaw's and Lope's
    treatment of the Nativity.

31 *Christiados*, III, 73–76, 82–93. The Latin text is quoted from *Marco
    Girolamo Vida's The Christiad: A Latin English Edition*, ed. and trans.
    Gertrude C. Drake and Clarence A. Forbes (Carbondale: Southern Il-
    linois Univ. Press, 1978). I have preferred my own less graceful but more
    literal English renderings for reasons explained in the following note.

32 Ibid., 616–24. Drake and Forbes translate *Et mirum in morem celeri
    proludere coetu* by "their swift band forming a frolicsome interlude in
    marvelous fashion." I can see no basis here for "frolicsome" in a context
    which seems to depict the angelic host in the performance of complex,
    formal, quasi-military maneuvers across the sky. Obviously "frolicsome"
    alters the tone. Similarly Drake and Forbes render *ardua Olympi* by "the
    height of heavens." To be sure, *Olympus* is a poetic term for "heaven,"
    but such a translation does not convey the continual allusiveness to pagan
    classicism which pervades Vida's biblical epic.

33 See also Jacopo Sannazaro's *De Partu Virginis* (1521), II, 379–89, in *Prose
    e Poesie Latine di Scrittori Italiani*, ed. Ugo Enrico Paoli (Firenze: Felice
    Le Monnier Editore, 1926), pp. 161–62, for a passage in which the storied
    ox and ass are defined, by way of contrast, with a setting of pagan myth:
    "Hic illum mitia anhelo/Ore fovent iumenta. O rerum occulta
    potestas!/Protinus agnoscens Dominum procumbit humi bos/Cernuus:
    et mora nulla, simul procumbit asellus/Submittens caput, et trepidanti
    poplite adorat. / Fortunati ambo: non vos aut fabula Cretae/Polluet, anti-
    qui referens mendacia furti, / Sidoniam mare per medium vexisse

puellam: / Aut sua dum madidus celebrat portenta Cithaeron, / Infames
inter thyasos vinosaque sacra / Arguet obsequio senis insudasse profani." I
have noted already in chapter 1 the infiltration of Geraldini's sacred
pastoral by this classicizing epic mode, and Leonard Grant's account in
Neo-Latin Literature and the Pastoral, pp. 258–89, suggests that such was
the usual tendency of the devotional form of the neo-Latin pastora. See
also Thomas M. Greene, *The Descent from Heaven: A Study in Epic
Continuity* (New Haven and London: Yale Univ. Press, 1963), p. 144–75.

34 A phrase which pleased Crashaw enough that he also incorporated it into
the new 1648 version of "The Weeper," stanza 15: "O wit of love! that
thus could place / Fountain and Garden in one face."

35 *Forms of Discovery*, p. 92. For a similar attitude, see Wylie Sypher, *Four
Stages of Renaissance Style* (New York: Doubleday, 1956), pp. 238–39,
242–43. Louis L. Martz, *The Wit of Love* (Notre Dame, IN: Notre Dame
Univ. Press, 1969), p. 135; and Robert T. Petersson, *The Art of Ecstasy*
(New York: Atheneum, 1970), p. 140, are among the few critics who have
perceived the humor and detachment of Crashaw's treatment of Teresa's
childhood escapade: "In this poem," writes Martz, "the rational presence
of the speaker with his tone of familiar conversation, controls the Baroque
extravaganza and makes one of Crashaw's perfect poems."

36 Most critics agree that the poem falls into three parts. Exceptions are
Stephanie Jauernick, "Crashaws Hymne auf Santa Teresa," *Die Neuren
Sprachen*, N.F., 14 (1965), 454; and Arno Esch, *Englische Religioese Lyrik
des 17. Jahrhunderts* (Tübingen: Max Niemeyer Verlag, 1955), pp. 128–
29, who both mark off the first fourteen lines as an "introduction" or
statement of theme. There is general agreement upon a division between
lines 64 and 65, but not about the beginning of the last section of the
poem. Esch, Jauernick, and Anthony E. Farnham, "Teresa and the Coy
Mistress," *Boston University Studies in English*, 2 (1956), 236, all argue
that it begins with l. 105. Petersson, *Art of Ecstasy*, p. 130, singles out l.
121. I would put the break at the dash at the end of l. 117. Here the
rapturous flow of the verse describing Teresa's ecstasy ends abruptly, and
the more subdued manner of the final part begins.

37 The information on San Hermenegildo and the circumstances of his
death is taken from *The Catholic Encyclopaedic Dictionary*, ed. Donald
Attwater (New York: Macmillan, 1939); and E. Allison Peers, ed., *Spain:
A Companion to Spanish Studies*, 5th ed. (London: Methuen, 1956), p. 33.
The contest, of which Lope was named secretary and judge by its Carmelite sponsors, was held in the garden of the Church of San Hermenegildo.
This setting accounts for the subject of Lope's poem, which was not
entered in the contest. See Joaquín de Entrambasaguas, "Lope de Vega en
las justas poéticas . . . ," *Revista de Literatura*, 22 (1967), 17–18.

38 Antonio Rodríguez-Moñino, ed., "Las justas toledanas a Santa Teresa en
    1614 . . . ," in *Studia Philológica: Homenaje ofrecida a Dámaso Alonso* . . .
    (Madrid: Gredos, 1961), III, 257. This poem and the others written by
    Medinilla for the contest honoring Santa Teresa remained in manuscript
    until published by Rodríguez-Moñino. Although it is therefore almost
    impossible that Crashaw was familiar with these poems, they are a good
    example of the enormous quantity of verse written about Teresa in
    seventeenth-century Spain. That Crashaw's own work so closely resem-
    bles, in some points, poems he probably never saw is an indication of how
    deeply he was influenced by the general Spanish sensibility. With the
    exception of changing "c" with a cedilla to "z," I have reproduced the
    Spanish text exactly in my quotations. The punctuation in the transla-
    tions has been added in the interest of simple intelligibility.
39 Ibid.
40 Ibid.
41 Ibid.
42 *Richard Crashaw: A Study*, p. 141.
43 See the references in nn. 8-10, 23 above. Entrambasaguas, "Lope de
    Vega en las justas póeticas," pp. 16-20, helps to substantiate my specula-
    tions about the nature of the siglo de oro "poetic tournaments" and their
    potential effect on poetry. The Spanish scholar points out that the influ-
    ence of Lope on the development of the contests was crucial, since he had
    a hand in organizing many of the largest and most extravagant which
    were held in the seventeenth century. For Lope the contests were a means
    of projecting "his power and influence upon the criticism and literature of
    the Spanish Golden Age." As such they were instrumental in his bitter
    rivalry with Góngora and, ironically enough, what Lope considered the
    excesses of the "nueva poesía." The fact that the contests were vehicles
    for literary polemic and that they were shaped under the impetus of
    Lope's flamboyant personality would be of great consequence for the kind
    of poetry produced in them. The intense rivalry between the religious
    orders which often sponsored them also must not be overlooked. See also
    José Manuel Blecua, "Villancicos de Lope a Santa Teresa," in *Sobre
    poesía de la edad de oro* (Madrid: Gredos, 1970), pp. 233-40.

CHAPTER 4

1 Austin Warren, "The Mysticism of Richard Crashaw," *The Symposium*,
   4 (1933), 135-55. Another early sympathetic treatment of Crashaw's
   handling of mysticism in his poetry is by Helen White, *The Metaphysical
   Poets*, pp. 235-38.
2 Wallerstein, pp. 146-47, questions whether Crashaw "fully realized his

whole self in expressing the abstract ideas" of the hymns on the Epiphany
and the Name of Jesus; Itrat-Husain, p. 22, finds "little evidence of his
ever having attained a direct vision of God in illumination"; Martin Tur-
nell, pp. 107–09, is concerned that Crashaw's use of erotic imagery in
mystical subjects represents excessive compromise with the age; Robert
Ellrodt, I, 417, 423, finds Crashaw's treatment of Santa Teresa's mystical
death unconvincing, and his preoccupation with the miraculous unsatis-
fying in the Epiphany poem; and Anthony Low, *Love's Architecture* (New
York: New York Univ. Press, 1978), p. 156, leaves the question of
whether "Crashaw knew mystical experience at first hand" undecided,
but curiously finds most evidence for it in the prayer-book ode.

3   "The Night," l. 50, in *Complete Poems of Henry Vaughan*, ed. French
Fogle (Garden City, NY: Doubleday, 1964), p. 325. See also Bush, p. 150:
"The question whether an indisputable poet is also an indisputable mystic
cannot be settled by rule of thumb, and perhaps does not need to be
settled. As for the poet, the reader may feel uneasy when the authentic
motives of adoration and self-surrender issue in an undisciplined fervor
which has never been rational and never ceases to be sensuous and
excited; he may think that larger and clearer glances of the One were
granted to the quiet Vaughan."

4   *A Catholic Dictionary*, 3rd ed. (New York: Macmillan, 1961). This same
definition is quoted from an earlier edition by Helmut Hatzfeld, "Problemas fundamentales del misticismo español," in *Estudios literarios sobre
mística española*, 3rd ed. (Madrid: Gredos, 1976), pp. 15–16.

5   "Problemas fundamentales," pp. 17, 20–23.

6   *Christian Mysticism in the Elizabethan Age: With Its Background in Mystical
Methodology* (1940; rpt. New York: Octagon, 1971), p. 17.

7   *Studies of the Spanish Mystics*, 2nd ed. (London: S.P.C.K., 1951), I, xvi,
xvii.

8   Cf. Hatzfeld, "Las profundas cavernas: estructura de un símbolo de San
Juan de la Cruz," in *Estudios literarios*, p. 319, n. 3.

9   Cf. Hatzfeld, "Influencia de Raimundo Lulio y Jan van Ruysbroeck en el
lenguaje de los místicos españoles," in *Estudios literarios*, pp. 37–121; and
Peers, p. 102.

10 In Crashaw's hymn this vision is treated as a recurrent, not an isolated
event, just as it is in the *Vida:* "The Lord willed that here I might
occasionally [*algunas veces*] see this vision..." (*Obras*, p. 131). Cf.
Petersson, *Art of Ecstasy*, p. 39.

11 *Colección de las obras sueltas* (Madrid: Antonio de Sancha, 1777), XIII, 89.
See also Teresa's own poem, "Mi Amado para mi": "When the sweet
Hunter / Shot me and left me wounded / In the arms of love, / My soul

surrendered. . . ./ He wounded me with an arrow / Anointed with love /and my soul has been made/One with its Creator" (*Obras*, p. 499).

12   *The Oxford Book of Spanish Verse*, ed. James Fitzmaurice-Kelly and J. B. Trend, 2nd ed. (Oxford: Clarendon, 1940), pp. 213–14. This poem was never printed during the seventeenth century.

13   *Obras sueltas*, XIII, 89.

14   Rodríguez-Moñino, ed., "Las justas toledanas a Santa Teresa en 1614 . . .," p. 258.

15   Ibid., p. 259.

16   Cf. above, chap. 2, n. 51.

17   For more on the knowledge of Santa Teresa, and mystical writers in general, among Lope and other Spanish poets, see Manuel de Montoliu, "El beato Juan de Ávila y Lope de Vega," in *Miscelánea filológica* (Barcelona: Instituto Internacional de Cultura Románica, 1960), II, 155–58; Robert Ricard, *Estudios de la literatura religiosa española*, trans. M. M. Cortés (Madrid: Aguilar, 1964), pp. 226–45; José Rubinos, *Lope como poeta religioso* (Habana: Cultural, S.A., 1935), pp. 19–24; E. Allison Peers, "Mysticism in the Religious Verse of the Golden Age," *Bulletin of Spanish Studies*, 21 (1944), 217–23, and 22 (1945), 38–45; and Otis H. Green, *Spain and the Western Tradition* (Madison: Univ. of Wisconsin Press, 1968), IV, 215.

18   *On Christian Doctrine*, II, vii, Robertson, p. 40.

19   Anthony Farnham, "Saint Teresa and the Coy Mistress," p. 232.

20   For an exposition of the structure of the *Moradas*, see Peers, *Studies of the Spanish Mystics*, I, 129. In the *Vida*, chap. 40, there is a comparison of God and the soul to mutually reflecting mirrors.

21   Cf. Petersson, *Art of Ecstasy*, pp. 20–21.

22   The four stages of prayer correspond to irrigation by means of (1) a well with a hand-drawn bucket, (2) a well with a windlass and aqueduct, (3) an adjacent river or spring, and (4) rainfall. The point is that prayer becomes more efficacious as the soul becomes more passive—an idea not missed by Crashaw: "Love's passives are his activ'st part" ("The Flaming Heart," l. 73).

23   See chapter 2, above. For an account of how Crashaw removed inappropriate mystical imagery from *A Letter to the Countess of Denbigh*, see Young, "Truth with Precision," pp. 3–17.

24   *A Literary History of Spain, The Golden Age: Prose and Poetry*, pp. 87–88. Hatzfeld, "Problemas fundamentales," p. 14, similarly emphasizes the connection between sacred parody and the literary development of mysticism during the siglo de oro.

25   St. Bonaventure, *Itinerarium Mentis in Deum*, esp. chap. 2. Cf. St. Au-

gustine, *Confessions*, X, 6, 9, in which aspects of the material creation are *nuntiis corporales;* Louis L. Martz, *The Paradise Within*, pp. 18, 56, 68, 71-72, 78, 81, 146; and Edward Cuthbert Butler, *Western Mysticism*, foreword by David Knowles, 3rd ed. (London: Constable, 1967), pp. 20-24.

26 *The Wit of Love*, p. 145.

27 *Image and Symbol*, p. 54.

28 For similar phrasing, see "Este sol que se hiela y arde" (p. 1252) and "En el trono de zafiro" (pp. 1276-77).

29 In "Desnudito mi Niño" (p. 1256) Lope compares the infant Christ to a naked Cupid with arrows in his eyes.

30 "Mysticism in the Religious Verse," 22 (1945), 43.

31 See the comments on this passage by Butler, *Western Mysticism*, pp. lv-lvii.

32 *Apollo and the Nine: A history of the Ode* (Baltimore: Johns Hopkins Univ. Press, 1960), pp. 352-53. See also Ellrodt, *L'Inspiration Personelle*, I, 387-88. R. O. Jones, ed., in his "Introduction" to *Poems of Góngora* (Cambridge: Cambridge Univ. Press, 1966), pp. 9, 32, suggests that the purpose of Góngora's "generic imagery" is "to capture the essence that lies behind the particular," and he argues that Góngora's "thought had a Neoplatonic cast," especially in the *Soledades* and the *Fábula de Polifemo y Galatea*. He draws attention to frequent references to music in the former poem which seem to symbolize the harmony of the natural universe manifest in the music of the spheres. Here the parallel to Crashaw's "Hymn to the Name of Jesus" is obvious, and we shall explore the metaphysical basis of the similarity of Crashaw's style to Gongora's in chapter 6.

33 Warren, *Richard Crashaw: A Study*, p. 148. See references above, n. 2.

34 For a superb discussion of how Crashaw blends liturgy and mysticism in this poem, see A. R. Cirillo, "Crashaw's 'Epiphany Hymn': The Dawn of Christian Time," *SP*, 67 (1970), 67-88.

35 This is Warren's view. See *Richard Crashaw: A Study*, pp. 147, 151.

36 *Mística, plástica, y barroco* (Madrid: CUPSA Editorial, 1977), pp. 29, 45-47.

37 Ibid., 50-52.

38 *A Reading of George Herbert*, p. 65.

39 *A Reading of George Herbert*, passim. An English poem which, in a sense, joins Christmas and the Passion together for contemplation is Robert Southwell's "Burning Babe"; but its tone is altogether different from Crashaw's.

40 See Santa Teresa, "Pastores que veláis," "Nace el Redentor," and "Navidad," in *Obras*, pp. 504-05; and Lopez de Úbeda, *Cancionero gen-*

eral, ed. Antonio Rodríguez-Moñino (Madrid: Sociedad de Bibliófilos españoles, 1962), pp. 198–99: "Gui[llen]. Y dinos a que ha venido?/Bras. A librarnos de prisión, /con sufrir muerte y passion/sin auerla merecido."

41 The word *tinieblas,* which I have here rendered as "darkness," is also the Spanish equivalent of *tenebrae,* the office of matins for the last three days of Holy Week. Hence, the word gives the passage an important but untranslatable resonance. See below, n. 46.

42 "Spark" in Crashaw's day already had the familiar secondary meaning of "gallant" or elegant young fop. See OED: "Spark," sb.2, 2.

43 There is some ambiguity regarding the subject of the verb *hería* ("wounded") and the antecedent of the possessive pronouns *sus* and *su* ("his/"hers"/"its"): is the subject *aire* ("breeze")? If so, then Helmut Hatzfeld, "Los elementos constitutivos," p. 389, interprets the stanza correctly: "This gust of wind with hands that caress the betrothed even unto ecstasy can only be God, whom she embraces at the same time." Or is "el aire del almena" merely a descriptive phrase, with *Amado* as the understood subject of *hería?* I am not convinced that we are supposed to be certain; the ambiguity adds an appropriate note of mystery.

44 Cf. Cirillo, "Crashaw's 'Epiphany Hymn,'" p. 84: "While continuing to develop the symbol of the darkened sun as the revelation of the true way of God, the Magi's song begins to move to the contemplative mode which is the true object of the poem. The darkening of the sun becomes the darkening of the world, a renunciation of the flesh in order to meditate on Christ and join in the mystical advent. . . . Thus the Dionysian system of the via negativa alluded to in lines 192ff. . . . is not a new element imposed on the light-darkness motifs of the poem, as Wallerstein states, but serves as a cumulative reflection and transmutation of what has preceded."

45 See above, n. 41. The only other possible translation would be the obviously redundant "dark" or "obscure darkness." On the Holy Week office *tenebrae,* see Tuve, *A Reading of Herbert,* p. 66.

46 The story of Jonah is, of course, a traditional type of Christ's Passion and Resurrection, as our Lord indicates (Matt. 12:38–41).

47 On the generic uniqueness of San Juan's work, see Karol Wojtyla (Pope John Paul II), *La Fe según San Juan de la Cruz,* trans. (into Spanish) Alvaro Huerga (1951; rpt. Madrid: BAC, 1979), pp. 11–12. This work, little-known until the sudden emergence into international prominence of its author, contains excellent comments on the relation between the mystical via negativa and the ordinary faith of the Church (esp. pp. 99, 177–79). An English edition of this book has recently appeared: *Faith According to Saint John of the Cross,* trans. Jordan Aumann (San Francisco: Ignatius Press, 1981).

48 Cf. McCann, "Oxymora in Spanish Mystics," pp. 23–24, who remarks

that there are similarities between Crashaw's use of the "light/dark paradox" and San Juan's, without elaborating on the observation.

49 Alonso, *La poesía de San Juan de la Cruz*, p. 174.

50 *Love's Architecture*, pp. 120–21. Cf. Wallerstein, *Richard Crashaw: Style and Poetic Development*, p. 39. Low, p. 121, uses precisely this passage to question the mysticism of Crashaw's poetry, because "by suggesting that God can be caught by leaps of violent effort it contradicts the observations of most mystics, who insist on passivity." Yet the lines from San Juan, a genuine mystic who "insists on passivity," suggest, as Crashaw does, that "Love's passives are his activ'st part." Cf. above, n. 22.

CHAPTER 5

1 Williams, *Complete Poetry*, p. 258. See also Maris Stella Milhaupt, *The Latin Epigrams of Richard Crashaw with Introduction, English Translation, and Notes* (Ann Arbor: University Microfilms, 1963); Kenneth J. Larsen, "Richard Crashaw's *Epigrammata Sacra*," in *The Latin Poetry of English Poets*, ed. J. W. Binns (London: Routledge & Kegan, 1974), pp. 93–120; Martin, p. xxi; and Warren, *Richard Crashaw: A Study*, p. 23.

2 Among the more recent discussions of the liturgical aspects of Crashaw's poetry are A. B. Chambers, "Christmas: The Liturgy of the Church and English Verse of the Renaissance," in *Literary Monographs*, ed. Eric Rothstein and J. A. Wittreich, Jr. (Madison: Univ. of Wisconsin Press, 1975), 6, 109–53; A. R. Cirillo, "Crashaw's 'Epiphany Hymn': The Dawn of Christian Time," *SP*, 67 (1970), 67–88; Anthony Low, *Love's Architecture* (New York: New York Univ. Press, 1978), pp. 118–24; Paul G. Stanwood, "Time and Liturgy in Donne, Crashaw, and T. S. Eliot," *Mosaic*, 12 (1979), 91–105; and Elizabeth Hageman, "Calendrical Symbolism and the Unity of Crashaw's *Carmen Deo Nostro*," *SP*, 77 (1980), 161–79, a numerological treatment of Crashaw's posthumous volume. See also A. R. Cirillo, "Recent Studies in Crashaw," *ELR*, 9 (1979), 186.

3 This definition is adapted from the entry "Hymn" in the *Princeton Encyclopedia of Poetry and Poetics*, ed. Alex Preminger et al., rev. ed. (Princeton: Princeton Univ. Press, 1974).

4 The hymns are those on the Name of Jesus and the Epiphany, and "The Flaming Heart," as well as the translations of the medieval Latin hymns. The Assumption poem is first identified as a hymn in the 1648 edition.

5 See S. L. Bethel, *The Cultural Revolution of the Seventeenth Century* (London: Dennis Dobson, 1951), pp. 35–36; and Christopher Hill, *The World Turned Upside Down: Radical Ideas in the English Revolution* (New York: Viking, 1972), pp. 148–207.

6   *The Century of Revolution, 1603-1714* (1961; rpt. New York: Norton, 1966), p. 82. See also p. 99.

7   "Wit and Mystery: A Revaluation in Medieval Latin Hymnody," *Speculum*, 22 (1947), 310-41.

8   *Love's Architecture*, pp. 118-20.

9   *The Art of Ecstasy*, p. 130. There is some mention of Teresa's own visions of the afterlife in the *Vida*, chap. 38. Her account of the glorification of a Dominican priest suggests the scene of her own apotheosis in Crashaw's poem: "Another time I saw our Lady placing a very white cape on the master (*presentado*) of this order" (*Obras*, p. 173).

10 *Obras sueltas*, XIII, 90.

11 Ibid., 91.

12 Ibid.

13 For reproductions of many of these paintings, see Erik Larsen, *El Greco and the Spanish Golden Age* (New York: Tudor, 1969), passim.

14 An oil-on-canvas study for this ceiling is reproduced by Raymond Cogniat, *Seventeenth Century Painting* (New York: Viking, 1964), pl 19.

15 "Textos teresianos aplicados a la interpretación del Greco" in *Estudios literarios*, pp. 251-52.

16 This particular theme is almost the whole substance of Crashaw's "Apologie."

17 *Obras sueltas*, XIII, 144.

18 *Obras poéticas*, ed. José Manuel Blecua (Barcelona: Editorial Planeta, 1969), I, 355.

19 Rodríguez-Moñino, ed., "Las justas toledanas a Santa Teresa en 1614...," p. 259.

20 *Historia* (Madrid, 1641), n. pag.

21 Even as the Mass in Christ's sacrificial death on the cross continued in unbloody form on the altar, so Baptism is death to sin and rebirth in grace. Hence, mystical death is an extension of the sacramental idea.

22 "Crashaw's 'Epiphany Hymn,'" p. 68. Curiously, Chambers, "Christmas," p. 131, does not notice that the "Hymn to the Name of Jesus" is part of this same liturgical sequence.

23 *Richard Crashaw: A Study*, see also p. 166. Wallerstein, *Richard Crashaw: Style and Poetic Development*, pp. 38ff., 145-46.

24 Two important exceptions to this statement are Louis Martz, *The Poetry of Meditation*, pp. 62-64 and esp. pp. 331-52; and Mario Praz, *The Flaming Heart*, pp. 255-57. The former analyzes the structure of Crashaw's hymn in terms of the meditative method set forth in the *Rosetum* of Joannes Mauburnus and later in Joseph Hall's *Arte of Divine Meditation*. Praz maintains that the hymn is an "exquisite string of variations" on the medieval Latin *De Nomine Jesu*, long attributed to St.

Bernard of Clairvaux. Crashaw may have known the medieval hymn, but, as George Williams points out (*Complete Poetry*, p. 30), "the variations are so extensive and have gone so far from the original as to eliminate the possibility of even Crashavian 'translation.'"

25 Alcalá, 1616.

26 The text given here is basically that of Sainz de Robles, but in the interest of simple intelligibility I have made several minor emendations of punctuation and capitalization, and in the eleventh quoted line I have changed *y existencia* to *la excelencia*. All of these changes are based on the edition of Alcalá, 1616.

27 *La Divina Commedia*, ed. C. H. Grandgent, rev. Charles S. Singleton (Cambridge: Harvard Univ. Press, 1972), p. 904. The relevance of the passage was drawn to my attention by Claes Schaar, *Marino and Crashaw*, pp. 94–95, who cites, in addition, Claudian as a classical source.

28 Carlos [Karl] Vossler, *Fray Luis de León*, trans. Carlos Clavería, 3rd ed. (Madrid: Espasa-Calpe, S.A., 1960), p. 30. Fray Luis was also praised as a poet by Cervantes in *La Galatea* (1585).

29 *Obras completas castellanas*, ed. Félix García, 4th ed. (Madrid: BAC, 1957), I, 774–75. All quotations of Fray Luis are taken from this text.

30 *Fray Luis de León*, pp. 56–57. The point is made in less condescending terms by Leopold Sabourin, *The Names and Titles of Jesus*, trans. Maurice Carroll (New York: Macmillan, 1967), pp. xiii–xiv.

31 Cited by Vossler, p. 56.

32 *The Flaming Hart* (Antwerp, 1642), "Translator's Preface," n. pag. I follow the common assumption that the "M. T." who signed the dedication is Sir Toby Mathew.

33 Cf. "Introduccion" by García, *Obras*, I, 394–95.

34 The Spanish word *salud*, which I have here rendered as "health," may also mean "salvation" or "state of grace."

35 "Names" here evidently refers to Rev. 2:17: "To him that overcometh will I give to eat of the hidden manna, and will give him a white stone, and in the stone a new name written, which no man knoweth saving he that receiveth it." This text is cited and discussed by Fray Luis in *Los nombres de Cristo*, in *Obras completas castellana*, I, 423.

36 Cf. Curtius, *European Literature*, p. 545; Alonso, *Poesía española*, pp. 178–80, 619–21; John Hollander, *The Untuning of the Sky: Ideas of Music in English Poetry, 1500–1700* (Princeton: Princeton Univ. Press, 1961), p. 266, passim; and Leo Spitzer, *Christian and Classical Ideas of World Harmony*, ed. Anna Granville-Hatcher (Baltimore: Johns Hopkins Press, 1963), passim, esp. pp. 111–14 on Fray Luis, and p. 134 on Crashaw. Sir Thomas Browne furnishes contemporary testimony of the pervasiveness

of the notion in *Religio Laici* (II, 9), in *Sir Thomas Browne: The Major Works,* ed. C. A. Patrides (Harmondsworth: Penguin, 1977), pp. 149–50: "for even that vulgar and Taverne Musicke, which makes one man merry, another mad, strikes in mee a deepe fit of devotion, and a profound contemplation of the first Composer, there is something in it of Divinity more than the ear discovers. It is a Hieroglyphicall and shadowed lesson of the whole world, and Creatures of God, such a melody to the eare, as the whole world well understood, would afford the understanding. In briefe, it is a sensible fit of that Harmony, which intellectually sounds in the eares of God."

37 Salinas was a professor of music at the University of Salamanca and author of the treatise *De Musica libri septem.* For further occurrences of the motif of music in the poetry of Fray Luis, see "Canción al nacimiento de la hija del Marqués de Alcañices" (II, 749ff.), "Noche serena" (II, 758ff.), and "Morada de Cielo" (II, 779ff.).

38 Wallerstein, *Richard Crashaw: Style and Poetic Development,* p. 146; Low, *Love's Architecture,* p. 123.

39 *The Poetry of Meditation,* pp. 340–41. For the recantation see Martz's notes to the hymn in *The Meditative Poem* (New York: Doubleday, 1963), p. 280; and in *The Norton Anthology of Seventeenth-Century Verse* (New York: Norton, 1969), I, 250. In a review of *The Poetry of Meditation* in the *Church Quarterly Review,* 156 (1955), 333–36, E. I. Watkin took issue with Martz's original hypothesis and urged—without furnishing any reason—that the occasion for the poem was August 7, feast of the Holy Name according to the Sarum use. Apart from the lack of positive evidence, this notion clashes with the obvious association between "Hymn to the Name of Jesus" and the other Christmastide poems in *Carmen Deo Nostro.*

40 *The Golden Legend,* ed. and trans. Granger Ryan and Helmut Ripperger (New York: Arno, 1969), pp. 82–83. This book was still familiar enough in the seventeenth century for Jonson to make a mocking reference to it in "An Execration upon Vulcan" (l. 66), and in all likelihood Crashaw knew it. This and the association between the feasts of the Circumcision and the Holy Name by Fray Luis, Lope, and Valdivielso have been previously noticed in R. V. Young, Jr., "Jonson, Crashaw, and the Development of the English Epigram," *Genre,* 12 (1979), 151–52. This article deals with ll. 207–24 of the hymn as an "epigram" within the longer poem.

41 *Obras,* I, 775. A footnote cites Luke 1:31, but the reference is quite as likely to 2:21.

42 *Romancero espiritual,* ed. P. Miguel Mir (Madrid: A. Perez Dubrull, 1880), pp. 77–78.

CHAPTER 6

1 *Agudeza y arte de ingenio* (Huesca, 1648), I, II, in *Obras completas,* ed. Arturo del Hoyo, 3rd ed. (Madrid: Aguilar, 1967), pp. 238, 239.

2 Ibid., II, p. 242; Joseph A. Mazzeo, "Metaphysical Poetry and the Poetry of Correspondence," in *Renaissance and Seventeenth-Century Studies* (New York: Columbia Univ. Press, 1964), pp. 44–59. See also Mazzeo, "A Seventeenth-Century Theory of Metaphysical Poetry," *Renaissance and Seventeenth-Century Studies,* pp. 29–43; and "A Critique of Some Modern Theories of Metaphysical Poetry," *MP,* 50 (1952), 88–96. Frank Warnke, *Versions of Baroque* (New Haven: Yale Univ. Press, 1972), pp. 22–23, 25, passim, argues that in the practice of baroque poets, the doctrine of universal correspondence leads to a poetry of "phantasmagoria" because it "enables the poet to speak of the unimaginable in terms of the phenomenal."

3 Martin, *Poems English, Latin and Greek,* pp. xci–xcii. See above, chap. 1.

4 Warren, *Richard Crashaw: A Study,* p. 237, n. 107.

5 My account is paraphrased from a rather typical description of the terms by Ángel del Río, *Historia de la literatura española,* rev. ed. (New York: Holt, Rinehart, & Winston, 1963), I, 392–93.

6 The landmark book is, of course, Rosemond Tuve, *Elizabethan and Metaphysical Imagery* (Chicago: Univ. of Chicago Press, 1947).

7 *Poesía española,* pp. 440–55.

8 Ibid., p. 376.

9 *Nueva poesía: conceptismo, culteranismo en la crítica española* (Madrid: Editorial Castalia, 1967), p. 85.

10 Ibid., pp. 88–89. Collard also supposes a large ethnic-religious element in the controversy (*feud* may be a better term) over culterano poetry. Góngora was thought to be a *converso,* a "New Christian" of Jewish ancestry, and members of this group were generally suspected of corrupting the pristine purity of the religion, manners, morals, and even the literature of old Castile. Collard believes that men like Quevedo looked upon the self-conscious erudition and refinement of Góngora's poetry as affectation and as an affront to Christianity and Spanish tradition. I have no firm opinion on the matter, but I would guess that Collard exaggerates. There was obviously an intense personal hatred between Góngora and Quevedo, fueled by literary rivalry; and it is not surprising that in seventeenth-century Spain (or anywhere else in Europe) Quevedo would seize upon his enemy's alleged Jewish lineage as a satirical weapon in the poetic quarrel. On the other hand, the thesis that Góngora's (presumably actual) Jewish descent did affect his poetry has been seriously advanced by a

contemporary Spanish critic, Guillermo Diaz-Plaja, *El barroco literario* (Buenos Aires: Editorial Columba, 1970), pp. 51–55. In any case, this aspect of the controversy could hardly have a bearing on Crashaw.

11 E.g., Joan Bennett, *Five Metaphysical Poets,* pp. vii–viii.

12 *Poesía española,* pp. 323, 368, 344. I have drawn general descriptions of the imagery of Góngora and Crashaw almost exclusively from Alonso and Warren respectively. The work of each of these critics has received wide acceptance, and I believe they give substantially accurate accounts of the poets they treat; therefore, it seemed wiser not to multiply references. For a very detailed analysis of Góngora's imagery which arrives at similar conclusions to Alonso's, see Eunice Joiner Gates, *The Metaphors of Luis de Góngora* (Philadelphia: Univ. of Pennsylvania Press, 1933). For an opposing view, see Jammes, *Études sur l'Oeuvre Poétique,* pp. 605–17.

13 *Poesía española,* p. 323. Cf. Alonso, "Claridad y belleza de las 'Soledades,'" in *Estudios y ensayos gongorinos,* 2nd ed. (Madrid: Editorial Gredos, 1960), pp. 73–74.

14 "Claridad y belleza," pp. 71, 73. Cf. Warnke, *Versions of Baroque,* pp. 21–51.

15 Cf. Alonso, *Poesía española,* p. 385: "The entire poem [*Fábula*] has a thematic musical structure, and these are the two themes, which, with a thousand variations, alternate throughout the length of the whole *Fabula.* . . . the theme of Galatea, the theme of Polifemo: beauty, monstrousness."

16 *Richard Crashaw: A Study,* pp. 179, 193.

17 Ibid., pp. 184–85.

18 "Claridad y belleza," pp. 78–79, 83.

19 *Richard Crashaw: A Study,* pp. 182–83.

20 "Alusión y elusion en la poesía de Góngora," *Estudios y ensayos gongorinos.* p. 104.

21 *Richard Crashaw: A Study,* p. 180.

22 Cf. Williams, *Image and Symbol,* pp. 82–83, n 90.

23 Cf. Martz, *Poetry of Meditation,* p. 347; and Maddison, *Apollo and the Nine,* p. 354.

24 "Alusión y elusión," p. 100.

25 Ovid, *Fasti,* V, 121ff. Góngora's association of the river with the Horn of Plenty may have been suggested by an alternate legend of Hercules and the river-god Achelous, *Metamorphoses,* IX, 85–88.

26 Cf. Alonso, "Claridad y belleza," pp. 70–71.

27 E.g., *Sancta Maria Dolorum,* st. 2: "Her eyes bleed TEARES, his wounds weep BLOOD"; and the epigraph to "The Weeper": "Is she a FLAMING Fountain, or a Weeping fire?" Similarly, in the stanza immediately fol-

lowing the one quoted in the text, Góngora writes that "Love" wonders if
Galatea is "snowy crimson or red snow."

28 *Poesía española,* p. 376.

29 I have emended an obvious misprint by Millé y Giménez in the fifth line
of this stanza, *mosquetes* ("muskets") to *mosquetas* ("musk roses"). Cf.
Obras en verso del Homero español, p. 134v.; and Foulché-Delbosc, *Obras
poéticas,* II, 78.

30 I have emended here another obvious misprint in the second word of the
third line of this stanza, *el* in Millé y Giménez to *al.* Cf. *Obras en verso,*
p. 121r.; and Foulché-Delbosc, II, 51.

31 *Poesía española,* pp. 385-92.

32 *Richard Crashaw,* p. 192. Cf. Warnke, *Versions of Baroque,* p. 31:
"Crashaw is here ["In the Assumption"] using imagery of the senses not
in a manner that significantly imitates or represents the world of ordinary
experience but in a manner that contructs a phantasmagoric heaven out
of chunks of sensuous experience regarded simply as raw material for an
artifact." See also Warnke, pp. 23, 37-38, on Gongora's "sensuous elabo-
rateness."

33 "Epístola I a Heliodoro o Soledad de Pedro de Espinosa, Presbítero," ll.
41-50, in *Poesías completas,* ed. Francisco López Estrada (Madrid:
Espasa-Calpe, S.A., 1975), pp. 129-30. López Estrada's introduction
gives a thorough account of the influence of Góngora on Espinosa and of
the latter's status as a "new" or culterano poet.

34 Ibid., pp. 136-37.

35 *Ad Sabinum Fuscum Tyrolensem: Inuitatur ad contemplationem rerum coeles-
tium,* ll. 81-92, in *An Anthology of Neo-Latin Poetry,* ed. and trans. Fred
J. Nichols (New Haven: Yale Univ. Press, 1979), pp. 620, 622.

36 *Carmina,* III, iv, 5-8, in *Horace: Complete Works,* ed. Charles E. Bennett
and John C. Rolfe, rev. ed. (Boston: Allyn & Bacon, 1962).

37 Much the same observations might be made about another famous depiction of poetic ecstasy by a Jesuit neo-Latinist and imitator of Horace,
Casimire Sarbiewski's *Odes,* II, 5, esp. 77-88. This poem is reprinted
and translated in Nichols, pp. 592-97.

38 The poems I have especially in mind are "Hymn to the Name of Jesus,"
"Hymn in the Glorious Epiphanie," "To the Same Party . . . ," "Hymn in
the Assumption" (two versions), "Ode on a Prayer-book" (two versions),
"A Letter to the Countess of Denbigh" (two versions), and "Charitas
Nimia." The poem to the Countess is written in couplets, but with
frequent and radical shifts in line length. The "Hymn to Sainte Teresa"
and "The Flaming Heart," also in couplets, have occasional shifts in line
length, but do not compare in irregularity with the others. The first two
poems named are the best examples.

39 *Richard Crashaw: Style and Poetic Development*, p. 39. Cf. Warren, *Richard Crashaw: A Study*, p. 230, n 43; and Low, p. 123.

40 *Richard Crashaw: A Study*, pp. 159–75.

41 Ibid., p. 237, n 107. Warren's further suggestion, that the shift in versification reflects a turning away from Santa Teresa toward Dionysius the Areopagite, is quite far fetched. In the first place, the mysticism of Teresa and Dionysius are not utterly different, as I show in chapter 4. Moreover, Warren's argument simply does not fit the quality of the poetry: why would a growing interest in the supposedly intellectual or philosophical mysticism of the Areopagite account for irregular verse? "Ode on a Prayer-book"—full of erotic imagery—is written in the irregular form, and so is "Hymn to the Name of Jesus" which, although probably among Crashaw's last poems, is characterized by sensuous imagery.

42 Cf. Warren, *Richard Crashaw: A Study*, pp. 161–62. Maddison, p. 371, n. 2, gives what is apparently intended to be an exhaustive list, but omits "Lycidas."

43 *Works of Herbert*, ed. Hutchinson, p. 153.

44 Crashaw may even have contributed to the volume; see Wallerstein, p. 26.

45 *The Italian Element in Milton's Verse* (Oxford: Clarendon, 1954), pp. 71–74, 81, 85–87.

46 *Apollo and the Nine*, pp. 331, 337–39, 346. Maddison studies the Italian ode extensively in this work (pp. 142–92) and never suggests that it was an influence on Crashaw. Her book does not deal with Spanish poetry.

47 Cf. Williams's headnote, *Complete Poetry*, pp. 588–89.

48 *Apollo and the Nine*, p. 338.

49 *Métrica española: reseña histórica y descriptiva* (Syracuse: Syracuse Univ. Press, 1956), pp. 235–36. For a thumbnail sketch in English, see "silva" in the *Princeton Encyclopedia*.

50 "Claridad y belleza," p. 66. In the Chacon manuscript (as edited by Foulché-Delbosc) the text of the *Soledades* is divided into stanzas—absolutely irregular stanzas whose limits are determined only by the ends of clauses or sentences, or by a shift in image or idea; and even these strictures do not always apply (e.g. the "Dedication" in which the break between the third and fourth "stanzas" falls between a verb, *besaba*, and its complement, *asta*). In a poem as difficult and as long as the *Soledades* (some 2,000 lines) such divisions are almost a necessity to preserve the reader's sight and sanity, and they are observed in modern editions. However, stanzaic divisions are omitted from the *Soledades*, except for the choral wedding hymn, in all the editions published by the time of Crashaw's death that I have been able to examine: *Obras en verso* (Madrid, 1627), *Todas las obras* (Madrid, 1633), *Todas las obras* . . . (Zaragoza,

1643), and *Obras de Góngora comentadas por D. García Salcedo-Coronel,* 3 vols. (Madrid, 1636, 1644, 1646). In all of these versions, the appearance of the *Soledades* on the page is very similar to that of "To the Name of Jesus" and the other hymns in *Carmen Deo Nostro.* Of course it is really impossible to determine the intentions of either author. Crashaw was not in England when *Steps to the Temple* was published in 1646 and 1648, and *Carmen Deo Nostro* (Paris, 1652) is posthumous. The *Soledades* is an unfinished work: four parts were planned, but only the first and 979 lines of the second were ever completed. Although widely circulated in manuscript during the poet's lifetime, they were never printed until his works were posthumously collected.

51 *Richard Crashaw: A Study,* p. 168. Warren uses a different passage from this poem as an example, but the style is basically the same.

52 Cf. Alfonso Reyes, "Contribuciones a la bibliografía de Góngora," *Cuestiones gongorinas* (Madrid: Espasa-Calpe, S.A., 1927), pp. 90-132; and n. 50 above.

53 *Lettres de Jean Chapelain,* ed. Tamizey de Larroque (Paris: Imprimerie Nationale, 1883), II, 72-75 (Letter 39, 21 Dec. 1659) and 204-05 (Letter 118, 16 Feb. 1662). I owe this reference to Collard, pp. 91-93. As a young man Chapelain had succeeded in adapting his severe classicism to the praise of Marino's *Adone.* See *The Continental Model,* ed. Scott Elledge and Donald Schier, rev. ed. (Ithaca: Cornell Univ. Press, 1970), pp. 3-30.

Index